HEAVEN HIGH — HELL DEEP

HEAVEN HIGH
HELL DEEP
1917—1918

BY

NORMAN ARCHIBALD

Illustrations by
ALLEN PALMER

ALBERT & CHARLES BONI, Inc.
PUBLISHERS   NEW YORK
1935

To

HAZEL AND EBEN

PART ONE

CHAPTER I

APRIL 6th, 1917. The United States declared war.

Since 1914 I had read with greedy interest every newspaper article, magazine story or bit of flimsy fiction which described the flights, battles or accomplishments of Allied aviators. The mere photograph of an aeroplane fascinated me; the drawing of an air battle hypnotized me.

Now one and only one thought raced through my mind. We are at war!—now I can fly! The idea obsessed me. It tired me. In a burning circle it chased around my brain until I felt on fire.

April 7th. This is my birthday. I am twenty-three today.

At dinner that night I said very little. No one noticed. The conversation was tense with every sentence pertaining to America's entrance into the war. When the dessert was served a cake with twenty-three red candles gleamed before me. The word JIM, outlined in uneven letters made of red seed candies, seemed to jump all over the cake. I remember I simply stared, thinking, "I am twenty-three—pretty old now—twenty-three but I'm going to war—to fight in the air."

"Jim, what is the matter?" My mother was speaking.

"Come, come—cut the cake," interrupted my father.

"Blow the candles, Jim—blow the candles first," shouted my sister, "and make a wish—don't forget to make a wish."

I made a wish, the greatest wish of my life. I blew the candles and cut the cake.

"Tell me what you wished," begged my sister. "Please, Jim, tell me—"

"What did you wish, son?" asked my mother.

"That I would get my share of Germans!"

An ominous silence. Would no one ever speak? Seconds passed. I busied myself with the cake, but could hardly swallow. My father and mother were intent on their pieces, but my sister's eyes never left my face. Finally she opened the way.

"I know what you're going to do, Jim!— Fly!— You're going to fly—aren't you?"

"Yes! I'm going to join the Air Service."

"I knew it! I knew it! Oh, Jim."

Again the dreadful silence. Annoyed that neither of my parents asked a question, volunteered a remark or even seemed interested, I continued in a hurt tone, "I'm going to fly!"

Not a word.

"I'm going to fight in the air—"

Not a sound.

"I'm going to start *tomorrow*."

And that was the end of my birthday party.

·   ·   ·   ·   ·

Officers were stationed at Fort Lawton on the outskirts of Seattle, and the next morning I was on my way. Arriving, I inquired about enlisting in the Air Service.

"I know nothing about it," a captain told me, "but if you go to the recruiting station they will probably have the information."

I wandered through the grounds of the Fort. It was a beautiful spring day and the trees swayed in a gentle breeze that drifted over the jagged cliffs of Puget Sound. I sat down in the shade. The water glistened a bright, bright blue and the whitest clouds were drifting across the sun. There I sat staring into the sky, and dreamed of flying through just such clouds.

A few hours later I was telling the recruiting officers of my desire. Eagerly I awaited their answers.

"Well!" drawled one, "I don't think there is an Air Service."

"If there is," chimed in another, "I don't know how you would join it."

They advised me to write to Washington and apply for enlistment. I was discouraged but posted a letter that very night to Newton D. Baker, Secretary of War, applying for enrollment in the Air Service.

Two weeks of impatient waiting passed before the reply came. My application did not comply with army regulations; it was necessary to fill out the enclosed form and with three letters of recommendation return it. No time was lost. Before the day was over I possessed the missives endorsing my character and moral fitness. In highest spirits I filled in the application blank and, with the precious letters, mailed it.

Three weeks passed. Each day seemed a year. Then the postman handed me a letter.

"I sure hope this is what you've been expecting."

"It is, thanks!" And I ran into the house—up two flights of stairs—shut and locked my door and, panting, tore open the envelope. The letter said that before enlisting in the aviation section it would be necessary to report to San Diego, California, for a physical and mental examination.

A few days later I was on a steamer bound for San Diego.

Arriving, I boarded a launch for a flying base at North Island. Filled with the mystery of army routine I sat down beside a sophisticated-looking soldier. His willingness to talk and answer questions clarified many details. Asking where to go, whom to see and, most of all, how to conduct myself properly in the presence of officers, made the trip across the bay seem short. Soon we were walking towards the Headquarters Building.

The sun was blazing. The day was hot. Planes were flying. They passed within forty or fifty feet overhead and the sound of humming motors filled the air. With highest hopes and pounding heart I entered the building and my companion pointed to an officer.

He read my letter from the War Department, asked numerous questions, then directed me to a medical officer. Five minutes later, stripped naked, I stood, with three other applicants, before an army doctor and two assistants. Hearts and lungs were tested, teeth and throats examined, exact measurements and weights taken. Feet were all-important. Never had I imagined that feet, mere feet, could be so thoroughly inspected or discussed. It seemed stupid that feet, flat or otherwise, should or could play such a stellar role in the flying ability or instincts of an aviator.

"What have flat feet got to do with flying?"

An assistant, surprised at my stupidity, stared but did not answer and the great interest in feet continued. After several minutes, I boldly repeated the question. The assistant glared at me.

"You evidently do not understand."

His tone was technically supercilious.

Seated in a revolving chair with instructions to hold tight, I was spun round and round at a terrific gait. Suddenly the two assistants caught the chair and the doctor held a pencil, sharply pointed, before my eyes.

"Follow the point of the pencil," he instructed.

Slowly he moved it back and forth, up and down and, repeating the movements faster—faster—faster, intently watched my eyes.

Dizzy, groggy and half-sick with disappointment, I imagined failure. This was a mistake.

One aspirant, after this test, was told he could not fly. He stood in blank amazement, shivered, and almost burst into tears. He could hardly dress. As in a trance, carrying his collar and tie, he tiptoed toward the door and disappeared.

Blindfolded, I was told to put one foot firmly on the other and hop in a straight line. Seated, hot water alternating with cold was poured into one ear, then the other. Again, I was dizzy and afraid.

"How do you feel?"

"Very dizzy."

"Good! Good!" he smiled, "you should be."

During the hearing test the officer, standing fifteen feet away, told me to repeat whispered words. His lips moved but the roar of a passing plane drowned his voice.

"Well?"

"I cannot hear with that engine roaring."

"Fine!"

Another failed and two of us were left. Countless questions pertained to health, habits, hygiene, and the examination ended with a regulation hospital test for blood, urine and so on. During this period each man was alone.

Outside the building stood the other "successful" chap.

"Well, you and I are lucky to have passed those tests."

He did not answer but offered me a cigarette.

"Thank you, but I've decided not to smoke for awhile—want to be fit as possible when we start training."

"I've no reason to stop—I won't be training—not for flying, anyway."

"What's the matter? I thought that you and—"

"Me? Oh, I'm swell!" he said bitterly. "A perfect man, almost. No flat feet, nothing, but they think my great-grandmother had lumbago. Lumbago! Sure! But —good luck to you." He grabbed my hand, pressed it and hurriedly walked away.

The next morning the medical officer reported my physical condition excellent, said he was recommending me to Washington, and there was nothing further to be done but wait for instructions from the War Department.

"Physically fit," but with small hope of flying in the near future, I went home.

.   .   .   .   .

Ten days later, with instructions from Washington to enlist as Private First Class in the aviation section of the Signal Corps and to proceed to the ground school at the University of Texas, I again rushed to the recruiting station.

Still they knew nothing. Furthermore, although my orders were explicit, they refused to follow them and tried to dissuade me, in fact, insisted on enlisting me as a private in the Signal Corps. I flatly refused. An argument ensued. An elderly major read the order and, shaking his bald head, said that he personally would wire Washington for further instructions.

More days of waiting.

Later I learned that many, certain they were signing up for the Air Service, were doomed to build roads, lay wires, dig ditches, but never fly. Had I left the matter of enlistment to the recruiting station this would have been my lot.

Finally, on July 9th, enlisted as Private First Class in the aviation section of the Signal Corps, I packed a suitcase and started for Texas.

. . . . .

Reporting a day late, I was greeted with an oration on 'Discipline' and told to purchase army clothes in Austin. Under the impression that once in the Army all wearing apparel was furnished, this surprised me but, completely subdued by my recent experiences, I felt no desire to argue.

That afternoon an order to drill was issued.

There I stood, serious and erect, in my first formation. My two extremities, the only reminders of the garb of a private citizen, stood out in bold relief, for on my head sat a swank, greyish-green cap and my feet were giddy in pointed tan shoes. In between there was a colorful display of my recent and hasty purchases—baggy, voluminous, olive drab breeches; ill-fitting brown canvas leggings and a golden-yellow cotton shirt.

"Attention!"

Had I realized my pathetically droll appearance it is doubtful if I would have drilled at all, for my cap and shoes proved targets for the drill sergeant.

"Hey, you in the green cap—step lively!" or "You, in the swell shoes—get in line!"

. . . . .

We studied the rigging and construction of aeroplanes, motors, transportation, astronomy, meteorology, telegraphy, drilling, calisthenics and army discipline. Many said that the rules and regulations at this ground school were as strict as at West Point, and, fresh from the freedom of civilian life, the confinement and routine were a hard task.

Days were full. Reveille at five-thirty; a run around the campus (the distance depending on the inclination of the regular army sergeant who led the chase); breakfast; classes until noon; luncheon; more classes until late afternoon, then drill; following the evening meal a study period until nine-fifteen and at nine-thirty lights were out.

Saturday afternoons were set aside for vaccinations and inoculations which left us weak, with no ambition or strength to enjoy Sunday—our one day of freedom.

July in Texas is hot! It was a common occurrence for those from cooler climates to collapse while drilling. Falling, they were dragged to a shady spot and left to recuperate while the survivors continued.

Each week the student body assembled on the campus. This was always an occasion of intense interest. We listened with breathless apprehension as the names of students, who had failed in studies or had broken any one of a number of regulations, were solemnly read. These were discharged and could no longer hope to become flyers. Owing to the dreadful uncertainty I decided that if this happened to me I would join the Canadian Air Force, known to be more lenient.

At the end of the third week, passing from the junior into the senior class, each student was called before the "Benzine Board" which consisted of civilian instructors and Army officers whose duty it was to judge each student as to his personal qualifications to become an officer. Every attempt was made to embarrass us. The questions asked by this high and mighty council seemed without sense, rhyme or reason.

"Who was the Queen of Sheba in 400 B. C.?"

"Why is a cow?"

"What is a tree?"

"Describe the different gaits of a horse."

One student was asked, "How old are you?"

"Twenty-one and a little over, sir," he answered nervously.

"How much over?"

"A year and three months, sir."

"That is all. Report to the adjutant this afternoon at three o'clock."

He was discharged.

Early in September the course was finished. We were cadets! Each was given ten days' leave and this afforded many the opportunity to return to their homes before commencing actual flying training. Impossible to travel to Seattle and back in the allotted time; I remained in Texas.

When the other students returned it was rumored that seventeen of us were to be sent direct to France. To be ordered to France without preliminary training in the States was a great honor, as but a few from each school were picked for preliminary flying instruction across the sea.

What news? Who would go? I was radiant when told that I was one of the seventeen.

I was going to FRANCE!

We packed our belongings. What a business it was! What baggage! Bags, packages, bundles, clumsily thrown together; fingers were feverish with excitement and I remember my small grip and leather suitcase.

"We'll train under French instructors who have actually flown in the war."

"Say, we'll be at the Front before we know it."

Then how I wanted to see my parents and my sister—how I longed to say good-bye! It was impossible. Going to France—to fly—to war—without a word of farewell.

CHAPTER II

NEW YORK.

We hurried to the Battery, boarded a launch for Bedloes Island, and there, beneath the Statue of Liberty, our detachment of cadets, numbering one hundred and twenty and chosen from every ground school in the country, assembled.

None had had any flying training. All eagerly awaited the great adventure. We slept in tents; lined up for meals, awkwardly using our recently issued mess kits. We sensed the great excitement of men who leave their own country to fight, on foreign soil, against a common enemy.

The Quartermaster's department, seething with activity, issued clothing suitable for cold weather. Scrambling for woolen overcoats, uniforms, shoes, shirts, underwear, socks and hats became a ritual. As we invariably received the wrong size, there was a continual exchange of clothes. A misfit for one cadet was a perfect suit for another and in a few days we felt presentable.

Hurried trips were made to New York. We never stayed more than a short time as orders to sail were ever rumored, expected and hoped for.

"What's the delay now?"

"Heard any news?"

"Why don't they send us?"

Stimulated with excitement it was almost impossible to think sanely.

The first week in October was raw; early one damp, chilly morning we were abruptly awakened.

"You're leaving for France!"

At last it had happened. The day had come. Half awake we hurriedly dressed, prepared for inspection, lined up beside the rows of little tents and—waited. A major appeared. He looked us over. His expression was one of utter disgust.

"Attention!" he roared.

We stood there, stiff as ramrods.

"Prepare for inspection. March!"

Arrogant, he strutted down the opened ranks and gazed into our startled, sleepy eyes; lashed each man with a caustic remark and said we were, without a doubt, the poorest looking crowd of men he had ever inspected. He told us that it was necessary to pass through New York on our way to Montreal.

"You are anything but soldiers and I doubt if you ever will be. You can't fool me but when we go through New York for God's sake try and fool the public."

If any of us had felt, before, the slightest degree of importance he quickly changed his mind. But—we were leaving for France! What did it matter? What did anything the major said or thought matter? Nothing mattered! We were off!

Our train arrived in Montreal. Trucks carried us to the pier where the *S.S. Megantic* was docked and, without a moment's delay, we boarded the steamer, already crowded with soldiers of machine gun companies. The *Megantic*, not yet refitted for the transporting of troops, was clean, comfortable and furnished as in peace times.

Oliver Beauchamp, a graduate from the Cornell ground school, was assigned with me to a large outside stateroom. Cornell was my college. This additional bond strengthened a casual acquaintance into that rare and sacred friendship known to men in times of war only.

.   .   .   .   .

The trip down the St. Lawrence was one of absolute freedom. Our commanding officer, not aboard but arranging for baggage left behind through error, was to join us at Halifax. The steamer became a casino. Staterooms were riotous with varied forms of gambling. High stakes, low stakes, depending on the number of the room.

In Halifax harbor, the *Megantic* was joined by twelve other ships. The convoy complete, it steamed forth on its wartime mission. An English battleship bade us God Speed. Sailors, in a straight white line, stood along the decks of this massive man-of-war while the soul stirring music of national anthems floated across the grey water.

Silent men, thinking men, pulses quickening with the realization of it all, stood hushed and strangely solemn.

Twelve ships at sea—twelve ships of steel—twelve ships in close formation, is an inspiring picture. Brazen by day; black by night; onward-onward-onward close together; a moving panorama that one watched with interest hour after hour.

The days were filled with life-boat drill, poker games, submarine watch, crap shooting and talks on discipline. The possibility of a submarine attack caused vague expectations. Warned that not a ray of light must escape at night, definite announcement was made that any man found responsible for a showing light would be tried as a spy. Smoking on deck after dark was prohibited and submarine watch was assigned to the cadets. As far as I knew each cadet, with one exception, fulfilled this task earnestly and seriously. My roommate Beauchamp, a firm believer in fate, had an utter disregard for danger, rules or army regulations.

"What's going to happen will happen," he would laugh.

His mere presence brought such an atmosphere of lightheartedness that to be near him was to forget care and worry.

Two A. M.

He was on watch and, scheduled to relieve him, I crept in the pitch dark along the top deck.

"Beauchamp!" No answer.

"Beauchamp! here I am." Not a sound.

"Beauchamp—where are you?"

Only the swish of the waves broke the black silence of a black night. Was this the wrong part of the boat?— surely it was the place.

"Beauchamp! Beauchamp!" I shouted, and a horrible fear gripped me. Could he, in the dark, have lost his footing and fallen overboard? Standing by a lifeboat, trying to think, listening intently—a slight noise, the sound of heavy breathing, became audible. There at my feet, in the shelter of the lifeboat, lay Beauchamp peacefully sleeping. Forcibly, I roused him.

"All this red tape is a pack of nonsense," he yawned. "What's going to happen will happen."

.   .   .   .   .

Thirty hours from Liverpool our convoy was met by twelve torpedo-boat destroyers. Safe in the harbor, on the evening of the 17th of October, we disembarked.

A light rain was falling as we boarded a typical fourth class European train. A feeble whistle, a jerk, the train moved and, with baggage and cadets overcrowding each compartment, bumped over the rails to an unknown destination.

Noon of the next day. Cramped and weary after a miserable night, we marched three miles to an abandoned English camp near Borden and spent the night in a water-soaked field. Twelve tents, askew in the mud, some half up and many down, were shelter for one hundred and twenty men. Food, all-important, necessitated the use of mess kits forgotten on our luxurious trip across the ocean.

Some attempted to fix the tents, others foraged for bread which, with hot soup made in discarded tin cans, was our supper.

We crowded into the tents, lay down and, without blankets or covering, tried to keep warm. The wind blew a gale, rain fell and the cold made sleep impossible. Suddenly, with a howl, the wind tore the tents from the pegs, leaving us with no protection against the storm. The rest of the night was spent building fires and huddling around them for warmth. At daylight, after managing to make some tasteless coffee, we left for the railroad station.

On the outskirts of Southampton, our next stop, was a row of tents—a so-called "Rest Camp." Again, twelve to a tent, we crowded in, lay down and tried to be comfortable on cold, damp ground. Rations here were soup, bread and cheese. Always hungry, frequent trips were made to the city but as war regulations made it impossible to eat enough in one place to satisfy our appetites we visited several restaurants, eating all that was allowed in each. Confronted with the lack of food, we saw how England carried on.

A few German prisoners dug roads and now and then an aeroplane flew above.

Several days later, in the early afternoon, we prepared to leave. Although constantly cold, hungry and sleepless there was never a complaint. Everyone was in good humor and full of enthusiasm, for we were nearing France where flying would commence.

Men, women and children lined the streets as we marched through.

"God bless the Americans!"

"Cheerio! Good luck!"

Cheers and tears on every side; they tried to shake our hands and touch our uniforms.

How much they knew of war and we—how little!

Food was still the major thought and, at the pier, we bought jam, canned meat, cheese and crackers. The steamer sailed late that afternoon and from that moment we gorged on cheese and crackers, corned beef and crackers, jam and crackers,—then more crackers.

As darkness came we anchored in the harbor of Portsmouth. A high wind whistled through the rigging. The only light was an occasional beam of searchlight sweeping the sky. Now and then its rays revealed a captive balloon, tossing about, and, from the ends of long ropes, a basket, with its human parcel, whirled and swung before the gale.

Our boat, small and filthy, had recently been used for transporting cattle. Crowded with British troops in full war equipment it was difficult to find space to sit down. The hold was assigned to the cadets and with our baggage stacked around the beams we set sail on a blackened sea, made rough by ever increasing winds, for France.

No lights.

The ship pitched and tossed. The stench was unbearable, so Beauchamp and I decided to go above for a breath of fresh air. Stumbling blindly over a carpet of sleeping men we reached the main deck and were climbing a narrow gangway to the top . . .

"No one allowed on the top deck," a guard spoke sharply.

"We are," I began, "because . . ."

"Because we're going on watch," supplemented Beauchamp and pushing past we reached a spot by the funnel.

The wind was freezing; we hugged the warm smokestack and the gale was fresh on our faces. The ship groaned, creaked and tossed like a cork as waves smashed against her sides. We had difficulty holding on. The shadowed glimpse of an escorting destroyer, nosing through the rough sea, was swallowed up and hidden from view by a gigantic wave.

The night, the dark, the heavy sea and howling wind made real the actual danger of submarines. Everything loose was washed overboard; packs and rifles were swept from the deck and in one jumbled mess dumped into the sea.

Discussing our fortune to be in the fresh air . . . we yelled simultaneously, "Hold on! Hold on!" and clung to the stack with all our strength. The ship lurched and seemed to roll completely over. Icy waters surged around us; back she rolled and, drenched to the skin, we clung together, desperately. Certain that the hold was, after all, at least safe we made our way down through the darkness.

The cadets, huddled together, were sea-sick. The jam, crackers and cheese had taken effect.

A terrible impact!

The boat trembled, seemed to stop and a submarine attack was a mental reality.

"We're hit!"

"We're sinking!"

Pushing, crowding and thinking a torpedo had struck, all started for the gangway. Stepping back to avoid the surging mob I noticed one chap lying very still, and shaking him I said, "Get up, the boat may sink."

"Think so?" he gulped. "Sink? Thank God!" He rolled over in a dead stupor.

A seemingly endless night and at nine o'clock the next morning we anchored in the harbor of Le Havre. The men, cold and sick, were motionless and speechless . . . filth, dirt, the odor of vomiting. An hour later we stood on the dock in a slight rain wondering what the next move would be.

A Red Cross train, carrying wounded soldiers from the front, rumbled onto the pier. Hundreds of men, on stretchers, were unloaded. We watched. Bodies under blankets, heads swathed in bandages, vacant eyes staring but not seeing, helpless, they were carried to a hospital ship. Sailing back to England. We made no comment. Silently watching, we had our own thoughts. France, we were in France, all right. Maimed, mutilated, blinded, quiet, they were second rate cargo from a first line trench. The war did not seem very far away, now. These stretcher cases, our first evidence of battle, made an indelible impression.

Our own physical exhaustion was, by contrast, momentarily forgotten. We lined up, roll was called and we marched along a muddy road. Black French troops yelled at us.

Three miles away, high upon a hill, circular, dirty-grey, weather-beaten tents, like ghosts of a deserted camp, stood pitched in a sea of sticky mud. The day was dismal and cold rain drizzled on us as we stood, in groups of three and four, like bewildered sheep in a storm, on the narrow duckboards. Uncertainty and bewilderment smothered us with suppositions. How long would we be here? What next? When would we start flying? Speculation became a perpetual epidemic.

Noon. We lined up before a small, wooden building nearby. A single French soldier, with a flowing black mustache and a frayed, faded-blue uniform, silently handed out corned bully beef, mustard pickles and thin slices of bread. His amused yet sympathetic smile clearly bespoke his veteran's mind. . . . Another bunch of ignorant, uninitiated Americans in France to fight a war.

Supper time. Another hand-out of corned bully beef, mustard pickles, thin slices of bread and bitter, black coffee. Plainly, food was scarce.

Twelve men to a tent. The sputtering light of a single candle and the twelve bedding rolls, close together on the wet floor boards, were like sections of a huge, soggy pie. The smell of damp clothes, the mustiness of a rain-soaked tent and the odorous reminders of bully beef and pickles were far from conducive to slumber as, pulling off our shoes, we crawled in for the night.

Sleep came in fitful snatches. Squirming in our cramped quarters we tossed from back to side and side to belly, until the grey morning. The same monotonous drizzle of rain. Cramped, with stiff muscles, we struggled to haul on our wet shoes.

Charged to keep in constant touch with the camp for sudden orders, we were allowed to go to Le Havre. British troops back from the Front for reorganization or rest and troops from England on their way to the Front were our only contacts with our Allies. Officers in the cafés nodded at us. Although they were pleasant enough we accredited their condescending bows to the knowledge of experienced soldiers against the ignorance of a mere handful of recruits, fresh and ambitious, arriving in France to throw the balance of power against Germany. We knew we were green. But, give us some training. Send us to the Front and we'd show them.

Children in wooden sabots played in the streets. Men, too old for service, looked at us stupidly and women haggled in the market shops for fish. We read the French signs and "Chocolat Meunier" was pasted everywhere. We were in France but it was far from interesting. Back to camp. No orders yet. A second night in the crowded tents and we felt like a bunch of cattle. Dumped at Liverpool, herded to Borden, unloaded at Southampton and now packed in at Le Havre, where were we going? A hell of a 'rest' camp this was! But it was only October, 1917, the arrangements would be better later.

The third morning, early and in a driving rain, we entrained. A rumor that we were bound for Issoudun—the great Aviation Center—and talk of flying was rife. This, the last leg of our journey, would bring us to a flying field! We changed trains at Orléans and arrived at Issoudun just after dark. We were tired, dirty and had never had our clothes off nor enjoyed a good night's sleep since arriving at Liverpool, over ten days before.

Army trucks lined the depot. With thirty men in each, they bumped and careened over twelve miles of rough road. Nothing could be seen in the black night, and jumping out we landed knee deep in a sea of mud.

"Get together and march."

Sheeplike, stumbling and groping we followed and soon came to a newly constructed barracks. Inside were rows of double-tiered bunks; two beams with burlap stretched between. Dry and clean, they were a welcome sight, for here at last was a place to lie down alone, in comfort, and Beauchamp and I appropriated two together.

What a good feeling to stretch out at full length. Issoudun—at last. A good night's sleep was before us and we felt contented. We might start flying tomorrow. For we had reached our dreamed-of destination, a flying field in France.

Fifteen minutes later the Major ordered us out. We lined up in front of the barracks and in single file, on a narrow wooden walk marched to the door of a small building where a captain was issuing blankets from some new bales.

"Give these men five blankets apiece," said the Major.

"I am only going to give them three."

The Major flew into a rage. "Give these men five blankets," he roared. "I don't want any damned captain telling me what to do."

The Major, although strict and exacting, did everything possible to care for us and now at the end of a tiresome journey he saw that we had a good rest—we received the five blankets.

CHAPTER III

Issoudun.

Our fondest dream since graduating from ground school.

It was not yet much of a flying field. Only three barracks were erected at the main part of the camp but about half a mile away two hangars housed a few Nieuports which were examined with great interest. The camp site was a veritable sea of mud, making it almost impossible to get from place to place. We did not think too much of this so-called "American Aviation Center," but we were anxious to start flying.

Our Major, receiving orders to proceed to Paris, turned his command over to another officer who was none other than the Captain who had issued the blankets. As the Major bid us good-bye he complimented us highly on our conduct and apologized for some of his scathing remarks. This, we felt, was a rare thing for an officer to do.

Put to work immediately, we helped build the camp; laid miniature railroads, dug ditches, constructed roads—every sort of manual labor. This we resented. It broke our spirit and we became sullen. We had gone through grueling weeks of ground school, lived up to every requirement, studied and successfully passed all problems pertaining to flying and as a reward of merit were sent to

France for special training. But, here we were wallowing in a sea of mud, carrying rails, shovelling dirt and performing countless offensive jobs entirely foreign to aviation. Our morose attitude was clear to the camp authorities.

Being ordered to answer roll call every morning at five o'clock was insult added to injury. What, we thought, has all this to do with flying?

In the middle of November, early mornings were cold and dark. At five A. M. a solitary figure tramped through the barracks pounding lustily on a large dishpan. This jarring noise summoned us to assemble outside the barracks and wait in the dark and cold until someone came along, read our names and, with great authority, dismissed us. We were supposed to kill time until seven o'clock breakfast, then go to work.

We saw no necessity nor sane reason for getting up at five with nothing to do for hours, and the consequence was that during the dishpan racket about twenty-five angry men lined up while the others rolled over. Faces could not be seen in the darkness and answers of 'Here' came from every direction. Some, shivering in line, generously answered for four or five friends who lay snuggled in warm blankets. Others lustily called from their bunks and in desperation the officer would dismiss the few stragglers. As time went on fewer and fewer responded to the sonorous noise of the dishpan.

We grumbled and became disobedient. Discontentment permeated the barracks and the long evenings dragged heavily. Slight quarrels about nothing became heated arguments and ugly threats invited fist fights.

One fellow plagued us all. Sitting on his upper bunk, feet dangling over the side, he would buzz-buzz-buzz on a wireless set. Learning the code with his buzz-buzz-buzz. Practicing to send twelve words a minute with his buzz-buzz-buzz. This devil's tattoo, incessantly buzzing hour after hour, grated on our already raw nerves.

"Say! cut out that damned racket!" . . . "Take that buzzer outside or I'll rip it to pieces" . . . Abusive language and threats made no impression. There he sat, smirking, with his buzz-buzz-buzz.

Nine o'clock. Defiantly he drummed away. The fellow on the bunk beneath, big feet dangling in his face every time he moved in or out, blew up.

"Say, practice in the day time, will you, some one might want to sleep."

"It's only nine o'clock, *dearie.*"

"Nine o'clock or twelve o'clock, *CUT IT OUT!*"

No answer but the provoking buzz-buzz-buzz.

"Stop that, hear me? or I'll throw you and your damned machine outdoors."

"Oh! and do you own the barracks, *sweetheart?*" he was sarcastic.

It was *his* bunk, it was *his* set and he'd do what he damn well pleased.

The fellow in the lower bunk jumped out and grabbed at one dangling leg. A kick in the chest sent him sprawling. Swearing, he got up, clutched a firm hold this time and, with a mighty jerk, slammed him whacko on the floor.

Stunned, the buzzer struggled slowly to his feet and as he staggered another wallop full on the jaw sent him reeling. Down he went with a thud.

A fight! Like bees to fresh honey we swarmed around.

The wireless man was on his back. His eyes showed white as his assailant, straddling his stomach, pasted him in the face.

Better separate them. "Oh no you don't," a tall, rawboned cadet from Texas drawled. "You fellows all been *talkin'* fight now I guess we'll *have* one."

They struggled for a hold. They fought in dead earnest. They rolled over and a strong arm encircling the wireless fellow's throat was pressing tight—tighter—tighter.

"He's got a strangle hold!"

"Never you mind," said the Texan, "I'll handle this."

The buzzer's body rose and then slumped back. His hands dropped to the floor, his eyes were glassy and his tongue hung out.

"Guess that's about enough," the Texan grabbed them both by the neck and, with angered strength, shoved them apart.

That was the end of the buzz-buzz-buzz.

We were put on guard duty. Some had never even carried a gun so this was not alone strange, but maddening. But as we knew that guard duty, in time of war, is a serious thing we performed it to the best of our ability.

Although resentful, when we heard about a cadet who lost his chance to fly because he had been lax in this affair, we decided to guard the camp as it had never been guarded before.

"Those cadets are no good," complained an officer. "Why, I could walk right up and take the gun away from any one of them."

We heard this boast, hoped he would try it and decided to foil him.

Seventeen posts were stationed around the hangars. We plotted that Post Number One was to challenge this bragging officer and, if he did not obey the command to halt, the guard would shoot into the air as a signal for the remaining sixteen to fire in rapid succession.

Two days later the Lieutenant who had belittled the cadets was Officer of the Day. An exceptionally black night offered a splendid opportunity. He approached Post Number One.

"Halt! Who goes there?" rang out the voice of the guard.

No answer. The figure was advancing.

"Halt! Who goes there?"

Still no response from the approaching officer who was, he thought, going to walk up and boldly take away the guard's gun.

"Halt! or I'll fire"—Bang! The sharp report of a rifle rang out in the still night.

BANG! BANG! BANGETY-BANG! BANG! echoed sixteen more rifle shots consecutively. The officer not only halted but, face down, lay prone on the ground to escape the deadly bullets.

After that episode no one hesitated to halt. We had won our laurels and—stupid cadets—were guarding the camp. Because of our efficiency and as we were receiving one hundred dollars a month, we were sarcastically dubbed "The Million Dollar Guard."

Another duty was to guard Americans who, for petty offenses, were locked up in the guardhouse. For two hours at a spell we paced back and forth.

One afternoon, not on duty, but merely talking flying with a friend I happened to be in the guardhouse. A cadet, who had previously attended a military academy in the States and, for the day, was given the rank of Sergeant of the Guard, passed by Post Number One when he noticed a general and a colonel, evidently on a tour of inspection, approaching.

"Turn out the guard!" he called, wanting to appear military.

We inside heard him but knowing nothing of the situation and, not on duty, paid no attention. Suddenly, flushed with excitement, he rushed in.

"Where are the guards?"

The room was practically empty.

"Where's everybody? A general is coming for inspection—Archie! come on out! Hurry, you be the guard."

Barely understanding, but realizing there should be six or eight guards lined up for inspection, I ran towards the door—stopped—ran back—grabbed my campaign hat, a gun and, trying to button my coat, managed to get outside. The General and the Colonel were twenty feet away and I could hear my friend inside laughing. Closer and closer came the General and the Colonel. Expecting a line of men at strict attention, they found instead a boy with hat askew, coat half buttoned and a gun trailing carelessly on the ground. Their faces—no wonder—showed surprise. The Sergeant, sensing the impropriety of the situation, stood at attention and saluted in his best military school fashion.

"Sir! We beg your leniency," he apologized. "We have never had this formality before."

The General looked at the Colonel, the Colonel looked at the General; they both looked—at me.

"Dismiss the guard," commanded the General without a moving muscle but, withal, there was a twinkle in his deep blue eyes.

"Beat it, Archie," whispered the Sergeant and, trailing the gun behind I turned and re-entered the guardhouse. Conversation outside, and seconds later, as the officers walked away, the sound of low laughter could be heard.

We had a collection of German prisoners sent here for construction work. Something was wrong. Did our commanding Captain, of the blanket episode, favor these prisoners or did we imagine it?

It was raining at Issoudun. We cadets, in soaking uniforms and our own shoes, worked in the mud and continual downpour. The German prisoners were issued slickers, sou'-westers and even rubber boots to keep them warm and dry. Why this favoritism? Needless to say we took offense. They worked from eight to five while we, with no regular working hours, did twice the labor and all the menial jobs.

The Germans were ordered to clean the latrines. They refused. Then we were ordered to clean the same latrines. We refused. Real trouble began. A near rebellion ensued. Cadets were confined to barracks but no punishment whatever was given to the disobedient Huns.

In an attempt further to lower our morale this Captain would assemble the cadets and say, "You are now in the service of the Government. You belong to the Government. Your souls and bodies are no longer your own. Your superiors can do with them as they see fit. You are nothing but material. You will be used by your country when and where it wishes. When your Government sees fit to take your life you have nothing to say. You cannot even think for yourself. You have lost all claim on your mind, your soul and your very life. They all belong to the Government."

We discussed these lectures in our barracks and decided that in the heat of his orations the officer spoke with an accent. Was this imagination? What was going on? We were upset, suspicious and fearful of the future.

Later this Captain, transferred to another camp in France, was given full and absolute control. Soon afterwards, although he had been in the American army for eighteen years, we heard he was arrested as a German spy and taken to America.

.   .   .   .   .

The last of November.

No flying. Nothing but guard duty. Our morale was low—we were dejected—we lived on rumors—we had been sent to France by mistake and were going to be shipped back to the States. So persistent was this rumor that heavy wagers were made and some professed to have actually seen the orders.

Issoudun was an advanced flying field boasting only of Nieuports, the fastest of planes on which only qualified pilots were allowed to train. We also heard that all preliminary flying fields in France were filled to capacity and there was no chance of being sent to any field for at least four months. We were crushed and despondent. Enlisting to fly, we had passed all the tests, lived up to requirements and here we were pacing, pacing, back and forth on guard duty. How we had been envied when, as honor students, we were sent to France! Now our classmates in the States were envied for, we felt sure, they were flying.

On November 30th seventeen cadets were ordered to report to the Commandant. Beauchamp and I were included. The officer greeted us with a smile and, responding meekly, we wondered what was coming for we had lost faith in everyone and everything.

"As you men probably know there is no chance to start training in France for some time to come. The preliminary schools are filled to capacity."

This confirmed the dreaded news but, patiently, we listened.

"I have decided to make an experiment. Seventeen of you have been chosen to start your training on Nieuports. This has never been done before. I have been told it cannot be successfully done now. Nieuports are advanced planes, never flown except by those who have first, on slower and safer machines, received their wings as pilots.

But—I believe in you. I believe you can learn to fly without the customary training. Report at the flying field tomorrow morning at eight o'clock."

We were dumbfounded. Going to fly! We were hilarious! Chosen to do something that had never been done before; to train on Nieuports. Nieuports! It was too good to be true. Nieuports! The swift, small, glorious machine considered too dangerous for anyone until he had earned his wings. What an adventure! We raced back to the barracks and shouted the good news. Everyone, with interest or with envy, was agog.

"Go ahead, train on Nieuports."

"Sure, go ahead . . . Kill yourselves."

.   .   .   .   .

The next morning, December 1st, seventeen happy men lined up outside the barracks. Bulky overcoats, knitted helmets and mittens furnished by the Red Cross, made up our flying equipment. As our names were called we answered reverently.

Marching to the flying field, where a month before we had gazed at the planes in awe, we reported to a French lieutenant who, with three other French aviators, awaited us. Three two-seated, twenty-three meter Nieuports stood on the field.

"Where did you receive your training? What type of plane did you train on? How many hours have you had in the air?" they asked us.

Ignorant, we simply said, "We have never had any flying. *We* are going to train on Nieuports!"

Amazed, they looked at us, then, with gestures such as only the French are capable of, continued, "Impossible! It is suicide to learn on Nieuports . . . Do you want to kill yourselves?" They flatly refused to take us up.

American officers were called and after much arguing, gesticulating and waving of arms the aviators reluctantly consented to take us for a "hop."

My turn came.

Climbing into the rear cockpit, I strapped myself securely in. Previously warned to TOUCH NOTHING I sat— rigid. The pilot, already in the front seat glanced back. "*Tout prêt?*" he asked. I nodded.

The motor roared. Tense—my two hands clung to the sides of the cockpit as the plane sped across the field. Then, with our speed noticeably lessened, we seemed to be floating. Excited . . . I leaned, very slowly, to one side. Fearful of shifting my weight I peered, cautiously, over the edge. The ground was beneath. Yes, we were actually off the earth. That slowing down, then, was merely a common-place sensation as the plane rose into the air. The ground was slipping further and further away. For the first time in my life I was in the air. Really in a plane. Flying. Again, gingerly, I looked over the side trying to locate the hangars. I could not see them, in fact I was unable to find the flying field at all. Everything looked strange. I was completely lost. The ship tipped on its left side. Nervously, to help balance it, I leaned to the right but my weight had no effect. The ship leveled out again, then tipped again, and still I was completely lost. Suddenly, the motor either stopped or was throttled down. The plane, pointing downward, was sliding fast and, for the first time, I spied the flying field. The ground seemed moving up to meet us. We were going to land, I felt, and it was all strange. The earth, slipping away under us, seemed, simul-taneously, rising fast, fast, faster and I braced myself for a terrific jolt. A slight bump, another, and we rolled to a stop.

"*Restez là,*" I was told.

Keep my seat? Was I, perhaps, going up again? This was wonderful! Excited. Thrilled. I could hardly believe my ears as in broken English the pilot instructed me to put my hands on the control stick, gently, very gently, and follow its movements but *to keep my feet off the rudder*.

We were ready to go.

Lightly, so very lightly, I placed my hand on the stick. My fingers, encircling it, were just barely touching for I had been warned how very tricky these sensitive Nieuports were. The motor roared and, beneath my loose fingers, I felt the stick move. We sped across the field and rose into the air. The stick, except for several spasmodic jerks, held a normal position. Then, as my relaxed hand was tipped to one side, I realized we were making a turn. Back again, but the movements were so slight that, excited, I was quite in a haze and not sure of anything.

The motor, throttled again, seemed silent. My hand moved but, without the protecting roar of the engine, I felt hanging aloft with no underpinning and, letting go of the stick, I again tightly grabbed both sides of the cockpit. We landed.

"Bon! Bon!" The instructor looked back and smiled. Good? Good for what? I, most certainly, had done nothing.

Several days passed. We made no progress. We wanted to learn, we wanted to know so many things but, with our limited knowledge of French, could hardly ask a single question. Their explanations, (if indeed they were explanations) of the technical points of flying, rattled off in a foreign language, were completely over our heads. And their effervescent *"Bon!"* about nothing exasperated us.

These experienced French flyers were skeptical, and rightfully, about our ability to learn to fly on Nieuports.

"Ah! Here ees the Su-ee-cide Club!" was their cheerful greeting whenever we appeared at the field.

Fearful—they were taking no chances. Wary—they had no intention of allowing us sufficient, if any, handling of the controls. We were not, as anticipated, learning quickly to fly. The mystery of the controls was as baffling as ever. In fact, we were not learning at all. Our "lessons" were merely rides in the air. We felt restless, ignorant and depressed.

Two Americans, experienced from both flying and instruction in the States, arrived at Issoudun. They were detailed to teach us. The Frenchmen, relieved to be rid of us, were delighted. But their obvious gratification could not approach ours for here were men who spoke our language. In plain English we could understand their directions, ask questions and, in turn, be understood. We were elated. We felt so secure.

The first lesson was mere repetition. Hand limp, following the stick. Feet flexible, obeying the rudder bar. But, we had our teeth in the bit. We were raring to go!

The controls of the plane—rudder, elevator and ailerons —are operated by a stick and rudder bar in the cockpit. Those in the student's rear cockpit are connected to a duplicate set in the instructor's seat by tubular, solid lengths of rubber. Therefore, if a student "freezes" to the stick the instructor can still, by force, be master of the ship. For, as the rubber necessarily stretches, the rear controls become useless.

The rudder acts the same as the rudder of a boat. It is for directional control. A push, with the right foot, on the right side of the rudder bar and the nose of the plane swerves to the right and vice versa.

The elevator, really a horizontal rudder, attached to the tail of the plane, causes the ship to go up or down. A forward movement of the stick depresses the elevator and as the rush of wind hitting it raises the tail of the plane her nose, simultaneously, tilts downward. A backward movement on the stick and, naturally, the nose is raised to a climbing angle.

The ailerons, flexible pieces hinged into the trailing edge of the wings at their extreme ends, are so connected that when the aileron, on one side, tilts down, the one on the opposite side tilts up. A movement of the stick to the right raises the right aileron, depresses the left, and the plane tilts to the right, i.e., the right wing drops and the left wing rises. This we call banking.

A plane, at rest on the field, sits on its wheels and tail skid. Its nose points up as the tail skid rests on the ground. When taking off the motor is opened wide. Then to lift the tail of the plane safely off the ground and bring the plane to a horizontal position so that the skid will not drag, the stick is held fully forward. As soon as the tail is clear the stick must be eased back. For, if it is held forward too long the plane will go over on its nose. Then while rolling along on the ground, speed is rapidly gained and as the body of the plane becomes level the stick is gradually brought back to a neutral position. The rudder is manœuvred to hold the ship on a straight course ahead. With sufficient speed gained the stick is gently pulled back, the nose now points up, and the plane rises from the ground.

Then in the air.

To effect a right turn, the stick is moved to the right, the right rudder bar is pushed slightly forward and, simultaneously, the plane banks and turns. For a wide turn, the movements are slight. For a sharp turn, identical movements but more pronounced. To climb, the stick is pulled back. To glide down, it is pushed forward. Straight cruising, when in the air, apparently needs little guiding.

Finally, to make a landing.

Purposely heading into the wind, the motor is throttled, the stick is shoved forward, the nose dropped, and we are gliding down. With the roar of the motor almost stilled, the wind whistles past the wings, through the rigging and around the body of the plane. The ground is coming up. Objects, below, grow larger and larger. The field looms closer and closer. Then what? For the movement of the stick, as it is pulled back, seems so slight, as the plane levels off and skims along just above the surface of the field. With a slight bump, the plane is on the ground and, rolling along, gradually loses speed until it comes to a stop.

It was cold in December.

A flurry of dry snow sprinkled the earth and, chilled to the marrow after a few hops in our makeshift flying clothes, we would huddle around the fire in a near-by G.I. can.

"Well, Archie, how'd it go?" Beauchamp, holding his hands to the can, blew on his cold fingers.

We wondered who would go up next, when our turn would come again, and, shivering, poked up the blaze.

Some days we would have one turn. Other days two or three and it was bitter cold. We would land, feeling almost frozen and with hand so numb from its enforced motionless position on the stick that to pry it open was painful. Rushing to the fire, our feet and hands stinging as we thawed out we were, nevertheless, exuberant. For, we were training to be real aviators.

The succeeding days brought more flying. We now were relaxed while in the plane. And, although still only following the duplicate controls . . . we began to see the light. I could tell, by the horizon, if the ship was level or not. When only the sky was ahead, we were climbing, slightly.

If the ground could be seen we were gliding, slightly. And when in normal, straight flight the ship's nose was outlined against the horizon. Turns seemed natural. Stick to the right, rudder on the same side. I no longer resisted the resultant banking of the plane. At ease, I rode with it. Secure and content I felt as, with my hand following the stick back, my feet straightening out with the rudder bar, the ship levelled out.

But still the landings were strange. I knew that when the motor was throttled the stick went forward to put us in a glide. That was to maintain our flying speed. "Always keep your flying speed!" we were admonished. I knew, also, that the stick was pulled back again to level out as we neared the ground. But, I could not get the *feel* of it. I could not tell, damn it all, just *when* the stick was pulled and just *how much*. It must not be so difficult, though. We always got down all right. I'd get it. Maybe next time.

The days went on. No longer "lost" I could see the hangars, planes on the ground and other ships in the sky. No longer tense or nervous I was now "at home" in the air.

One afternoon after we had climbed to a goodly altitude, Armstrong, my instructor, motioning for me to take the controls, held up his arms as proof of my sole responsibility.

I held the stick, firmly. Then, as I moved it slightly to the right, the plane banked. Again, as I moved it to the left, the plane easily responded. Well, that was simple. What fun! Then, with the rudder bar held straight and a forward pressure on the stick to keep the nose level (for, with a wide open motor a ship has a tendency to climb) we flew in a straight line. I again lightly tipped the stick, gently pressed the rudder bar, and attempted a wide turn. Around we sailed. I was doing it. Elated, I flew for a bit and then, banking too severely I turned too sharply and the plane, whipping in a half-circle, was pulling away. My God!— I could not handle it! Armstrong grabbed the controls, straightened out the ship and motioned for me to start all over. A bit panicky, vowing never again to make that mistake, and wanting to make a good impression I went at it.

Armstrong, signalling for me to land, crouched low in his cockpit and was out of sight. Fearful, but determined to do it, somehow, I started to glide down. Well—down we went. Good Lord! My brain was wondering, *why* did he take such chances? Fast, faster now, heading for the earth and then, about to hit the ground, up he bobbed, grabbed the controls and made a perfect landing.

Annoyed at myself, and wondering what Armstrong thought, I climbed out. This landing business, damn it all, I could not get the hang of it. The feel, the real "feel" of the ship was not yet mine.

The barracks hummed with activity.

To while away the long, winter evenings, we played poker, red-dog, black-jack or squatting on the floor, yelled "Come on baby! . . . roll a seven for your papa!" This wild hilarity was intellectually balanced, however, by serious games of chess and a note of real genius supplied by one who, blindfolded, could play and unfailingly win five games at once.

Our real "intelligentsia," frowning above the racket, concentrated their cultured brains on "good" reading and some gentlemen pedants ostentatiously taught incongruous French to the "illiterate."

"Stove" flying, however, was the most popular pastime.

"No stove flying!" Armstrong instructed. "When you leave the field forget flying. Don't let me hear of you fellows 'flying' in the barracks."

He did not want us to become confused. He wanted all flying to be done in the air. He did not want us intimidated by the frightening experiences of others or deluded by fanciful tales which carelessly diverged from the truth.

But to forbid us to breathe would be just as effective for we thought, talked, dreamed flying and "stove" flying was an irresistible narcotic.

"Now here's the way to take off."

"Get the stick!" and a sawed off broom handle was produced.

The "flyer" erect in a straight backed chair, his feet on an imaginary rudder bar, his hand on the broomstick, is ready.

A groaning, guttural, terrifying noise as one fellow, his face red and distorted from some gizzarding strain, appears to be having a fit.

"What in hell's the matter?" we yell. "Stop that!"

He quiets down. "Oh, pshaw!" he is plainly irritated, "I was just imitating the engine."

Relieved he is not an epileptic, we tell him to "Roll over and imitate a dead dog." Squelched, he pouts in a corner. "One more yap out of you!" . . . and we return to the "stove" flying.

Again, with his hand between his knees on the broom stick, his feet on the visionary rudder bar, the "flyer" is ready. He takes off properly, and then "in the air" moves the "stick" and, as we critically watch his every motion, banks the imaginary plane and turns in supposable air. Sitting close to the cherry red stove he calmly soars into the heavens.

"Now . . . a sharp turn!" He moves the broom handle, pushes his foot, leans over. . . . "Hold her nose up, you fool, you're slipping!" he is reprimanded. Nervous, he levels out, gets around and . . . "All right, now *land*," we direct him.

With his left hand in space he cuts the phantom motor, pushes on the "stick" and, gliding now, is nearing the non-existent earth.

"Pull your stick back!" "Pull it back!" we warn.

"Not yet," he is dogged. "I'm not down yet . . ."

"Pull it back!" we yell. "You'll break your neck!"

Far into the night "stove" flying held sway. Some boasted they were ready to "solo." Others told of flying without assistance. They bragged, with belying confidence, about their skill, while I, gullible and aware of my own meagre knowledge, was discouraged at their swift progress.

Our lessons continued.

Several days passed but no one, as yet, had "soloed."

One day, about to take off, Armstrong turned saying, "Now, Archibald, you do it all. Take off, circle, and land by yourself. I'll give you complete control."

I felt a bit hollow. He opened wide the motor, held up his hands, and, as I guided the speeding plane across the field an unforgettable thing happened. Something deep inside me seemed to snap and the "feel," the unexplainable "feel" of the ship came—like a flash!

Exhilarated, I felt suddenly reborn as the plane, docilely obeying my slightest directions, rose into the air, sailed in a straight line and circled. I—at last—was master, and buoyant with confidence I throttled the motor, dropped the nose into a glide and made a fair landing.

"Well, what was wrong that time?" Armstrong questioned.

"Slipped a little on the right hand turn."

"That's right. Go up again, you'll do better this trip."

A second flight. We landed and Beauchamp came running over. Armstrong got out, stretched himself, and said, "All right, Archibald, you're going to 'solo.'"

Astounded, I did not speak.

Beauchamp, with a broad grin, whispered, "I'm going to 'solo' too."

"What about the others?" I asked, climbing out. "Everyone going to 'solo'?"

"Hell, no!" he laughed, "just the clever ones."

"Who?"

"You and me."

"Who else?"

"No one else," he chuckled excitedly, beaming with enthusiasm.

I stood stock still.

"Come on, Archibald, let's go," said Armstrong and we three walked toward the solo field. Armstrong was visibly nervous. His encouraging words about how easy it was, how well I was doing and his constant repetition to do *exactly* as I did when with him, belied his inner misgivings.

A twenty-three meter Nieuport stood on the solo field.

"All right, Archibald, take this ship," said Armstrong.

I climbed in.

Armstrong, after minutely examining the plane, saw that I was securely strapped in. But he seemed fearful to let me start. As I was his first pupil to solo in a Nieuport, he felt the responsibility of using me as an "experiment."

A mechanic swung the propeller, the engine barked and Armstrong, standing alongside, throttled the motor and listened attentively to the engine.

"All right?" he asked.

"Fine!"

He stepped clear of the ship and, smiling, waved me off.

With the motor wide open I sped across the field and, before quite realizing it, was in the air—alone. The free joy of it was intoxicating! Up I went, climbing . . . climbing . . . climbing . . . until glancing at the altimeter, I levelled out at a thousand feet. How easy it was! How simple, really. How could anyone think flying was difficult? Then something whipped me right in the face. Blinded—and snatching at it frantically, I shoved the bib of my knitted helmet into my mouth and clenching my teeth with the tenacity of a bulldog, flew along. Calm again, sailing aloft in the clear, blue sky I longed to slip away into the distant horizon but remembering Armstrong's anxious face turned into the wind, glided down and landed. It was as simple as that.

He ran over. "Splendid," he said. "Go up and do it again."

My happiness was complete.

That night the "stove" flyers had a long session. Beauchamp and I took turns at the broomstick while fifteen eager embryo aviators asked countless questions about our first solo flights.

What a wonderful day it had been!

CHAPTER IV

FLYERS now, we associated with the more experienced pilots. But we knew just enough to realize there was a long road ahead before we would be skilled, finished, fighting aviators. With interest we watched the planes from the Formation, Acrobatic and Combat Fields. Their activities beckoned, for, if the different flying tests were successfully passed, we, too, would be doing these stunts.

A few advanced students were quartered in our barracks. A test pilot's bunk was across from mine and far into the night we talked of flying, its thrills, dangers and, most of all, the requisites necessary to be a finished pilot—ready for the Front.

One morning he left for the aerodrome about half an hour before me. I walked happily across the field. Clear weather—plenty of flying. Planes in the air—blue sky— silence, except for the whirr of motors overhead.

It was a good life. Reaching the field I heard someone say a plane had just crashed and the pilot was instantly killed.

"Who was it?"

"The test pilot, that fellow in your barracks—I think."

Killed! He was an excellent flyer, cautious, experienced

and reputed to be one of the best pilots in Issoudun. "A faulty plane," they said.

Two hours later, my own flying finished, I went to verify the news. A small wooden building, about fifteen feet square, was the morgue. I went in. There, on a narrow table, lay his body. The boy undertaker doubled the legs, twisted the arms and shook the loose head.

"He's sure smashed up, this one," he said and prepared the corpse for burial.

Nearly every bone in his body was broken. Why!— just talking with him—now he is gone. Dead. My eyes blurred and, turning away, my feet stumbled against something. I looked down and saw, through a mist, the body of another acquaintance.

The next day there was a double funeral.

In a field, beside the road and about half a mile from camp, they were buried. The volley of rifles; the sound of taps; the body of a comrade lowered into its last resting place, is something never to be forgotten. Then and there, a resolution was made. Never again—while flying—would I attend another funeral and for the first and last time my eyes witnessed the burial of a friend in France.

.   .   .   .   .

Every man, now, was his own protector. Experience was our only benefactor and each was on his own resources. Those who survived the following days of training must profit by mistakes of the less fortunate. Anxious to get into the air at all times, to try something new; each flight taught a different lesson; each was a new sensation.

With courses on the twenty-three meter planes finished, we were ready to fly the eighteen meter Nieuports: single-seated machines with less wing area and slightly faster than the twenty-three meters. The requirements were good take-offs; landings within a certain distance of a predetermined point; spirals and correct handling of the plane while in the air.

At this stage one's flying ability was carefully judged and the choosing of pilots for various branches of the Air Service began. Seasoned French flyers observed our flying with keen and critical eyes. Take-offs must be good. Turns in the air must be executed without slipping or skidding. Three-point landings (wheels and tail-skid touching the ground at the same instant) must be practically perfect. "Pancake" or bumpy landings were black marks. Air performance was facilely judged by these veterans of the air. They could spot true flying "instinct." Those who noticeably lacked this "instinct" could not continue on Nieuports or ever become *Chasse* pilots. They were transferred to other schools for further instruction on larger, slower and more easily handled two-seated bombing or observation planes. Then, if not qualifying as pilots, but fit to serve in the air, they were chosen for observers and bombers. Others were taken from flying altogether and given ground jobs.

Issoudun was a school purely for *Chasse* pilots. Only those who showed a fitness and tendency to fly single-seated fighting planes were allowed to remain. To make *Chasse* was to achieve the last word in flying—the pinnacle of aviation—the height of success in the flying world. Our one goal was to become pilots of these sensitive, single-seated, fighting planes. Individual success alone could fulfill this ambition.

Three "hops" were made in the eighteen-meter planes. If take-offs, flying and landings were satisfactory the French instructor would yell, *"Lachez."* This meant proceed to the next field. We were now ready for spirals. Straight flying only had been done so far and this was our first attempt at "Stunts."

The instructor, standing near a plane, was watching several students manœuvring in the air as I walked over. He demonstrated with the controls how to do a spiral and sent me up. Climbing, I went to an altitude of five thousand feet (fifteen hundred feet higher than I had been told to go) for plenty of room to fall in.

Throttling the motor and pushing the control stick to the right, my plane tipped on its side. Lower and lower the right wing dropped. Steeper and steeper the plane banked until the rudder and elevator controls became reversed. Holding the stick way over I pulled it back—at the same time pushing deeply on the left rudder—and started to whirl and fall with the nose swinging around the horizon. Around and around, holding the controls as they were until the altimeter registered two thousand feet, I then straightened out, pushed on the stick and the plane came out in a glide. Opening the motor the ship was again in normal flight.

A slight sensation of dizziness. With no idea of exactly what had been accomplished, if anything, and to make certain of getting credit for a spiral, I again climbed to an altitude of four thousand feet and repeated the performance. Coming out of this second whirl there was no feeling of dizziness. I felt quite normal, flew around for a moment, landed, rushed over to the French instructor to ask if my spiral was successful.

"I was not looking," he said nonchalantly. *"Encore un tour."*

Disappointed after trying so hard, but pleased at another opportunity, I again climbed, whirled, turned and fell into space.

"Too flat," he corrected. "Go up and do it again."

Suddenly I was unstrung and weary. To whirl, fall into

space and catch yourself is—for a new pilot—a great strain. Wanting to rest for a second—afraid of failure—but not daring to hesitate—I climbed, for the fourth time, into the air. Once more I pushed the controls over, once more fell in a whirl and, once more, landed.

"*Lachez*," he called.

Oh! the potent magic of that word "*Lachez*." It was over. I had succeeded. My lungs swelled with a deep breath and, renewed, rested, almost reborn, I walked towards the hangar.

A fifteen-meter plane, with a dead motor, glided into the field attempting to land. Several sacks of meal had been stacked on this field. Their contents, when spread over the ground, would make a smooth landing surface. The gliding plane struck a solitary sack of meal, flopped over and crashed. I ran to it. The plane was badly smashed and crawling out of the wreckage, covered with meal, and swearing, was Bill Russel.

"Bill! Hello Bill. Why, I had no idea you were in France flying and—"

"Flying—Hell!" He brushed meal from his face and clothes. "Look at my plane. Who started up this hay and grain business anyway?"

Training at Field Five, a few hundred yards away, something had gone wrong with his motor and, forced to land, he picked what appeared to be a clear field only to ruin his plane on a solitary sack of meal. He was furious.

"Well, Archie, you've seen my first crash—wrecked my plane on a damned sack of meal." How we laughed!

. . . . .

Ordinarily when a pilot finished his spiral work at the Eighteen Meter Field he was sent to the Fifteen Meter Field. But as we began on Nieuports we had actually flown very little and needed more time in the air. The Major who started this experimental training gave us a fair chance and a special order was issued to give each of us ten hours' flying on eighteen-meter ships.

To one who has never flown, ten hours of flying may not seem long but it gives a world of experience to a new pilot. Movements of the plane, indelibly stamped on his memory, become second nature. He gains confidence and the true air sense which comes from enough actual time in the air.

For five consecutive days six of us reported for flying, staying up two hours at a time. Permitted to go anywhere, within a radius of five miles, we could fly as we wished. The only requirements were to get in ten hours' flying time before we proceeded to the Fifteen Meter Field.

Our own bosses now, free to suit ourselves, we played Follow the Leader and Hide and Seek. In sheer fun we turned, dove, climbed and frolicked with glee in the lace-like channels of sun-tipped clouds. Youths, without care, on the wings of swift swallows.

.   .   .   .   .

Annamites worked near by. We would dive, swoop down, and these "Chinks," as we christened them, ran wildly in circles and flopped on the ground in terror. This became quite a game.

"Come on, let's scatter the 'Chinks.'"

Down the planes swooped—closer each day.

Down the "Chinks" flopped—faces buried in the earth.

The flyers became bolder; so did the "Chinks" and a reckless pilot curved dangerously near. One brave "Chink," accustomed to the game and knowing it was just to frighten them, did not fall to the ground as usual. He stood—upright. He stood—smiling. The plane swept earthward and—that was all.

The boy was nonplussed at what he had done. Tragedy ended a reckless game and the poor brave "Chink"—still grinning in death—was buried beside a knoll.

"Gosh!" said the boy, his eyes streaming tears, "I didn't mean to do it. Gosh!—but he always—fell down—before."

.   .   .   .   .

When not flying we practiced shooting pistols, rifles and machine guns. We learned the theory of shooting in the air and the method of taking sights on an enemy plane. We studied the mechanism of the Vickers machine gun, its construction and how to relieve jams due to faulty bullets. Our days were filled. We were gay and hopeful of making *Chasse*.

One morning when the instructing corporal was showing us how the mechanism worked as the bullets were extracted we crowded around a Vickers machine gun.

"These, of course, are dummy bullets."

He loaded the gun.

"This is the way a bullet is fired."

He pulled the trigger.

A dry, sharp, terrifying report. Startled, we looked at the instructor who simply fiddled with the gun. A jerk at my side.

"Good God! He's been shot—"

The chap next to me stiffened. His eyes were glassy; he opened his mouth; he tried to speak, shuddered, closed his eyes and crumpled at our feet.

It happened so quickly that, for an instant, no one realized he had actually been shot. The Corporal, looking inane, did nothing. We grabbed the unconscious form, laid it on the table, tore off the clothes and found his stomach and thigh streaming with blood.

"Get the doctor!"

Stiff—he lay and we wondered if he were dying. The Corporal, not stirring, looked stupidly on.

"You're a hell of a soldier," one fellow yelled. "Can't you even say anything? Dummy bullets are they? You dummy—"

In rushed a boy dragging a stretcher.

"Come on!"

"Where's the doctor?"

"Oh, *that* ass, I told him and he said, 'Are you *sure* he can't walk over?'"

The deathlike form we put on the stretcher, and took turns carrying it to an old shed called "The Hospital."

CHAPTER V

EIGHT fields were at Issoudun, all of which a pilot must pass through to become *Chasse.*

Field One: Initial flights with instructors in 23-meter Nieuports.
Field Two: Solo flights in 23-meter Nieuports.
Field Three: Solo flights in 18-meter Nieuports.
Field Four: Spirals in 18-meter Nieuports.
Field Five: Initial flights and various flying requirements in 15-meter Nieuports.
Field Six: Acrobatics.
Field Seven: Formation.
Field Eight: Combat.

But another Field had come into prominence. This, called Field Nine, was the last Field at Issoudun. Here one went but did not leave. It was at this Field I attended the burial of my two friends. During the last three weeks many were taken away. Killed in training—their flying days over—they went to Field Nine to stay.

.   .   .   .   .

Field Five.
Considered fair pilots and well on the road to *Chasse*

we felt like children who graduated from Kindergarten to Preparatory School. With bag and baggage, bedding roll and blankets, separated from other pilots in lesser or more advanced stages of training, we moved in.

The fifteen-meter Nieuport was small, wasp-like, speedy, most sensitive to the controls and equipped with a rotary motor balanced to withstand speed from 1200 to 1500 revolutions a minute. The pilot fitted so snugly into the cockpit that he felt a living part of his machine.

The sensation of the first flight in these planes was as keen a thrill as a first solo flight. These little aristocrats of the air—fast—powerful—climbed at a steep angle, responded instantly to the slightest touch. The machines we had just left were slow and cumbersome in comparison.

We worked at take-offs, landings and figure eights. Each point was a serious consideration. A pilot, to become *Chasse*, to fly and fight alone later, must have actual flying knowledge in his subconscious mind so that the conscious mind, free and alert, is left for fighting problems. Flying must be second nature.

Once a flyer had mastered these tiny, baby Nieuports, there was not a ship built which he could not handle easily.

Seated in my plane, waiting for the signal to take off, I saw everyone looking toward the Eighteen Meter Field. A plane, in a sickening spin, neared the ground.

"He's in a *vrille!*"

A hangar shut off my view. CRASH! Silence.

The instructor signalled me to take off. Finishing the flight, my fears were confirmed, for rarely did a man survive a smash resulting from a spin. Another pilot killed! Another for Field Nine!

So many deaths, since we arrived at Issoudun, so many fatal crashes! We never discussed them; no comment was made. Each man knew the dignity of silence. Each man thought it over—by himself.

In most cases the pilot was at fault. He became excited and lost control of his plane. At crucial times, and they were many, I would not allow nervousness but *made* myself feel, and did feel, that the plane was under my complete control. Each day I said to myself, "You must *never* get excited. You must *always* keep your head. *You* are master of your ship."

To learn the lay of the ground we flew over the field, glided down to landings and came to a full stop within a small circle on the ground. Here judgment was necessary. One must know just when to throttle the motor so that the plane would settle within the allotted space.

One day I took off with all the confidence of an experienced aviator. Circling the field, and approaching the edge of a road, two telephone poles about fifty feet apart were a surprise. To land within the given circle my altitude should be just below the level of the poles' tops so, planning to fly between them, I started across the road.

A terrific impact. My plane was thrown on its side. Instinctively I attempted to right it but the controls did not respond. Helpless, I cut the motor—grabbed a small iron bar on the instrument board—ducked into the cockpit—and waited. WHAM! CRASH! I shut my eyes. Dark. Light. I crawled from the tangled wreckage. Wires and wires, like thread on a spool, were wrapped around the propeller. Wires! When had wires been stretched between these poles? This was my first accident but I feared it would mean a black mark.

The ambulance, ever present at flying fields, sped over and the field officer, arriving by motor-cycle, ran to where I stood. First he seemed relieved to find me alive. Then I had a hard time to convince him of my lack of injuries.

"How did this happen?" he inquired harshly.

"I did not know those damned wires were there, sir."

Indignant, I felt justified in my opinion that wires should not be strung up over night without our knowledge.

"When you get to the Front there will be no one to tell you where wires are."

I felt that the accident was not my fault but I trembled at the thought of a black mark.

"Well," he said, at last, "there'll be no mention of this. Get into the ambulance and sit down—you're all to pieces."

In spite of my protests he pushed me bodily into the ambulance which started for the Hospital.

Elated, I jumped out and ran back to the field.

"I'm sorry, Archibald," said "Casey" Jones who directed the training. "It's my fault, not yours. I should have told you about those wires."

A plane landed and Jones turned to me.

"All right, Archibald, take that ship."

Surprised to be allowed to fly immediately after a crash, this surprise was mingled with nervousness and for the first time I lacked complete confidence. The crash was still vivid. The whole heavens seemed strung with invisible wires and in no hurry to take off I slowly walked toward the machine and slowly climbed into the cockpit.

Nerves! I too had nerves. They were plainly bothering me. The students and the instructor were watching. I fastened the belt, moved the controls, assured myself that everything was satisfactory and called—"Contact."

The mechanic twirled the propeller. The motor whirred. With caution I sped across the field and rose into the air. Flying in a wide turn, to gain time before landing, my nervousness blew away into the blue. Settling down—who was master of this plane or any other?—I flew with ease and not only glided into the marked circle but landed in the very heart of it.

How wise to send me up before I had time to brood; before anyone could question or discuss my accident! Many lost their nerve because such instant, proper action was not taken to eliminate fears of "what-might-have-been." Some talked it over, pictured fatal possibilities, lost their self-reliance and never flew again. But "Casey" Jones had saved me. Faith in myself was stronger than ever.

That night brought complaints of the telephone service. Someone expected a "special" call but Beauchamp laughed with glee.

"How in hell do you expect to get 'phone calls when Archie tears down all the wires?"

. . . . .

Tight spirals.

At an altitude of from six to eight hundred feet the motor was throttled and the spiral executed. Gliding down one must land with precision. Difficulties arose. Coming out of the spiral a plane often headed away from the field and if the altitude was not sufficient to locate your position and glide to a landing without opening the motor, credit for the stunt was cancelled.

The weird contortions planes were put through by pilots attempting to reach the circle without their motor were numerous and varied. Many, in a dogged attempt to succeed, were killed. Others, through the most miraculous of manœuvres, were saved. Two and sometimes three chances were allowed a pilot to perform this feat. If still alive, but unsuccessful, he was transferred to another branch of the Air Service.

Cross-country flights.

This constituted flying over unknown country to an unknown field about sixty miles away. A map, in an aluminum frame, enabled the pilot to locate highways, lakes, railroads and wooded areas on the ground below. There was a flavor of adventure in starting out over new territory but, in this instance, the field was easy to locate so it resulted in a joy ride. We would land and, with the commanding officer's signature as proof of the trip, start back.

.   .   .   .   .

The altitude test.

Flying, so far, had been done under four thousand feet. We longed to climb. A flyer always wants to do something different . . . something new. The limit of these toy-like Nieuports, because of their small wing area and type of motor, was about twelve thousand feet. Designed for lower levels, their controls had less effect at a high altitude and thus this particular height was the "ceiling."

The requirement for the altitude test was to climb in a circle and, at all times, keep over the field. The ascent must be constant and even until reaching the "ceiling" where, for fifteen minutes, the altitude, without a fraction of loss or gain, must be maintained. The descent, likewise, must be made at an even angle and a sealed barograph recorded the flight.

At twelve thousand feet, in February, it is cold.

Bundled in a fur lined coat, fur lined mittens and shoes fashioned of sheep skin I am ready. Climbing—the field is in view. Climbing—the barograph registers an even angle. Climbing—my altimeter reads ten thousand feet and, satisfied, I look down.

The roads are pencil lines, finely white across the earth; the houses and barns are dots; a toy train serpentines through a brown landscape and the world is reproduced in fascinating miniature.

A clear, blue sky above draws like a magnet and pulls, pulls, pulls,—but below are swift moving clouds which threaten to shut away the panorama. The cool azure beckons, beckons, and disregarding conditions underneath, I climb on.

A solid mass of dark clouds completely obliterates the ground but thinking instinct will keep me over the field I continue to climb. The controls are sluggish. It is difficult to keep the plane in flight and finally the altimeter, moving slowly, registers twelve thousand feet. The ceiling! I hold the plane's nose slightly up, she squashes through the thin air but, seemingly without speed, will not climb and feels about to drop. After fifteen minutes, with motor throttled, I glide towards the sea of tumbling black vapors. Just above them, at nine thousand feet, I open the motor and, hesitant to dive into this unknown darkness, fly around wondering how deep the clouds are and knowing my barograph will be ruined. Then, with no alternative, I plunge— into utter blackness.

The wind shrieks through the rigging. The steep dive brings a sensation of terrific speed. Blinded to all sense of balance, direction or view but knowing eventually the plane will come out of this oblivion, I continue in a vertical nose dive.

Light—I pull up. The beautiful sunny day is gone, it is pouring rain and the country is strange. Not a familiar landmark and my gasoline is low. Just as I plan to land, a circular wood, one of the marks on the cross-country flight, comes into view. Twenty miles from my starting point! In a driving rain pelting pebbles against my face, I head for home.

There are the familiar hangars and in another moment I am over the field. It is desolate and bare. Not a soul stirs, not a plane is in sight but as I land, soaking wet, cold and tired, two mechanics come out to guide my ship as I taxi in.

"Glad you're here—terrible storm."

Waiting for me in the hangar is Beauchamp.

"Where in hell were you in this awful storm?" he asks.

"In heaven—above it—no storms up there," and as we walk to the barracks I tell him, as always, about my experience. He whacks me on the back and laughs about my "sitting with the angels for protection." But I know he waited out in the hangar—alone—for me to return. My heart goes out to him stronger than ever.

The barograph registered a good ascent, even flight at twelve thousand feet, an even descent to nine thousand feet and then showed that the plane had performed every sort of gyration. This was, of course, due to storm clouds and the instructor, knowing the conditions I was forced to descend in, gave me full credit for the altitude test.

·   ·   ·   ·   ·

Acrobatics.

Severe and cruel, they made or unmade a flyer and if successfully performed the pilot was almost certain to fly "pursuit." The crucial test of ability, physical condition, nerve, nerves, daring and an adventurious disposition, it was the peak of our training and the height of our dreams. We had reached the Acrobatic school! The school where blasted hopes, loss of desire to fly, altered air careers and frequent deaths stalked on every side.

Beauchamp and I walked over to the Acrobatic Field. A fuselage, all that remained of a wrecked plane, was propped up on boxes. Sitting in the seat of this skeleton, grim reminder of some fatal accident, was Rabbit-Foot. We christened him "Rabbit-Foot" because of his many miraculous escapes from death. A smug smile of contentment lighted

his face as the instructor told him how to move the controls
to perform a certain stunt.

"Kick it hard . . . it won't come off . . . Hard. Don't
be afraid."

Rabbit gave a kick.

"Harder, why you act as if it would come off," said the
instructor.

Rabbit-Foot, giving the rudder a terrific kick, waited for
further instructions.

"That's right . . . that's fine. Now go up and kick it
that way in the air."

Rabbit walked over to a waiting plane, climbed in and
rose into the air. In silence we watched for the first acrobatic ever attempted by one of our group. At an altitude
of three thousand feet he turned and, as instructed, flew
directly over the field. He throttled his motor and was
ready to stunt. Without warning the plane went into a
vertical nose dive and we watched, breathlessly, as it dove
towards the ground.

"It's the end of Rabbit," someone whispered and then,
within fifty feet of the ground, his plane levelled out, flew
past us at a terrific speed and landed in a vineyard a
quarter of a mile away. We saw him, white as chalk and
gasping for breath, running towards us.

"Rabbit! What happened?"

"Rabbit! How in the world?—"

"Well . . . the . . . rudder *did* come off," he choked.

He kicked it hard, all right—so hard that he kicked it
loose from the ball and socket joint and only with the
rudder held parallel in space was the plane under partial
control. Again, by sheer luck, he had escaped a fatal drop.
Again—lucky "Rabbit-Foot."

.   .   .   .   .

The requisites of the Acrobatic Field demanded that stunts be performed to a nicety. The *vrille, renversement, virage* and *vertical side slip* were most important.

A *vrille.*

The motor is throttled, the plane loses speed and its nose, which now has a tendency to drop, is held up by gradually pulling back on the stick. With all flying speed lost the controls, almost inoperative, feel flabby. The plane is ready to fall. It flutters for a moment and when about to drop the left rudder is given a quick kick and held in that position while the stick is, at the same instant, pulled over and back to the right. The ship, now a free body in the air with no power to sustain it, must necessarily drop. The nose points to the earth. The plane spins rapidly. Altitude is quickly lost.

The rudder is straightened, the stick put in the center, slightly forward, and the plane stops spinning to come out in a glide. The motor is started, stick pulled back and normal flight is resumed. If the stick is not in the forward position the plane will immediately go into another spin. The *vrille* is finished but the pilot learns he has dropped eight hundred feet instead of an intended four hundred feet. Up he goes again, plans to spin for six hundred feet this time and, repeating the performance, comes out. The first *vrille* was a profitable loss and he realizes the necessity of quick thinking and prompt action.

The *renversement.*

The *renversement* requires more skill than the *vrille* since the Nieuport has a natural tendency to spin and it is difficult to perform this stunt without falling into a *vrille.* The pilot goes up to a safe altitude, usually three thousand feet, the plane is in full flight with motor wide open and the stick is given a quick short jerk backwards. The ship quickly starts up, the rudder is immediately given a sharp kick and the plane turns over on its back. Upside down, hanging by his straps, the pilot quickly throttles the motor and the nose of the machine, heavy with weight, drops. The stick is pushed forward and as the plane comes out in a dive the stick is pulled back, the motor is opened and the plane sails in an opposite direction.

Left and right *vertical virages.*

These are executed to change quickly the line of flight to an opposite direction. By putting the control stick hard over (to the left or the right as the case may be) the plane is thrown on its side into a vertical position. Pulling the stick back in a circular motion and to its former position the plane turns, owing to its speed and wide open motor, without slipping. This is a quick, effective movement and no altitude is lost as in the case of a *renversement.*

The *vertical side slip.*

With preluding acrobatics mastered the pilot is ready for this final and most difficult stunt of all. The motor is throttled, the stick slowly moved to the right and as the control is pushed over the plane tips more and more onto its side. Owing to this position the elevator and rudder are reversed. The elevator acts as the rudder and the rudder acts as the elevator. As the plane continues to topple on its side, "top rudder" must be given to hold the nose from dropping. Thus, with the top of the rudder pushed to its limit and the stick forward and over as far as possible, the plane's wings are perpendicular instead of parallel to the earth. The wings present no supporting surface so the plane suddenly, with the speed of a rocket, drops in a death-like slip. The pilot's body, held only by straps, hangs from the plane. The rush of air caused by this sudden descent has the force of a hurricane, sufficient to rip off his goggles and even tear off his helmet. Altitude is so instantaneously lost that no sooner has the hazardous slip begun than it is time to come out. Pulling back the stick in a circular motion to a position of normal glide, the plane is brought out in a spiral. Should the rapid descent be halted suddenly and the machine not allowed to come out in a spiral the wings would be ripped off by the terrific strain.

Dear was the price paid by many trying this *vertical side slip*. Unaware of the terrific speed and sudden loss of altitude they crashed to their death.

.   .   .   .   .

A plane landed. Its propeller was still and a mechanic rushed out to start the motor.

"Contact," he called.

"Wait a minute," answered the pilot who crawled out of the cockpit and stood vomiting and deathly sick by the side of the ship. He tried with all his might to overcome this illness and went up again and again but to no avail. Heartbroken, he was transferred to observation where he could do straight flying but never fly "pursuit." His physical condition would not stand the strain.

Acrobatics had finished them. Many hopes for *Chasse* were crushed. Many others—had enough! They had lost their courage and were through. These were severe, sometimes sad and often fatal ends . . .

"Stove" flying reigned supreme. Stories were told and retold; flights flown and reflown; some loved the thrill, others were silent, still others, frightened by some recent experience, had become overly cautious and one by one many disappeared. Frightened by acrobatics they asked to be transferred to schools where only straight flying was demanded. Happier and more ambitious than ever were those who remained.

.   .   .   .   .

Finished with acrobatics we are moving to Field Seven. A truck waits. Beauchamp, Follmer and I climb in. We arrive at a barracks, about a mile from Field Five, jump out, and throw our baggage on some empty bunks.

Early the next morning we report. A leader is selected. Five men are chosen and told their respective positions. The leader ties a white cloth to the strut of his plane to distinguish him from the others. A rendezvous is named. We are to meet at a certain altitude over a lake, woods or town as the case may be.

We take off, gain altitude and fly towards the place of assembly. When all planes have arrived we fly, one following the other, in a circle. The leader starts in a straight line of flight, with motor slightly throttled, and the others fly into their designated positions. Number one on the left is in the rear, above and to the left of the leader. Number two, on the left, is in the rear, above and to the left of number one. Number one and two on the right are in corresponding positions on the right of the leader.

The five planes are now in a V. Straight flying only is done in this first flight so the pilot may become accustomed to holding his position. For two hours we fly over the country. To keep a tight, close unit the motor is at times speeded up or at other times throttled, for to maintain perfect alignment the engine is as important as the controls.

The *circus*.

This is the defense manœuvre, originated by the great German Ace, Baron Von Richthofen. The leader signals by rocking his plane, turns and flies in a circle. In single file the other planes follow. Thus a tight circle is formed and maintained until another signal to resume the original formation is given.

To change directions as a unit the leader signals and

does a *renversement*. The two pilots flying positions one and two on the right perform *vertical virages* to the right. Pilots one and two on the left execute *vertical virages* to the left. They fly into positions behind the leader and are now headed in the opposite direction. Planes which were left are now right and those which were right are now left.

When a pilot finishes this training he flies by instinct more than ever, for his attention has been on other planes. Movements to alter his position from time to time become natural. Constantly near other planes in flight, noting their comparative speeds and manœuvring near them has made mere flying a simple performance.

CHAPTER VI

The Combat Field.

Early one afternoon Beauchamp and Follmer finished their formation flying and moved to Field Eight. I had one more flight to complete but by ten o'clock the next morning was on my way.

When I arrived at the field I saw mechanics, with upturned and astounded faces, standing in the hangar entrance. All the pilots, too, were gazing up with expressions of wonder and amazement.

Two planes were in the sky.

"There's never been flying here like this," said an officer.

"It's the greatest show ever put on at Field Eight," explained another.

The silhouette of an aeroplane, cut out of canvas, was fastened to the ground. The two planes roared over the field, turned and dove for the dummy. With the earth but a few feet beneath they zoomed, turned, soared and again swooped down. So dangerously near the ground they came, that we held our breath. Again, and again, they darted past, seemingly scraping the earth, then banked and soared into the sky. Their wings appeared to brush the hangar sides. Like wild things—unleashed for play—they flew.

What daring! What skill! Who were these two pilots?

What flyers could hold, spellbound, the mechanics, officers and pilots at a field where the most daring combat work is a commonplace and everyday occurrence?

The planes landed. Everyone ran over. Anxious and curious to see these great aviators I hurried along.

Out jumped one. His red face was wreathed in a familiar grin . . . Beauchamp!

Out jumped the other . . . Follmer! and a prickly sensation of pride ran through me.

"Archie!" yelled Beauchamp. "Talk about fun! Did you see that canvas dummy?"

"I saw *you*," was my answer. "Follmer and you were wonderful! Great! . . ."

"Oh shut up!" he laughed. "Come over to the barracks and talk."

Here we were treated as real flyers.

Not a word of air instruction was uttered and we each received a brand new plane with two mechanics to care for it. Each ship belonged solely to its operator, no pilot could fly another's machine, and, proud of our prize possessions, we were careful not to damage them. With a plane of our own, flying when and as we chose, we felt a new freedom and a new responsibility.

My plane, faster and more powerful than any former ship, was a treasure. With no orders, two mechanics waiting below, I, a new individual, flew in a new air world.

A gun camera was mounted rigidly on the front of the machine and speed, so necessary at crucial moments, made it easy to manœuvre. To aim the camera, the nose of the plane must be pointed in the direction of the target and the pulling of the trigger took a picture which showed a hit or miss.

We took pictures of the canvas dummy and examined the developed films. We dove on planes in full flight. Two pilots coöperated for taking pictures in "line of flight." One, with motor throttled to reduce his speed flew in a straight line while the other, flying at maximum speed manœuvred around him at will. We would zoom up from underneath, dive from the rear, front, side or above and each time took sight, aimed and pulled the trigger. A good "shot" now meant only a picture but later it would mean an enemy plane. It was thrilling. To "shoot" was fun. To be the "target" was different, for to fly calmly in a straight line, while an onrushing plane often came within a few feet before swerving away, took will-power and strong nerves.

.   .   .   .   .

Competitive flying.

The gun camera is loaded, we climb to an altitude of ten thousand feet and on an imaginary aerial path we guard an imaginary border from an imaginary enemy. A plane is seen in the distance. The "enemy," his gun camera loaded, approaches. "Foes" in the air, we "shoot" at one another. Closer he comes. Manœuvring to keep out of his "gun's" focus we try, at the same time, to aim our plane's nose at a vital spot. He does likewise, a combat ensues, all one's flying ability is needed and pride alone prevents each pilot from a second's cessation in the furious antics. The pictures will tell the story. There can be no alibi. This battle royal continues until all films are exposed or one flyer, from exhaustion, withdraws.

Combats with unknown pilots are excellent practice. Opponents usually know nothing of each other's air experience or flying personalities. Stiles, whom I had met at Field Seven, was picked for my first opponent.

At nine thousand feet I fly around, alone, and for thirty minutes patrol this fanciful battle line. When about to return to the hangar, a plane approaches. To get a favorable shot at its tail I fly in a circle. He does the same. Round and round we fly; smaller and smaller grows the circle, both planes are steeply banked, almost perpendicular, and neither pilot dares to straighten out for fear of exposure. Suddenly my controls become flabby and useless. My plane falls into an unintentional *vrille* but hoping to elude my pursuer I allow it to spin earthward. After dropping two thousand feet I pull up, glance back and there is the "enemy" diving on me, a perfect target. Defeated, for had he been using real bullets instead of a camera I would most certainly have been shot down.

Tired, weary and ashamed to be the inferior pilot I landed and entered the barracks, humiliated. Stiles, who had "shot" me, sat calm and rested on his bunk but made no comment. Nor did I. Later, unable to suppress my feelings, I nonchalantly referred to our combat and congratulated him. Still he was smilingly silent. On and on I talked about our antics and during this one-sided parley an instructor strolled in. He listened for a while then laughingly interrupted.

"I was your opponent, Archibald."

"You?"

So—I had been pitted against one of the best acrobatic aviators at Issoudun. My cheeks were hot with pride.

Some days, choosing a leader, we flew for miles over the countryside and, as he tried to elude us, did whatever he did. It was hilarious! We hopped hedges, hurdled stone walls, rows of trees, houses, barns and played Leap-Frog in the air. We "attacked" moving trains. Soldiers, riding on the roofs, lay flat and motionless. Flocks of sheep, attended by a lone herder, would huddle together for protection as we swooped down. One day the herder tied a white rag to his staff and waved a truce, so we bothered him no longer.

The two pilots who secured the best "shot" pictures and were the most proficient in outwitting air "enemies" were given week-end leaves with a plane to fly wherever they wished. Some returned with stories of Tours, of Paris, of visiting in French châteaux, but many never disclosed their holiday destinations.

.   .   .   .   .

April!

A new world is coming. Green leaves try to push through the winter's bark and lambs wait to be born. Dead grasses blowing . . . green grasses growing . . . a higher sun in the early morning and a pale peach moon in a dove-grey sky.

Our spurs are won! Qualified to fly "pursuit"—finished with the eight fields—escaped from Field Nine where so many friends now rest—we are *Chasse* pilots.

There were rumors of the great German offensive, driving back English and French Allies! Restless, we wonder if American troops arrived in France in time. We are like wild horses, waiting to break. But we must go through our paces. One thing more—the French aerial gunnery school at Cazeaux—then to the Front.

Cazeaux.

Again we packed our things, left Issoudun in trucks, boarded a train, changed at Bordeaux and continued about forty miles to Arcachon. There an army truck drove us to the barracks, about two miles from the flying field at Lake Cazeaux which is ten miles south of Arcachon and two miles from the Atlantic coast.

Russian soldiers formerly occupied these quarters. An army of fleas were now in active possession.

They ran up the walls in disturbed activity and, to escape our onslaught, scurried into crevices and cracks. Our bunks were alive with them. So were we. It was horrible.

"Is *this* a flea?" An enormous captive was exhibited.

"Perhaps, but it looks more like an elephant."

Beauchamp found some insect powder and ruthlessly scattering it in every direction sang lustily:

> "Oh my mother was an elephant,
>   My father was a flea,
>   So we kids are half and half,
>   What a hell of a pedigree."

Then, holding the can aloft, he chanted solemnly.

"Some day insects will war with men. They shall inherit the earth. But not while American Aviators still breathe . . . Get the hell out of here!"

. . . . .

The flying field, skirting one end of the lake, was dotted with observation planes, slow two-seated Caudrons and single-seated Nieuports. Hydroplanes of various sizes and designs rested on the shore and the lake's surface was spotted with racing motor boats.

Six balloons, approximately four feet in diameter, evenly spaced along the shore and fastened to the ground by cables, floated four hundred feet above. In Nieuports, with machine guns, we dove on the balloon from various angles and, when the balloon was hauled down, the hits were recorded.

A friendly rivalry existed between the French and American pilots. Our pilots had gained a reputation for excelling in accurate shooting from the air and we were anxious to maintain this distinction.

About to go up for my first shot at a balloon someone whispered.

"Sneak up on it . . . fly close . . . don't open fire until you're right on top of it . . . we've got to beat these Frogs . . . fill it full of holes . . . fly close."

In the air and ready to dive the advice was remembered. I dove straight toward the floating target, held my plane in a direct line, aimed the gun sights and when a hundred feet from the balloon opened fire, flew nearly upon it, then swerved away. A sudden lurch. My controls were useless. The expectation of a spill into the lake was certain when somehow my plane righted itself. He told me to fly close. I did, much too close, and when swerving away my wing tip struck the balloon and tore it open. Luckily it had been but a glancing blow with no damage to the plane, but the balloon, deflated, lay flat on the ground.

Small parachutes played a part.

At five thousand feet they were thrown out and shot at as we followed their drifting journey to the earth. Our speed, as we passed these targets, so easily tossed by the wind and so small, made a "hit" difficult. When they finally fell to the ground the number of hits, checked against the number of shells, proved the development of the pilot as a marksman.

For further practice a slow plane, usually a two-seated Caudron flying at a high altitude towed, about two hundred feet behind it, a circular sleeve, six feet long, twelve inches in diameter and tapering to four inches. As the sleeve was dragged through the air the rush of wind inflated it, thus presenting a round, full target. Several Nieuport pursuit planes, their speed more than double that of the slow Caudron, flew around and, from every angle, shot at the sleeve-target.

According to rule, no shots could be fired except in a direction away from the Caudron. This necessitated flying ahead, turning and firing as we sped past. Wanting to register as many hits as possible, without using time to re-fly before the target, we often shot at right angles, turned swiftly, dove and shot again.

The French pilots of the towing Caudrons had no confidence in our self-styled methods. Frightened at the reckless firing and with stray bullets whizzing near them, they would cut loose the target. Floating down, it would be lost in the woods and our hits unrecorded. We complained. Trouble began, and for a time this shooting practice was suspended. When it was resumed the wily French pilots flew in and about the clouds to hide the target.

Large observation planes; cumbersome, slow Caudrons; swift, small Nieuports, and hydroplanes, decorating the skies at all altitudes, made Cazeaux a scene of beautiful but menacing activity. There were numerous accidents. Mid-air collisions, machines diving out of control and countless mishaps from forced landings. Many were killed, others seriously hurt and still others fatally injured, but it was here, for the first time in all my training that I ever saw or knew of pilots surviving from a crash, in a Nieuport, resulting from a spin.

A plane when one hundred and fifty feet in the air went into a spin and with terrific speed nosed into the earth. We rushed over to pick up the body but the pilot crawled from the wreckage with only a skinned nose.

Beauchamp had a close call.

A ditch, recently dug on the edge of the field, had piles of dirt on its edges. Gliding into the field and levelling off to land, Beauchamp saw another plane gliding down, across his path. To avoid a collision he opened his motor. At full speed his landing-gear hit the dirt. The plane turned over, hurdled the ditch and with a resounding noise landed upside down. Rushing over we found Beauchamp crawling out blushing guiltily. He took the blame for the crashed plane but never thought of his miraculous escape. As the Major, in charge of our group, came up I knew from Beauchamp's expression that he expected a reprimand. Saluting, he stood, red-faced, at attention.

"Congratulations on being alive," said the Major extending his hand.

.   .   .   .   .

This aerial gunnery work was interspersed with other branches of learning. Classes were devoted to the theory of shooting. On the ground we shot rifles, pistols, carbines, machine guns and shotguns. Also, swift motor boats and hydroplanes skimmed us along the lake as we potted at floating, moving, and stationary targets.

Every minute filled, the days were busy, and we returned to the barracks tired and hungry. Time for mess. We sat at a long, wooden table and enjoyed simple but well-cooked food. Several girls, from the surrounding neighborhood, were our waitresses, and they were highly amused at our clumsy French.

"Encore du eggs."

He was promptly brought some more rolls and butter.

"Voulez-vous promener avec moi?"

A slender little thing, with red hair and black eyes, smiled knowingly. *"Oui, Monsieur."* She trotted off and returning with a glass of water said, *"Voilà!"* She was learning the ways of the American aviators!

One fellow, who had hurriedly picked up a few well chosen sentences laid down his fork, and, catching at the skirt of a buxom mademoiselle, said in a loud voice, *"Voulez-vous coucher avec moi?"* A resounding whack! She had slapped him plumb in the face for what he, honestly, intended as a joke.

Dinner over we sat around sampling different liqueurs and smoking. But, the days were full, we were tired, and after the customary routine of swearing and sprinkling flea powder on our blankets, turned in.

French Aces, distinguished for shooting down five or more enemy planes at the Front, were at this field. Arrangements were made to compare our skill with theirs. Two flyers took off—a French Ace and one of our pilots. At a predetermined height they approached each other. The show was on! At close quarters each tried to get on the tail of his opponent. Rolling, zooming, diving, they tossed and tumbled but neither gained an appreciable advantage. What an exhibition! Each demonstrated great skill; each was master of his plane.

A draw seemed certain until the American succeeded in getting above and in the rear. We were wild with enthusiasm and pride, for the French Ace, unless he escaped by diving, was at the mercy of our American. He dove. The American followed. Near the ground the Frenchman pulled up and climbed. The American still followed. To higher altitudes they soared in a continued battle for supremacy. Suddenly, without warning or apparent reason the wings of the American's plane collapsed and it fell—like a stone. A deathly roar. The nose of his plane dug deep into the solid earth and the pilot was instantly killed. One more—snatched away when so near his cherished goal . . . the Front—the longed-for Front—which he now would never know.

The French Ace attended his funeral. With feeling he draped the coffin, already wrapped in the Stars and Stripes, with his own revered tri-color.

"Un de nos frères aussi," he said. *"Un brave Americain! Un brave et glorieux aviateur!"*

.   .   .   .   .

Sometimes, we had leave for a day. Or, if extremely fortunate, our commanding officer allowed us thirty-six

hours' freedom.   Keenly aware now of what might happen
in a few moments in the air, thirty-six hours seemed a long
vacation.   We anticipated a whole day, evening and the
following day, of sheer fun and laziness.

"Going to Arcachon?"

"Yep!" and I polished my boots till they shone like glass.

"Thirty-six hours?"

"Yep!" . . . and I slicked back my hair till it shone
like my boots.   Stiles was shaving.   That was a ritual.
Slowly, carefully and peering into a cracked mirror which
hung outside the barracks, he scrapes off his stubble of red
whiskers.

"What you going to do, Stiles, play Post-Office?"

"Sure, and Musical Chairs and then some," laughs Stiles
splashing his smooth young face and neck with cold water,
"and *THEN SOME . . .*"

We were ready.   Our flying caps at a rakish tilt; our
uniforms pressed and franc notes in our pockets.

"Here's the truck, come on."

"All aboard for Arcachon!"

Stiles and I, laughing, climb in.

Beautiful Arcachon snuggling tight on the shores of the
Bay of Biscay.   A former playground for the idle French,
it was now a Paradise for the American aviator.   The air
was warm and sunny.   The breeze was cool and salty.   We
went to an hotel, rented a room overlooking the beach, and
laughed at each other as we preened ourselves before the
mirror before we started out for our destination, a café.

A few drinks.   We decided to have a swim.   In rented,
gaudy bathing suits we sprawled on the sand and swam
through the waters of the cool, green surf.

"This is the life!" we laughed and swam.

"Yes siree! This is the life," we repeated nonsensically,
but somehow it fell a bit flat.

For, although our leave had just begun, we could almost hear a clock tick-tick-ticking away the precious hours. We were alive and free as meadow-larks but, seriously mindful of what the next day at the flying field might bring, we wanted to be *terribly* alive. We did not want to rest for a moment. We wanted to hurry, to DO something, to crowd and jam every hour with activity and snatch at every crumb of silly pleasure.

It is mid-afternoon. On an open verandah, back from the street, we sit at a round, small table. Three other flyers join us. We order some drinks and talk and laugh.

Two girls at a near-by table attract our attention. One, about twenty-four, is far from bashful and her glances in our direction are certainly not unfriendly. The other, much younger, appears modest and truly shy. In naive innocence she watches her companion's every flirtatious gesture with profound admiration and then, plainly blushing, she, too, smiles at the American aviators.

"Whew! what a pretty girl," says Stiles.

"I *KNOW* her," boasts one.

"The Hell you do?" we question but, to our surprise, he joins their table and, after a few teasing moments, brings them back with him.

They are sisters. Madame—for the elder one was married some six years before—is a real beauty. Her dark brown hair is wavy and moist, young curls cling to her neck. When she laughs her brown eyes sparkle jet while her white teeth seem even whiter than her dress which has little puffed sleeves and is fashioned of stuff which is sheer and yet crispy. Hatless, she carries a soft blue scarf which now she throws over her arms and then drapes around her throat in studied carelessness. The "tout ensemble" would serve as a provocative inspiration for a modern Reynolds.

"She lives in a villa high upon the hill," someone whispers.

"And where is Papa?"

We order more drinks, in which she joins us while Guerlain, the *petite soeur,* who is just sixteen, has a lemonade made with Perrier water. "She says he's in Paris. A wine merchant . . ."

"Well, he better stay home," we laughed meaningly.

The young wine-widow revels in our attentions and conversation. She is a rascal and, although evidently a person of breeding and a certain background, is having her fling, thoroughly enjoying it, and probably excusing herself to *le Bon Dieu* with the old bromide *"C'est la Guerre."*

The little innocent just watches. Her eyes like saucers stare at us with guileless wonder. She is seeing life for the first time and her cheeks burn with excitement. She sips her lemonade and, choking, gets the hiccoughs. We all howl at that; the only one not drinking to get the hiccoughs and, ordering more drinks, we invite our new friends to dine with us.

"Mais non, Messieurs. You dine with *me."*

It is settled. All come, *oui,* and bring any other aviators . . . but *only* aviators. *"Moi, j'adore les aviateurs Américains,"* and they rise to leave. Seven o'clock, then, at the villa on the hill top and the little Guerlain claps her hands for joy.

"Au revoir" until seven.

Stiles and I stroll to the hotel. Another shave for we feel untidy after the early morning's scraping. Another drink. A bath. We chatter, laugh, dust our boots, change our linen and, as the sun slips into the Bay of Biscay, start for the evening's fun.

Her villa was white. Tight to the hillside it seemed held aloft by a spacious lawn attractively planted with shrubs and flowers outlined in the moonlight. Loud talking, singing, and raucous laughter sounded its way through tightly drawn blinds as we rang the bell. The door, noisily unlocked, was held slightly open and a maid pointed to another door where we were supposed to enter.

A small, square foyer was lighted by a chandelier of glistening, pointed prisms. On either side-wall hung matching mirrors with carved gilded frames, and directly ahead an arched doorway led into the main salon. This room was filled with aviators. We did not bring along any friends but, it was plain to see, someone had and as our hostess led the way into another room I counted sixteen.

"Just look at her, Archie," said Stiles.

She was standing, at the head of a long table, seating her guests. Her hair seemed raven black in the candle lighted *"salle-à-manger"* and her sleeveless dress, the color of a ripe peach, was cut so low that the neckline divided her high breasts. Encircling her throat was a diamond dog collar and she wore several diamond bracelets.

We are all seated. Two maids struggle in with a huge basket piled high with bottles of champagne and place it on the floor beside our hostess.

"You!" pointing to one of the guests, *"venez ici près de moi."*

He, lucky dog, is to sit by her and open the champagne. We give him three lusty cheers. Guerlain, sitting quietly beside her sister, is entranced and after childishly answering, *"Oui, oui, Monsieur"* to every comment, swiftly looks at her sister who nods approval.

The dinner is delicious. Champagne with the soup, champagne with the dinner and champagne with the fruit. Between rounds we sing and give toasts and the glasses seem bottomless for I drink and drink, yet my goblet is always full of fresh bubbles.

After dinner we wander around. The rooms are full of flowers and the furniture and draperies are in perfect taste. Upstairs or downstairs the place is ours. We peek into her bedroom. A large double bed, with deep turned-down sheets, is made up for the night and a flimsy flesh nightgown with green satin slippers is arrayed on a chair near by.

"Hot Po-ta-to!" says a thick-tongued individual.

Below the champagne still flows freely and we are certain now that her husband is a wine merchant. I feel dizzy and cannot find Stiles. Upstairs again and I lean against a bathroom door.

"Stiles! you in there?"

"Yep." He opens the door.

We grin at each other and, almost simultaneously, bend over the basin. It is four o'clock and we decide to leave. We will just slip out, we plan, not spoil the party. Tiptoeing down the stairs, a bit befuddled, we try a door. Locked. We try another but it is also locked tight. What the devil . . . Where the Hell . . .

Madame, with the flyer she honored at dinner is in a far corner of the room. Together—close together on a divan they are whispering while his hand slips far down her bare back.

Stiles and I weave over to say good-night.

"*Chéri* . . . *restez vous avec moi?*" she is purring.

Then, seeing us approach, she sparkles again, jumps up and with one arm around my neck and the other around Stiles' leads us to the piano and cries, "*Chantons!*"

We try to sing. To the seedy accompaniment of weary, uncertain fingers we yowl "Tipperary." One artistic fellow feels he must render "Roses of Picardy" and, yawning, we squat on the floor while his champagne baritone struggles over "Col-in-nette with the see-a blue eyes." Others, in from the dining-room, stagger around with champagne glasses dripping on the carpet and, all together now, we chorus a sour "Sweet Adeline."

Stiles and I mutter something about leaving.

"Mais non," she informs us firmly. *"Partir? Non, non."* No one ever leaves before five. So . . . that is why the doors are locked tight. She rejoins her *Chéri* on the couch and we loll about. Five o'clock. She unlocks the door. With gracious good-nights, and thanks, and many *au revoirs* and a great deal of bowing and saluting we make a stupid get-away.

Her *Chéri,* however, makes no pretense of going. We leave them, arm in arm, smiling in the doorway.

"Hot Potato!"

Will he show up at the flying field on time, we wonder, and straggle down the hillside. The morning air is cool and birds are chirping but we are sodden and need sleep.

Better not undress and really turn in, we argue, thickly. Might not get back in time for flying. A cold bath, a shave and a good long walk will brace us up.

We stride along the beach. The sun is well up and streaks of copper-yellow stripe the green water. Refreshed a bit, we quicken our pace and decide to hike through a near-by forest. Deep, deep breaths of salt air blended with the smell of pine trees and we decide that food will do the trick. Better get some breakfast. It is nearly nine o'clock and, starting back to the village, we see a hump of brown lying beside the entrance of a blue villa.

Something glistens in the sun.

"Well . . . I'll be damned!"

There, sound asleep, is *Chéri,* with *Madame's* diamond collar tight around his neck.

We shake him. He is quite drunk. We yank him up. We must get him in shape for the afternoon flying. Some one volunteers to return the necklace and, after some coffee,

a cold tubbing, and more coffee he is almost ready to return
to the barracks.

"Some party!"

Chéri is quiet. He does not look us in the eye.

"Hot Potato!"

"Oh, dry up . . ."

We are ready to go back. Flying was in our veins. Flying was our job. Flying was happiness and all else was a
maudlin existence.

· · · · ·

The end of May.

We were frothing to get to the Front. Not because of
war . . . not because it meant the gruesome thing of killing . . . not because of any heroism but because the Front
meant a culmination of our flying lives and progression to
our goal. It was the ideal, the purpose, the thing for which
we had worked and lived. Restless, ready, eager to fly to
the end of the trail; the trail which led to the greatest thing
in our lives.

We qualified at Cazeaux and on June 7th reported back
to Issoudun for orders. Strolling around grounds left but
a month before, everything was different for Issoudun had
become a veritable city. New barracks, additional hangars,
dry gravel roads in place of the old mud holes, showers,
mess halls, electric lights, Red Cross canteens, Y.M.C.A.
recreation huts and countless conveniences had been installed. The men were living in comfort, a sharp contrast
to the life we had known, and Field Nine, with long rows
of white crosses, was a well cared for cemetery.

"Not much like the old place is it?—feel like a stranger."

"Issoudun, *our* Issoudun, is gone forever."

"See the cemetery? Beautiful. Glad it's fixed up . . .
nicer place."

"Yes, so many new ones there, too."

An orderly appeared in the doorway with papers in his hand. Tense, we listened as he read.

"The following men will report to Headquarters at once: Oliver T. Beauchamp; Robert H. Stiles; Norman S. Archibald . . ."

Two more names completed a list of five. Why only five names? What did this mean?

We reported.

The Major, a recent arrival at Issoudun, greeted us, *too* cordially.

"Something queer up this bird's sleeve," whispered Beauchamp.

The officer cleared his throat and with a broad smile began.

"Well, gentlemen, you have made a splendid record. You have proved it possible to train on Nieuports. You are excellent pilots; better, I believe, than had you trained in the customary way."

We knew there was a reason behind all this and tried to interpret his flattering remarks.

"I know you are anxious to get to the Front."

Interrupting, we all talked at once and assured him it was our fondest hope. Impatiently, he continued.

"Owing to lack of fighting planes there is absolutely no chance to go to the Front for at least three months."

Without comment we listened to this disheartening remark.

"For this reason, and because of your exceptional record, we want you for instructors here at Issoudun."

Another smile. He paused . . . waiting for some response.

No one spoke. Crestfallen we looked at each other in amazement. Our feelings of discouragement, dislike and rebellion must have showed plainly for, sensing we would not commit ourselves, he asked each one separately to volunteer as an instructor. Each one flatly refused. Each answer was "No"—decidedly *"No."*

"Well, gentlemen,"—his manner now authoritative and domineering—"if you do not consent of your own accord an order will be issued commanding your services. That is all!"

We walked from the room.

"The old gooseberry," said Beauchamp. "Is he running the American Air Service?"

We knew that the Air Service was voluntary from start to finish. If a pilot were not feeling up to it, not in the mood, or did not think a plane was in proper condition he could refuse to fly. But, we were uncertain as to a code for instructors.

"That's the last straw!" Stiles' face was red with anger and the veins stood out on his temples.

This was a calamity. To be kept as instructors! My stomach felt hollow. Talk about an unexpected blow. They could command our services, too. And heretofore we had been so certain, so unquestionably certain, that once through training we would go directly to the Front. Finished aviators! And now, after all that grind, to be kept as instructors. My lips felt dry. Finished aviators, blah! We were slapped in the face. We were caught in a trap. Damn him . . . damn him . . . damn him . . . I felt my nails dig into my palms.

"Well, what can we do about it?"

"Why, hang the old buzzard by his necktie!" Beauchamp wiped the sweat from his forehead.

"Oh, don't talk nonsense."

"Well, believe me, I'm not going to sit around Issoudun and show some kids, still in their diapers, how to fly."

Depressed, but fighting mad, we discussed it from every angle and tried to scheme for a way out of this terrible situation. Here, after six months of intensive training for the Front, to be anchored as instructors. What should we do? What could we do? We hated Issoudun!

Still in debate we walked to the little town of Vatan, about eight miles away, entered a café and ordered wine.

"Well, here's to the Major!"

"Damn his soul!"

We were in a terrible predicament.

"Let's just refuse."

"Yes, all of us, absolutely refuse."

But, if we refused to be instructors we might be kept on the ground. If we became instructors we would be held at Issoudun. Either was a crushing situation. We drank the wine and ordered more.

"Again—to the Major!"

"Again—damn his soul!"

Raging, but helpless, we were sick with disappointment. Our high hopes for which we had worked so faithfully and successfully were, in that second, all knocked into a cocked hat. All this smart-aleck chatter of ours could change nothing. So, this was flying in France! So, this was to be our fighting the Huns in the Air! What a farce! Instructing some greenhorns in the gentle art of flying. Hell and brimstone! The disappointment of it.

We dragged ourselves to our feet. Eight miles over and eight miles to walk back. We returned some time after midnight. The stove was cooling, we poked the fire and slumped into chairs. Nothing more to say. We did not want to go to bed for we dreaded the morning which might seal our doom.

The door flew open.

"There's orders for a few flyers to go to Orly and you're on them," yelled a voice.

We did not stir. We doubted the rumor. The Major's words were still too vivid but, grasping at the last thread of hope, we rushed to Headquarters.

There on the bulletin board were our names. We were to proceed the next day to American Aviation Acceptance Park No. 1, at Orly, France.

Hurrying back to the barracks we yelled the good news. Everyone asleep or awake joined in. At dawn we crawled into bed and when I was half-dreaming Beauchamp's voice yelled out—"That damned old Major!"

All was quiet.

"Archie! Are you awake?"

"Yes."

"Well, I *said—That damned old Major* . . . trying to fool us into instructing. Good-night."

"Good-night, Beauchamp."

The sun shone bright the next morning. Beauchamp chuckled as he packed. We rushed about locating the others included in the list and went to the headquarters building for final orders.

Quentin Roosevelt, happy and smiling, stood on the steps.

He not only was on the list but, as officer in charge of this lucky little group of twelve flyers, held our orders in his hand.

We left Issoudun by noon, reached Paris late in the afternoon and went in trucks to Orly.

CHAPTER VII

ORLY was an ideal aerodrome.

There were hangars at one end, barracks and mess halls along the side, and in the headquarters building was a room furnished by the Red Cross, cheerful with chintz, easy chairs, magazines and a piano.

We had observation, combat, training ships of different makes and sizes: Spads, Nieuports and single-seated Sopwith Camels, the English combat plane. Planes delivered to the American Government from France, England and other countries were officially tested and accepted here. Pursuit pilots were sent from this Park to fighting squadrons at the Front.

We reported to the officer in charge.

"What are you cadets doing here?" he demanded roughly. "Only officers fly at Orly."

"We trained on Nieuports, sir."

That was sufficient. Wherever we went we were known as the "Crowd who trained on Nieuports."

"Oh! I know all about you boys," he complimented us highly, "but you cannot go to the Front until you have your commissions. I'll get them for you as soon as possible. Just hang around and kill time until they arrive or, if you wish, you may ferry some ships."

Here we were at Orly, eager for action, ready, successful, but ahead of the Army's routine. We must wait until the regulation red tape unwound enough to catch us in its network.

Was this road to the Front endless? Could we, as commissioned officers, with Sam Browne belts, fight better? Would we, with silver bars on our shoulders, fly better?

.   .   .   .   .

Bill Russel was here.

Awaiting orders for the Front he bought a large police dog which he continually trained and proudly paraded along the Champs Élysées.

"Why the dog, Bill?"

"Well . . . no one would look at me in Paris," he joked, "so I got this hound. And—how they stare! Oh! that *lovely dog! 'Regardez ce beau chien avec l'aviateur!'* "

.   .   .   .   .

No routine of flying duties but we ferried planes to different aviation centers in France. We would leave Orly at noon, fly to Issoudun, deliver the plane and return by rail that evening. Trained on Nieuports we were trusted with all makes. The large, slow planes bored us, but we saw new country and were "in the air."

A Sopwith Camel arrived in Orly. About the size of a Nieuport, it differed greatly in design, for an extremely short fuselage brought the elevator control within a few feet of the trailing edge of the wings. This caused a quick response to the slightest movement of the controls and because of a tendency to buck like a broncho, if flown by anyone not familiar with its peculiarities, it was known as the "Hump."

Eager to try this tricky machine my request to deliver it at Issoudun was promptly granted and I took off. The

"Hump," like a sensitive galloping goose leaped, jumped and cavorted, so climbing to ten thousand feet for safe altitude and plenty of room, I dove, rolled, zoomed and purposely let it "hump" until we understood each other.

Two hours later, proud of the machine and my ability to make it behave, I decided to "show off" over my old training field and did all the stunts, acrobatics or flying tricks possible before landing. Pilots and mechanics, much to my delight, surrounded the first Sopwith Camel ever seen at Issoudun.

An improved type of Nieuport was delivered to Orly and all were anxious to fly the new plane. Swift and easy to handle, it climbed quickly. Sturdy qualities, however, had been sacrificed to make it light and agile. A pilot took off, circled the field, flew away and returned at low altitude near the aerodrome and over a wheat field. A terrific, unfamiliar noise! The loosened motor, ripping through the aluminum cowl, scattered in every direction. With difficulty he guided the light-nosed, motorless plane and, forced to glide into the tall wheat, flopped over and crashed.

The pilot, his face streaming blood, crawled out.

"I'm through flying until after the harvest," was his only comment.

He blamed the wheat, never referring to the disastrous mishap which almost proved fatal.

We flew French Sopwiths to England and returned with Sopwith Camels. The course usually flown, was from Paris along the Seine (for forty or fifty miles) then north to Marquis, where the plane was refueled for the flight across the Channel.

Amiens, seventy miles north of Paris, was at this time the furthest western point of the Front. Obviously it was imperative to keep well to the west. A pilot left Orly for England. A light rain made it difficult, in the mist, to check his location by landmarks. As Marquis was about one hundred and forty air miles due north he chose the shorter route and skirted the lines. Clouds, drifting in from the English Channel, completely shut off his view of the earth. Doubtful of his whereabouts he dove down to check his location. Emerging, the air was instantly filled with bursting shells. He had unknowingly drifted across the lines and was a perfect target for the anti-aircraft.

Bewildered, surprised and in the center of a heavy barrage, he must do something, and do it quickly. His one thought was to get down. Flopping and floundering in excitement, he landed and jumped from his plane. Machine gun bullets whizzed past and spattered on the ground. Grenades burst in the air. Confused, with no idea which were the French trenches and which the German, he crawled under his ship. Peeking from the shelter of a wing he saw a French soldier beckoning. Through a raining torrent of bullets he ran and, headlong, fell into the friendly trench —safe. His plane, the next second, was blown to atoms.

"For the first time in my life, I knew why Frenchmen kiss each other," he said when relating his experience. "I sure felt like kissing that Frenchman."

.   .   .   .   .

A friend, in the British Air Force, was stationed at a field in England where planes from Orly were delivered, and hoping to see him I asked permission to ferry one over.

That morning a British aviator arrived. He was returning to Marquis, was familiar with the route, and to eliminate the bother of flying by map I arranged to follow him. As we circled over Paris he headed due north. Remembering the latest episode I let him go, watched his plane disappear, then steered a lone course further west along the Seine.

High above Rouen my motor suddenly stopped. Attempts to start it proved futile. There was no choice but to land, so gliding down in a wide circle I saw only one possible spot, a wheat field flanked by tall poplars.

To land in tall grain one must level out above it and "pancake" after all speed is lost. If one glides into grain it wraps around the landing gear and turns the plane over on its nose. Near the ground I turned, headed into the wind and was gliding towards the field when telephone poles, with masses of wires stretching between, came into view. Below their level and remembering my experience with wires, I pulled up and soared over them. With a dead motor my speed was barely enough to clear the wires. To avoid falling the plane must dive quickly and gain momentum so—I dove. The increased speed changed my previous calculation and skimming over the wheat tops at a rate rapid enough to crash into the poplars ahead I could never "pancake" now. To crash into the poplars or glide into the wheat? The wheat was best and, as expected, the landing gear caught, the plane nosed over and settled on its back.

Nearby was an English Aircraft Supply Depot. I wired my Commandant. While awaiting further instructions I spent four days with some of the most charming English gentlemen it has ever been my privilege to meet.

.   .   .   .   .

At Orly again Beauchamp, resplendent in a new uniform, greeted me.

"Hurry up, Archie. Get your uniform. I am Lieutenant Oliver T. Beauchamp, and cannot be seen talking with a cadet," he grinned in his inimitable fashion.

A Sam Browne belt encircled his slender waist; bars
of a first lieutenant gleamed on his shoulders and a trim
little flying cap perched snugly on the side of his head.
So! our commissions had arrived.

Officers now. A matter of days before the great adventure. Prepared for the Front, even dressed for battle.
We talked Front, lived Front, dreamt Front, and, to while
away the snail-like hours, Beauchamp and I went to Paris.
Soldiers saluted us as we passed. The cadet days were
gone. As officers we carried a burden; as lieutenants we
realized we would soon be in a fighting squadron.

.   .   .   .   .

June in Paris.

Warm, sunny days, clear, moonlit nights, nature, in innocence, showering her gifts, ignorant that man had decided
to have a war. Paris, knowing her allure, masquerades as a
city of pleasure. A playground for the restless, diversion
for the weary, an intoxicant for the broken-hearted.

Cafés are crowded. Theatres are jammed. Girls, tempting with joy and amusement, swarm everywhere. A frivo-
lous whirligig of life—good, bad, gay, sad—the explanation
is ever the same: *"C'est la guerre."*

War!

Sipping old white port on the sidewalks of the Café de la
Paix—it is a distant dream.

War!

Wounded soldiers pass, the blind—it is a grim reality.

War!

Air raids, at night, prove it all too near this mock scene
of pleasure.

A moon and glistening stars are dreaded. The clear sky
is a perfect setting for the Gothas which quickly, and with
little warning, come to destroy.

Ten o'clock—Paris is playing.

"Let's go to the Folies Bergère."

We watch the show.

A girl in red, with thin, young legs and pointed breasts, dances, not too graceful but, wanting to applaud, we applaud—loudly.

A "funny man," with a huge cigar in his mouth, grotesquely rides a bicycle, not too funny but, wanting to laugh, we laugh—uproariously.

"*Alerte!*" a man calls from the foyer.

Instantly, the stage curtain is lowered. The audience leaves the theatre, files into the street, orderly but talking rapidly.

"*Les Boches viennent.*"

The ever watchful listening-posts outside the city have reported enemy planes passing over and headed for Paris.

"*Les Boches viennent.*"

In a few minutes the avenues are deserted. Everyone, except ourselves, has sought refuge in subways, *abris* or other bomb-proof places. We do not take the raid seriously, want to see the spectacle, and look for a taxi.

Empty, they stand in empty streets—their drivers, too, have fled into the cellars.

We start walking.

Except for an occasional beam of dull light from a lamp-post covered with blue glass, the streets are black. Quiet . . . dark . . . deserted. Paris is a ghostlike city of ghostlike shadows. We walk alone in a depopulated world.

A roar. Defense guns belch. Muffled sounds of shells exploding high in the air. The sky is alive with twinkling flashes of light. The thunderous barrage over the city is deafening. Hundreds of anti-aircraft fill the sky with more exploding shells. Shrapnel, in a shower of steel fragments, rains upon the streets and sidewalks. A distant flash of light is followed by the stunning noise of a terrific explosion.

BANG! CRASH! The Gothas are dropping their bombs.

BANG! CRASH! Another . . . then another, long, slender and feathered, hits the earth.

The Gothas, unloading their cargo of destruction, are still on the outskirts of the city and dare not enter the sea of protecting shells. The barrage is successful. No more bombs. The Gothas have passed.

"My God!" ejaculates Beauchamp, "are they through or are they coming back?"

"*Voulez-vous promener avec moi?*" Stiles takes his arm.

The boisterous defense bombardment of the heavens ceases. Searchlights are turned off. The silence, after the terrible din of guns, is more deathlike than ever.

Clump, clump, clump, we three walk down the avenue. Clump, clump, clump, our steps resound on the bare pavement and Beauchamp sings:

> *"Three musketeers in iron boots*
> *Guarded old Paris town.*
> *The shrapnel fell; so they did too*
> *And painted the city brown."*

The eerie far away note of a siren. The listening posts report the Gothas' return to "Das Vaterland." A fire truck, with siren screeching, races through the streets. Paris knows the raid is over. People bob from every nook and corner. Lights glow. Cafés and theatres reopen their doors and patrons return. The raid is over, the heart of Paris beats again.

The humdrum life at Orly was fraying on our nerves. No longer contented on the ground we flew whenever possible.　Two two-seated Salmson observation planes were destined for a squadron near Château Thierry.　Although large and slow they presented a way of seeing an aerodrome at the Front.　Leaving Orly at three o'clock the other pilot and I arrived, thirty minutes later, at our destination.　A few hangars and some observation planes were of no interest so we were ready to return.

Arrangements had been made for an automobile to take us back to Orly but it was not to be found.　Compelled to spend the night, motor-cycles whisked us to a small French settlement a few miles distant.　We found a place to sleep and walked around the village, a pathetic drab little place with the stillness of a tomb.

"Nothing doing here," said my companion.　"Let's have a nap before dinner."

We returned to our room and flopped on a large feather-bed.　It was ten o'clock before we awoke and still tired but ravenously hungry we went out in search of food.　The absence of light made it difficult to find our way.　Drugged with untimely sleep we stumbled over the cobblestones but could not find a café.　Every house and building was tightly shut.　Finally a window, through which we could distinguish several tables, attracted our attention.　The door was open.　We walked in, groped our way to a table and sat down.

"*Madame!*" we call.

Not a response or even a footstep breaks the black silence.

"*Madame!*"

We light matches.　A table, covered with a checkered red and white table cloth is set with cracked, spotlessly clean dishes.　More matches reveal the life-size portrait of a young man.　His yellow hair is slick.　His cheeks are rosy pink and his lips vermilion. His uniform, of horizon blue, is giddy with medals and their attached ribbons.

It is a devilish Chromo.

We look at him.

Calmly, he gazes back at us.

The unskilled daubs of color melt into the canvas. A pale oval face with firm features speaks of bravery—one medal is the *Croix de Guerre*. His eyes, wide apart, are cool and clean with outstanding courage—another medal is the *Médaille Militaire*.

Mute, we stare at the picture.

It is a god-like masterpiece.

"Dead?"

"Suppose so—"

A sound. The bent figure of an old woman crooks in the doorway. She carries a small kerosene lamp, the wick so low that it might be a firefly in a bottle. Without a word she places it on our table. Her face is lined, the muscles hang with sorrow as well as time, she stands by us, phantom-like, dumb, the personification of pent-up misery.

"*Avez-vous quelque chose à manger?*" we inquire.

Her keen blue eyes look through us but she utters not a word. Further attempts at conversation are useless so we boldly suggest meat, eggs and hot chocolate. She turns away without a single response and hobbles through a doorway which leads into an open court.

A bright moon fleetly sifts through the sky. Other doorways, from different parts of this rambling old house, all leading into the same court, are seen. The moon hides and our voices so resound in the uncanny stillness that conversation seems a sacrilege.

We light cigarettes . . . and wait.

Madame returns and after placing jam, bread and two bottles of wine on the table, goes out.

We turn up the lamp wick.

She appears again, glares at us, turns down the wick, grunts her disapproval and is gone.

Are we too extravagant with the kerosene? Is she annoyed with our presence? Does she live in this house of despondency and gloom alone, or, perhaps, with the ghost of a dead son?

In almost total darkness we eat the bread and drink the wine.

WHAM! A bomb explodes in the distance.

BANG! Another, closer this time and the whirr of aeroplanes overhead.

Machine guns, accompanied by the tremendous noise of exploding bombs, rattle. Two more bombs, in rapid succession, explode with their bursting missiles uncomfortably close. A second later the aeroplane that dropped them zipps over. Above the roar of the plane's motor is the constant firing of machine guns defending the town. We expect more bombs but not knowing where to seek protection do not move.

"Might as well die eating as any other way," scoffs my companion.

We spread jam, in thick, dark patterns, on our bread.

WHIZ . . . ZZ . . . ZZZ . . . BANG!

An explosion shakes the house. Chairs topple over. The painting of the soldier rattles against the wall. It sounds and feels as if the bomb struck into the very center of the room. We jump up, run to the door, into the courtyard and look for shelter.

Where is Madame? Where can we go? Standing in the court we scan the sky for enemy planes.

BANG! . . . more bombs . . . but further away. The rat-tat-tat of machine guns sputters and stops.

Quiet—the dreadful, ominous silence.

We walk around the courtyard. Where has Madame hidden herself?

We must pay before we leave. A cellar door, almost at our feet, opens. Six or seven frightened people, by the faint light of a shadowed moon, hesitantly and with caution, crawl out of an under-ground retreat.

Why had we not been warned of this expected air raid when our lamp was extinguished? Why were we not invited to join them in their cave of safety? No one spoke a word of caution to us then. No one speaks to us now. Perhaps, seeing the wings of aviators on our uniforms they feel we should be in the air flying protection above instead of eating their bread and jam.

Our supper, half-eaten, waits on the table but our appetites are not as keen. Also, we are plainly not wanted in this house of gloom. We pay the Madame who, counting, nods her approval of the number of francs, and grope our way to the black streets.

Wide awake, refreshed by our nap and disturbed by the thought of another raid, we toss and turn on our feather-bed.

Morning.

Strolling through the square of the town we hail a passing truck.

"Where are you going?" we call to the driver.

"Paris," he yells.

Running, we jump aboard and, amid cased goods, bump over a rough road to the city.

Bastille day.

The 14th of July. Paris is celebrating.

We stand in the *Place de la Concorde*. It swarms with

people waiting for the parade in commemoration of their national holiday. The Champs Élysées, spotless and clear of all traffic, runs like a ribbon of pavement fringed with masses of humanity to the Arc de Triomphe. Soldiers are passing through the arched center of that majestic sentinel of triumph. Slowly, the line of marching men moves in simple splendor, reaches the *Place,* swings in a semi-circle and marches on.

With colors flying at the head of their respective columns, the uniforms of France, England, Australia, Italy, Belgium, Canada and the United States pass by. Infantry, Cavalry and Artillery troops are in full war regalia, as if marching into battle.

The rhythmic sound of clocklike steps; the beat of horses' hoofs; the singing, grinding noise of gun carriages rolling on the pavement are the only sounds.

The people are silent.

This is a parade of serious minded men. Their faces show determination, strength and courage. The countless masses gaze with admiration and respect but no outward signs of enthusiasm. They, too, are serious minded. All troops of all nations are veterans of battles for hotly contested territory. The American section includes hard visaged veterans of Cantigny, Bois de Belleau and Château Thierry. Troops who have met the Prussian guard and vanquished them. Young Americans who have saved and are saving this very city from the Invaders.

Boys of all nations. Haggard, tired, aged before their time, they look straight ahead with eyes that have seen too much. Marching monuments of unconquerable will, human pillars of indomitable courage—a breath-taking, inspiring and victoriously sad processional.

On . . . on . . . on . . . the line of march filters through the city.

No one calls "Hurrah!" No one shouts. No one cheers. They stand—in silence. They stand—in simple reverence. They stand—without a word to signify love of country, until the last moving column has passed. Then, without demonstration or loud talking, they disperse.

Patriotism is lived, not cried out.

About six o'clock the next morning, July 15th, startled by the violent noise of an explosion, we jump from our beds, throw on our clothes and run out to unravel the mystery of this sudden blast. A shell from a Big Bertha has landed in Paris. The Germans have started a drive on the Marne River. Yesterday we saw the faces of men who had known battle. The night before we were in a terrific air raid. Today Big Berthas are shelling Paris.

War . . . war . . . war . . . we are in it.

CHAPTER VIII

"Archie! Hurry!" Beauchamp, stuffing his clothes into bags and with his bedding roll already in a neat bundle on the floor, greeted me, on my return to Orly. "Pack your things! We're going to the Front!"

"Are you sure?" I questioned.

"Sure! Positive! Hurry up, I'll help you."

Dame Rumor had been so active that I rushed to headquarters. There on the bulletin board in bold, black letters:

BEAUCHAMP and ARCHIBALD—to report immediately to the First Pursuit Group.

It was true! God! How wonderful! Hilarious with joy I ran back and started to pack.

"Hurry!" said Beauchamp, "hurry! Let's get out of here."

Throwing my things together he fretted at a moment's delay.

"That's all right—here, I'll arrange that—come on!— fix it in Paris."

My excited fingers, trying to tie my bedding roll and jam personal belongings into a full bag, fumbled. Beauchamp laughed, talked rapidly, stuffed my extra things into his pockets and, inside of fifteen minutes, we left Orly.

That afternoon, at a hotel in Paris, we carefully read our orders.

"Imagine! The First Pursuit Group."

"Why, it's the most talked-of fighting group at the Front!"

Nothing was lacking now. Our joy was overspilling. Talk about luck! This group contained some of the veteran airmen of the war. Two, known to us by reputation were Raoul Lufbery and David McK. Peterson, both former members of the immortal Escadrille Lafayette.

Lufbery was dead. With eighteen victories to his credit this American Ace of Aces attempted on May 19th his nineteenth victory over the Toul sector. A few moments later his plane fell in flames. At one thousand feet he jumped into the air apparently hoping to land in the river below, but his body struck the earth.

Peterson, already an Ace, now commanded the 95th squadron.

We—members of this famous fighting group!

Paris that night was not the same. Nothing amused or held our attention; everything was drab, useless and unimportant. We sat in our room talking, talking, talking. Happy, proud, ambitious, we talked all night and in the morning boarded a train for Coulommiers.

With plenty of room and many seats unoccupied the trip was a contrast to previous ones in France. Two other men, also ordered to the First Pursuit Group, were aboard— Grandville Woodard and Frank Luke. We four sat together. Four men in the same uniforms, four men with the same goal, four men with the same thoughts . . . the First Pursuit Group . . . *Chasse* pilots . . . The Front!

The slow train stopped frequently. Every five minutes of waiting was unbearably long. About four-thirty in the afternoon we jerked into Coulommiers, a peaceful village about thirty kilometers southwest of Château Thierry. A truck from the Group met us. Twenty minutes later we drew up before the headquarters tent and reported for duty.

An officer, seated behind a desk in the corner, looked up and, smiling, greeted us. We handed him our orders and received a questionnaire. We must fill in the blanks: our parents' names . . . home address and whom to notify in case of death . . .

Fully a dozen times had I answered these same questions, filled in these same blank spaces and it always seemed a useless, red-taped procedure. But now—WHO SHALL BE NOTIFIED IN CASE OF DEATH stood out. It was, after all, necessary and important. For the first time the question seemed sane and logical.

Quickly and with little conversation we were assigned to our squadrons. Beauchamp and Luke to the 27th; Woodard and I to the 95th.

All in the same group, the squadrons but a stone's throw from each other and yet, I wished with all my heart that Beauchamp had been assigned with me. I looked at him. He smiled, but it was not his real smile—different somehow.

The First Pursuit Group comprised four squadrons. The 95th, 94th, 27th and 147th. The 95th and 94th had been fighting on the Toul sector during the month of May and most of June. Early in June the 27th and 147th had joined them and these four had been on the Château Thierry Front about three weeks. I knew that the 94th and 95th had been equipped with new French Spads while the 27th and 147th still used the Nieuports. The Spad was considered the finest fighting plane on the Front, superior to the Nieuport in construction and performance.

To fly a Spad! Luck was surely my constant companion.

But Beauchamp—I wanted Beauchamp to have a Spad, too.

Our baggage, piled in trucks, was taken to our respective destinations. The 95th was billeted at the village of Saints, half a mile away, and the 27th an eighth of a mile further. We four started down the road inquiring for directions as we went.

"Guess we leave you here," said Woodard.

I felt as if someone had hit me. For the first time since we sailed away from the Statue of Liberty Beauchamp and I were to be separated. Not far apart to be sure but—damn it all—why couldn't we have been assigned together?

Wanting to say—something—I tried. Why didn't Beauchamp smile? He always did.

"Come on Beauchamp," said Luke.

Beauchamp looked at me, forced a grin and grasped my hand.

"Archie! Show the damned Boche! . . . you can do it. . . . and . . . come over . . . often." Then he slapped me on the back. "Good Luck—"

"Good Luck to you, Beauchamp," I managed to say. "See you soon."

．　　　．　　　．　　　．　　　．

Woodard and I, assigned to connecting rooms on the second floor of an old house, climbed its creaking, misshapen stairs. Doors were askew; the roof sagged; cement and plaster had fallen in numerous places. In one room was a marble top dresser and a feather bed piled high with softest quilts. The other room, except for a low rocking chair, was void of furniture. Who would occupy the luscious bed? We tossed a coin. Luck again! But as Woodard began to set up his folding cot I assured him of the feathered nest every other night.

On the lower floor lived the owner, a dear old lady of eighty. An accident two years before had left her badly crippled, with one arm not properly set, bent in an awkward position. Unable to go about she had not crossed her threshold since the mishap. Kindly neighbors brought warm food, gossiped and cared for her tenderly during the declining years of tedious old age. Happy and courageous, but with trembling lips, she told in vivid terms of 1914. Germans had occupied this village and Prussian officers, living in this very house, had forced her to prepare their meals and obey their commands. Her eyes sparkled as she thanked the *"Bon Dieu"* for the young Americans who now shared her home.

Another house, further along the road, was the mess hall for the 95th. We went up, met Captain Peterson, our squadron commander, and were introduced to the other pilots.

During dinner the light-hearted, gay conversation of plans for the evening—a bridge game the previous night, trips to Paris, surprised us. We knew of the victories won and of the pilots lost, but not a word was spoken of flying nor of war.

．　　　．　　　．　　　．　　　．

The next morning, at seven-thirty, we arrived for breakfast. The cook, a French woman, told us the others had left for the aerodrome. Hurriedly eating we started along a winding road to the 95th hangar, less than half a mile away.

It was a warm, sunny day.

Five beautiful little Spads, with motors humming restlessly, were lined up. A few pilots put on light cotton coveralls to protect their uniforms from oil and dirt while others added only helmet, goggles and gloves. They were ready to start.

"My motor is not turning up well. Climb slowly, will you, so that I can keep in formation and give it a chance to warm up," said a pilot.

"If you're having trouble don't come at all," answered the leader plainly provoked.

Excuses were not tolerated in the 95th. If a pilot felt his plane was not in perfect condition he should not fly. Or if for any reason he was not inclined to fly, he need not. It was final. No explanations were needed nor wanted.

For a final test the pilots pulled the throttles of the motors wide open. The planes, held by blocks under both wheels and with mechanics holding each wing, quivered with restrained power. The leader signaled, his mechanics removed the blocks, and he was off.

Five Spads, one after the other, rose gracefully into the air, roared and were lost in sunshine. Away for the day's work. Away to the front lines. The pull, the longing to be with them!

As new arrivals no one paid much attention to Woodard and me. Walking towards the operations tent we saw Captain Peterson and Bill Russel sitting on a bench. We saluted. Captain Peterson quickly informed us that no saluting was done by officers here. However, we all so loved and respected him that we saluted, always.

Bill Russel and Quentin Roosevelt had been assigned to the 95th.

"Where is Roosevelt?" we asked.

"He's been missing since July 14th," said Bill quietly.

What! Quentin gone? So soon! Why, it seemed but yesterday he stood, thrilled and happy, holding our orders. They tried to keep him at Issoudun as an instructor, but he insisted on the Front—nothing less. The Front! Well, he got here . . . but, how quickly—how terribly quickly it had claimed him. At Orly, the last time I saw him,

Hamilton Coolidge and he were on a motorcycle. Quentin, in yellow, cotton coveralls, his tawny hair flying in the wind, steered through the gate and streaked it for Paris.

Replacements! How exuberant we had been when sent here as replacements! Now—how plain, how ugly the word! So—men must die that other men may fly. Replacements—yes, we stepped into dead men's boots.

Inside the operations tent, bulletins posted on a board told many interesting things. There was a list of German aviators, the color of their planes, the number of victories to their credit and their method of fighting. It told if the Hun were reckless or cautious, aggressive or defensive and whether he fought alone or with protection. The characteristics and attack methods of several German Aces were described. How was all this detailed information received? How could they know that a certain man flew a certain plane? We never asked questions but we realized the importance of each scrap of information.

The aerodrome was approximately square. Two sides were flanked by majestic poplars. A road bounded the third side and on the fourth an open field, studded with barbed wire entanglement, was a reminder of early war days. Looking across the field we faced the hangars of the 27th and 147th squadrons and to the left was the 94th.

Waiting for the patrol to return I examined the Spads. Strong and sturdy, they were equipped with 220-horse-power Hispano-Suiza motors. The exhaust pipe extended along the side of the plane with the opening just back of the cockpit. Two Vickers machine guns, mounted side by side and resting on the motor, were synchronized to shoot between the blades of the propeller. A wire from each gun, running through a flexible tube, was attached to two triggers on the control stick, which enabled the pilot to shoot either gun separately or both at once. In a white circle, painted on the side of the fuselage, was a kicking mule, the insignia of the 95th, "The Kicking Mule Squadron." A small live donkey, the squadron's mascot, was tied to a post outside of the hangar.

The hum of a motor. A plane appeared in the distance, circled, landed and two mechanics steadied it up to the hangar. One of the pilots back from the Front! Did they have a fight? What would he have to say? Tense and eager for the least bit of information from a flyer who returned, after two hours at the real battle line, I watched him.

Nonchalantly he crawled out, took off his goggles and with placid unconcern walked towards the operations tent. Where were the others? Another plane lands. Why did they not return in formation? Another, then finally a fourth and fifth with each pilot as complacent as if he were returning from a tea party.

With avid interest I read the leader's report. They crossed the lines at fifteen thousand feet, received heavy anti-aircraft and, while patrolling, sighted a formation of seven enemy planes further back in Germany. Without further events, they continued the patrol and were about to return when they saw seven Fokkers, above them, approaching. The enemy dove for an attack and, when still some distance away, fired. The Spads broke formation just as the Fokkers turned and headed back. The patrol finished, they came home, receiving heavy anti-aircraft again when crossing the lines.

Judging from the pilots' attitudes this forced breaking of formation, being attacked by Fokkers and receiving heavy anti-aircraft was an ordinary, unimportant occurrence. How envious I was to go on a patrol! The next day they took off, returned and the report told of a real battle. When over the lines they encountered a formation of German planes, all Fokkers. A combat followed. No victories were claimed and none of our men were missing, but holes in the wings of the Spads were evidence of enemy bullets. Heavy anti-aircraft was again mentioned but the entire report was short and simple. A real skirmish, but no intimate details, and my desire to get over the lines was so strong that to wait another day was anguish. However, as the squadron had no additional planes, Woodard and I must wait.

CHAPTER IX

THE morning of the third day a brand new Spad arrived.

What a beauty it was! How the wings of doped fabric glistened as it rested in splendor on the sunlit field. Two mechanics, assigned to keep it in condition, were all admiration. Gently, I touched the wings and peeked into the cockpit.

"That's your plane, Archibald," said a voice behind me.

Whirling around I faced Captain Peterson, but before I could express my delight he walked away.

Mine! This little, new, glorious Spad was mine! Happier than a child with a Christmas toy I stood, close, beside my new possession. Heinricks, an old member of the 95th, came over.

"Captain Peterson asked me to take you to the balloon line and show you the Front. Want to go now?"

"Now?" I repeated. "Now? Right now? Great!"

Heinricks laughed at my enthusiasm.

"Meet me at five hundred feet over the field," he said.

"May I go along?" asked Gill, another pilot.

"Certainly, come along," said Heinricks.

Hurriedly borrowing a helmet and a pair of goggles I ran to my plane, climbed in and settled into the cockpit. How comfortable it was! I moved the stick. The control

wires were tight. The elevator, ailerons and rudder answered to the slightest touch. Everything was in perfect
order so I motioned to the mechanic to start the motor.

"*Coupez*," he called.

"*Coupez*," I answered, holding the ignition switch in
the off position.

Four times he turned the propeller and then stood free
of the blade.

"*Contact*," he yelled.

"*Contact*," I yelled back and switched on the ignition.

With a swift downward stroke he swung the propeller.
The motor started. Adjusting the *manettes* I listened to
the rhythmic whirr of this perfectly running motor with the
rapt attention of a musician listening to a symphony. I
fastened the safety belts and, securely tied in the cockpit,
thoroughly tested the motor, then motioned the mechanic
to remove the blocks.

Ready to go!

I taxied out, turned into the wind, opened the motor,
pushed on the stick and sped across the field. This Spad,
heavier than a Nieuport, required a longer distance to take
off, but it rose without a flutter, climbed quickly and was
more stable.

Circling the field my thoughts tumbled from happiness.
I am really in a Spad! It is mine! We are going to the
lines! A fighting pilot of the First Pursuit Group! Here
at last . . . in a Spad . . . a member of the 95th. Adventure—combats—the Front—everything—Death, perhaps—what matter? Here I am . . . here I am! At last.

A fighting institution was here to do its part in the
war. The soft wind seemed to know, to respect the ground
over which it blew. The direction of the Front! Calling
. . . with hidden things which beckoned me on. Soon I
would know.

A few hangars and tents dotted the field in a new scene. Fresh sensations. The very air was different . . . quiet . . . still . . . yet it demanded action.

Heinricks and Gill in two Spads took off, reached my altitude and Heinricks headed for the lines. Pulling up behind and above him on the left, Gill in the same position on the right, we climbed to nine thousand feet. I watched the surrounding country.

Small wooded areas; a little lake; rolling land and the River Marne, like a silken cord. The remains of a city—Château Thierry—in ruins. Bridges built to span the river proudly were in toppled, grey heaps. Buildings were masses of debris, the earth a honeycomb of pitted shell holes. All was grey. All was desolate. All was devastation.

Floating in the air, to our left and in a row, were large sausage balloons—the Allied balloon line, watchful for enemy movements. Ahead, to the right, black puffs of smoke filled the air. Above the roar of the motor muffled sounds of explosions could be heard.

WOOF!

The sound followed each black gust of smoke.

WOOF! WOOF! WOOF!

A small area of air was filled with bursting shells.

What were they aimed at? Could it possibly be us? If so the results were poor as the explosions were above and to the right.

Observation balloons at the left, bursting shells at the right, war-torn country below, so much to see that my searching eyes hurt. Watching . . . watching . . . afraid of missing something . . . when, as a flash, Heinricks turned and dove straight down. Gill turned left, dropped and disappeared. What was I supposed to do—dive after

Heinricks? Down—down—Lord! how this Spad could dive! Where was he? Against the earth's dark background he could not be found so climbing to five thousand feet, still worriedly looking for Heinricks, I started for home and soon, far below, saw his plane sailing peacefully along.

Gliding down to position behind him, my body slumped with relaxation from a tense strain, hitherto unfelt. Reaching the aerodrome I asked Heinricks the reason for his sudden dive. His vague answer revealed that he had, purposely, tried to lose me. He never knew that, for a moment, he had been successful. This taught me how suddenly a Spad could dive, disappear and how necessary it was to keep formation.

Mid-day.

Content with the knowledge that I had sailed through the mysterious veil which heretofore had so jealously hidden the Front from my eyes, it elated me to see my name with four others, posted for a patrol over the lines at two in the afternoon.

Before the patrol my Spad was put through her paces. Responsive—she had faith in me. Understanding—my faith in her was boundless. She would play no tricks on me now.

A helmet, goggles, gloves and coveralls were given to me and with my plane inspected, refueled and the machine guns loaded with belts of ammunition I was ready—for my first patrol.

"You're number one on the left," said the leader. "We'll assemble at one thousand feet over that adjoining field."

No words of advice or suggestions. No instructions.

Knowledge of aerial warfare is learned only in aerial

warfare. A pilot is self-taught. This game cannot be learned on the ground.

The planes line up. We are ready. Fastening the safety belts I signal to my mechanics, take off, climb to a thousand feet and wait for the others. One by one they appear. In tight formation, each in his position, we follow our leader who heads for the Front.

Safe, free, winged on high, we are sailing along when the leader, with motor trouble, drops from the formation.

Now we are four.

One of the remaining four assumes the lead.

Another plane drops away.

Now we are three.

I know nothing of the etiquette in such a case but as the other remaining plane flies behind to the right of the leader, I fly behind to the left and, still rapidly climbing, we go on.

Over the Marne.

The altimeter registers twelve thousand feet and still we climb. Surely we are over the lines—where are the enemy planes?

WOOF! WOOF!

Anti-aircraft explosions pull my eyes to the right where puffs of smoke, black, hang in the air.

WOOF! WOOF!

More appear and more; closer now, above, to the right and the leader zigzags in his course to warn that we are targets for these enemy shells.

The smoke puffs and muffled explosions hold my attention as a great spectacle, void of danger. They break again, still above, but to the left this time. So! we are being fired at! The thought thrills me, thrills me to thumb my nose at their vain attempts. At fifteen thousand feet the leader levels out, continuing into Germany.

Suddenly, ahead and one thousand feet below, planes are silhouetted against a large, white, cumulus cloud. Not in formation but playing, diving, zooming and cavorting around this dense ball of whiteness.

Enemy planes!

Now—for excitement!

Our leader turns and starts back. Why are we running away? Are they, perhaps, Allied planes?

The leader, turning again, starts after them. Following —maybe he planned an attack but first made certain there were no other planes about. Closer now . . . counting them . . . One, two, three, four, five, six—seven! Seven Boche—Seven, jet black against the white cloud.

Waggling his wings for close attention we follow our leader as he glides toward them. Their topsy-turvy manœuvres cease. A wonderful example of perfect team work as, instantly, they assume formation with four in one group and three in another. Nearer—white crosses on their black fuselages. Nearer—they invite us to dive on the smaller formation and so place ourselves in position for an attack from the other four.

Our leader opens fire.

Guns, from the Spad on my right, shoot out streams of smoke. This is my cue so I, too, aim, pull both triggers and smoking tracer bullets speed in the direction of the Huns. They break formation, instantly become disorganized and, like black water snakes, squirm in a sea of air.

Pulling up we circle above them. They twist, turn, and their manœuvres to reach our level remind me of slimy animals, hideous and poisonous to touch. With such odds as seven to three our leader has no intention of seeking their level and keeps well above. Beneath, one black, evil body, with its nose pointed directly at me, leaps straight into the air.

Good God! Can these German planes climb straight up? If so, what chance have we? With my eyes glued on him he falls off into a dive. So! . . . he zoomed and took a pot shot at me. But he missed . . . Pooh! did he think he could get me and my Spad that way? Again we circle—again we dive—this time I fire both guns at the mess in general. Down they go through a layer of clouds and one, in a death-like spin, is lost to view.

The air is clear. Only our planes soar above the clouds and the leader starts for home. Crossing the lines more anti-aircraft welcomes us, warmly, as we zigzag a course to the Marne.

Why go home? Surely we could find more Germans! Is it all over? Safe across the lines I take off my goggles and helmet. The fresh air streams through my hair and fans my hot face. Oh! for another whack at them! Never have I felt more rested, alive or with more energy but I settle down in the cockpit to enjoy the ride back. Wonder if we got the plane—the one that went down in a spin?

My little Spad sails smoothly on, humming, humming with contentment and as docile as a thoroughbred jogging towards his stable after a race.

The ever faithful mechanics are waiting, eagerly.

"Did you see any Germans?"

"Did you have a fight, Lieutenant?"

As it was my first experience I did not know if it was anything out of the ordinary or not but waited to read the leader's report.

It told of heavy anti-aircraft; sighting seven Fokkers; keeping altitude because of superior numbers; forcing them down through the clouds and of one plane falling in a spin. No confirmation was asked for the latter because we could not be sure. Whether we "got" the plane or not no one but the Germans ever knew.

The report, except for "heavy anti-aircraft" seemed perfect. Was that a great bombardment of the air? Thought it would be far worse. So! I had been in this terrific anti-aircraft! Pooh! Then it was my least concern.

·　　·　　·　　·　　·

A pilot, missing for two days, returned to the aerodrome.

"Where have you been?"

"I have been in a hospital near the Front."

"What was the trouble?"

"I have been suffering from shell-shock from anti-aircraft," he stammered.

His story was taken with a grain of salt. He was ridiculed and laughed at. The Medical Officer, however, told us that he was really shell-shocked, quite ill, and we must recognize it. He was ordered back to Orly for a rest.

Shell-shocked by anti-aircraft? Good Lord! Ridiculous! he better stay in Orly and rest.

But—now I realize that a pilot's first flight over the lines might easily affect his flying attitude for all time.

The *WOOF* of anti-aircraft explosions means they are from two hundred to five hundred feet away. But when *CRACK* thunders in your ear, it warns that shells are exploding within a hundred feet. If one bursts beneath you, rending a hole in the air, the plane, tossed like a cork from the sudden gush of wind, drops helplessly and out of control through the created vacuum until thick air is reached.

Some pilots, who without warning, hear the terrific *CRACK*, forever have a dread of anti-aircraft. Others, if shells break close by and shrapnel tears their wings, cr if their plane is tossed by the sudden blast, become shell-shocked, "lose their nerve" and are sent from the Front. It

either does or does not happen. There is no way to fore-
stall it. The lucky gain confidence. The unlucky lose it.
Lucky, on my first trip to the balloon line I heard the
WOOFS. This initial baptism left an indelible impression.
The so-called "Archies" had broken far enough away not
to startle or terrify me and confident they would never hit,
I could not take them seriously but instead was filled with
contempt. This was not bravery. It was simply a first impression that all the CRACKS and WOOFS in the world
could never change. Filled with ignorant bravado, I pooh-
poohed all anti-aircraft stories.

"Do not worry about anti-aircraft," I scribbled in a letter
to my sister that night, "they're a joke."

Woody, assigned a plane, had been to the balloon line.
He was one of five slated for the next morning's patrol.
What news would he bring? What would be his first experience? The time dragged until two hours later the
mechanics, excitedly asking questions, steadied his plane
into the hangar.

Woody, with a broad smile, climbed out and looked at
his Spad. The wings and fuselage were riddled with German mementos of deadly intent.

"Woody! Why, Woody! Was the whole German Air
Force after you?"

"It sure looks like it," said one mechanic, sticking his
fingers through the bullet holes and gazing at Woody with
idolizing admiration.

Woody just laughed.

"Twenty-seven! . . . there's twenty-seven, Lieutenant!"
said the other mechanic and he stared at Woody with eyes
full of pride and wonder.

"Twenty-seven what?" asked Woody.

"Bullet holes! Lieutenant . . . bullet holes! . . . Look! count 'em yourself."

Woody laughed aloud as we started down the road to our billet.

"Hurry up . . . tell me . . ."

"Well," he began, "heavy anti-aircraft when crossing the lines."

At that, we both chuckled.

"After patrolling for an hour and a half we started back."

"Yes-yes-go on."

"More anti-aircraft as we neared the lines."

Again, we giggled uproariously.

"Not a damned German in sight and, thinking it was pretty tame, I suddenly realized I was separated from the formation and lagging behind. Rat-tat-tat-tat-tat, machine guns, and streams of bullets flew past both ears. They were close, so close I wondered why in the world they didn't get me. So . . . pushing on the stick and with my motor wide open I went into a vertical nose dive. DIVE! . . . did you ever think a plane could dive like these Spads? Her nose was pointed straight down and, hanging by the straps in the air, I said to myself, 'My God! this is too steep,' and pulled up. But three Fokkers were still on my tail and bullets whizzed by thicker than ever. 'Steep . . . hell . . . nothing's too steep,' and nosing her over I dropped. Down —down—Lord how a Spad can dive! Surely I've lost them . . . and pulling up I looked back. Not a plane in sight— guess that's about all."

CHAPTER X

Air battles were now our daily work. They were not re-lived nor discussed. Those in the patrols knew what happened and others, with their own personal experiences, did not question. A flight ended was a flight forgotten.

But Woodard and I joined the squadron together, were billeted together and, when alone, talked freely. At night, like whispering schoolboys, conscious of mutual understanding, we confided our reactions to each other.

"Life certainly hangs by a thread up here." I knew he referred to Nevins, killed but a few hours before. "Just back from a combat over the lines, back and alive, and then to crash up right at the aerodrome."

Nevins' motor had stopped just outside the field. In an attempt to make his customary landing, he was gliding flatly, lost speed, fell off and crashed to his death.

"Seems a damn shame to go that way," Woody was voicing my own thoughts.

But, we agreed, Nevins' spill was rather an accident. He should have, with a crippled plane, landed outside the field. Not tried to make it. Quick judgment, that was the main thing. We were realizing how, whether fighting Fokkers or not, a pilot's very life hung on instantaneous coördination of thought and action.

"You had a close shave, Woody."

We discussed the dangers over the lines. Death, just over there, was waiting for us. We must face it. Death, every morning, every afternoon, and we must remember it. Think quickly. That was the way to save your skin. Never, never would we lose our lives by a mistake. If we were out-manœuvred in a fight well, that was different. That was the way, we supposed, we would have to go. Death was very close to us. How did the rest of them feel, we wondered?

"The other pilots take it calmly enough" and that was one thing neither of us could quite grasp. The utter nonchalance of the others. In fact, we were both groping for a certain understanding. We were a bit bewildered by the whole affair. The mysteries of this Front business were still vague. Either we were gauche sentimentalists, we decided, or they were hard hearted devils. At any rate their cucumber coolness toward any situation whatever was getting under our skin. Were we different? Or were they steeped in a flying etiquette of which we were still ignorant? Anyway, we liked that phrase, "cucumber coolness"; that was certainly pertinent!

"I know," said Woody, "but is that a mask they're wearing?"

"Perhaps."

"Maybe they're in as much of a blue funk as we are."

We wondered. Perhaps this casualness was a pretense. Or, it could be merely inertia from the daily routine of flying. Maybe the time, the sectors to be patrolled, the inevitable casualties were an old story to these pilots. Just like going to a daily job. Yes, we guessed, that must be it. We were not quite in the harness, yet. It would take a little time. But, we argued, some of them had been here but ten days or two weeks before we arrived.

"And they seem just as indifferent."

Would we feel the same in, say, a week? Would we be real "veterans" in such a short time? Anyway, we agreed, we would not show our feeling to these older members of the squadron. How would we fit into this picture? We did not know. But, we would assume this careless, devil-may-care attitude, too. For, we must fit in. We would take it in our stride.

Beauchamp was ever in my mind.

Why had he not been over? How he would laugh at those seven Germans against the three of us! Must go to the 27th and see him—

Good old Beauchamp! . . . would arrange it . . . very soon.

During the great American July offensive the First Pursuit Group was stacked against the ablest antagonists. Famous German Aces and experienced, seasoned pilots of the celebrated Richthofen's Circus were among our opponents. We pitted our skill, green and scant, against brilliant flyers, canny and clever from long experience.

Baron von Richthofen, organizer of his famous Flying Circus, with eighty victories to his credit, was dead. Udet, another German Ace, was said to be in command. We knew these enemy Aces by the vivid colors of their planes. Bright yellow, scarlet or bold black and white advertised their importance.

The First Pursuit Group, when on the Toul sector, before I joined, got the impression that German planes, when attacked, ran. These older members said they used to hunt far across the enemy lines in search of even one solitary plane. It was, according to them, quite a tame, easy going war.

But, here, this was far from true. Never once, unless the odds were overwhelming, did I see a German pursuit ship run from attack. They did, to be sure, stay on their side of the lines and our combats were fought, usually, over German territory.

This air was alive, all right. Alive with enemy planes. Droves of them! Eight, ten, fifteen and sometimes twenty in a single formation. They were known to be flown by crack pilots, too. Whenever we encountered the enemy it was a bitter fight to a bitter finish. Tons of shrapnel were exploded in the heavens. We fought, before a whelming tide. Hell was let loose.

This was our initiation. We knew nothing different. This was our first Front. We had nothing to compare it with. Shell-torn country below. Towns literally blown off the map. Mile-long lines of observation balloons, artillery fire that seemed incredible and tremendous ground explosions which sent dust and smoke-clouds high into the air. Destruction. Chaos and destruction everywhere.

We expected enemy planes to fill the skies. Well, we found them! We foresaw them waiting to shoot us down. Well, they were!

To us, this was the Front! Who had control of the air concerned us not a whit. We were fighting pilots. We knew our job. To fly over the lines, shoot down as many enemy planes as possible, and try to get back alive. That was our business. The cause of the war, who started it or why, meant nothing to us. We had work to do. How we fitted into the general scheme of things we did not know nor care. We were at the Front! Who would "get it" to-day? Who would be missing tonight? Our squadron, we were proud of the 95th, must make a good record. Our own men and our own flights; that was our concern. If we returned, well, lucky we were alive for another day.

·   ·   ·   ·   ·

Luke was being talked about.

His own squadron almost ignored him. So, he would come over to see us, Woody and me, for he had known Woody in the States and I was an amused listener.

Luke. Light haired, stocky and just twenty years old. The tales he told!

"Well, got another Boche," he boasted and thereby began a recital of such flying and fighting as none could imagine.

"Did you get confirmation?" we parried.

Well, no, he hadn't but, hastily switching to the details of another victory, he so graphically described his personal triumphs, always against such terrific odds, that we would smile, insultingly.

But, Luke was undaunted.

He insisted he always left the formation. So, flying off somewhere all alone, how could anyone see what happened? He was a good flyer and a natural pilot. We knew that. He was fearless, too. But his commander, Hartney, had told him *not* to leave the formation so nothing hung together.

One evening in front of the operations tent, Luke again was narrating about his prowess. Said he left the formation, saw a German plane about a mile over the lines, had a terrible fight and his opponent went down in flames.

Another flyer was standing near by. "*Those* kind of victories are easy," he said with dry sarcasm. "You better go back and get confirmation."

Luke looked a bit hurt. But, launching afresh into another yarn, he novelized a hair-raising air battle in which, as always, he was the hero.

No one believed him. No one ever saw his conquests. Luke still came over. His stories, more self-trumpeting as time went on would have paled the "Penny-Dreadfuls."

Again and again after Hartney assumed command of the group and "Ack" Grant became his commanding officer,

Grant called him to account for deserting the formation. Always an excuse. He saw a German across the lines. He got lost in the clouds. He had motor trouble. Luke always had an alibi.

"I want to *do* things," he explained. "I just can't help going off alone. I'm a different person when I once get into the air."

The conceited jackass, we thought. His self-heroism sickened us. His cocky assurance made us fume. He had been too much for his own squadron, now we, too, were through. We would not tolerate such talk. We would not listen.

Luke, the towheaded kid from Arizona, was an outcast.

.   .   .   .   .

Orders specified low, high or intermediate patrols. A low patrol was usually flown at an altitude of six thousand feet, but we were often ordered to fly as low as fifteen hundred feet. Intermediates were from ten to twelve thousand feet and a high patrol from eighteen to twenty thousand. Villages and towns designated our boundaries. At this time we were flying northwest from Château Thierry as far as Soissons and northeast to Reims. The air space between, over German territory, was our hunting ground.

Previous to flying, during training and until now my thoughts, dreams and interests were solely in pursuit planes. Bombing and observation planes existed, to be sure, but, as mere names. My interest in them was negligible. For the first time, the three distinct branches of the Air Service were clearly defined and duly respected. Bombing, observation and pursuit squadrons each, now, had a definite theoretical mission with a personnel trained for respective tasks.

Observation planes carried a pilot and observer. They

went over the lines to direct artillery fire, take photographs and observe enemy movements. Photographs enabled the ground officers to compile data and correct maps. They disclosed locations of ammunition dumps, command posts, batteries, dugouts, communications, strong points, centers of resistance and showed if paths and roads were frequently used. In short they pictured the daily routine of the enemy. Troop movements and the increase of supply establishments in rear areas were observed and these disclosures made our artillery fire effective. An observer, obviously, must first know what to look for and then understand its significance. To give closest attention to his job and return with reliable information he must be able to perform his duties unmolested by enemy aircraft.

For defense purposes only, these planes were equipped with four machine guns. Two, mounted on the front, could be operated by the pilot and the two in the rear cockpit were manned by the observer. Rotary mounting allowed the rear guns to swing in every conceivable direction except through the bottom of the fuselage. Thus, an enemy attacking an observation plane, unless he approached by zooming up from underneath, was a perfect target.

The bombing planes carried a pilot and a bomber. Their guns were for defense purposes only. Their job was to bomb industrial centers, lines of communication, munition factories, ammunition dumps, large supply depots and railway heads. Cities and towns were visited but more for a political effect than actual damage.

Pursuit, the third branch, was the backbone of the Air Service.

Without it all operations, against an enemy strong in this essential, would be unsuccessful. Aerial combat was the sole reason for its existence. Observation and bombing planes, with speed far greater than an express train, were snail-like when compared to pursuit planes. We could literally fly circles around them.

The pursuit pilot must control the air.

He must destroy the enemy—he must reign supreme—he must sweep the skies clean—then, and only then, could bombing and observation planes operate in undisturbed peace. The pursuit pilot was, by every instinct, offensive. At times, when forced to fly escort to observation he was restrained, devitalized and out of his natural element. To throttle his motor and hover, in tight formation, above a slow observation plane was to lose his greatest asset—*speed*. The observation plane felt protected but it was a false security, for the enemy, knowing the escorting pursuits were leashed, could await a favorable opportunity and dive on them. How much better if pursuit pilots had definitely been ordered to follow their accustomed offensive role! All, in the long run, would have been more secure.

.   .   .   .   .

A patrol of five, flying high, was greeted with the usual anti-aircraft. We continued into Germany. At an altitude of sixteen thousand feet, about eight miles northwest of Château Thierry, the leader waggled his wings for attention, turned slightly to the right and glided gently down. Following—what was the reason for his manœuvres?

Suddenly—a speck.

Far below, it moved, swiftly, toward the Allied lines.

The leader apparently did not see it and was going on.

What a find!—The chance of a lifetime! Turning, I left the formation and glided down toward easy prey—an observation ship.

An instant and my formation was out of sight. Centering my attention on the plane below I glided nearer—nearer —and saw tell-tale German crosses on the wings. A blinding sun at my back. What luck! He could not see me.

My first Hun! I must take no chances of missing him.

My first real victory! Now, to grab this golden opportunity.

So, when over a thousand feet away, to make sure of a hit on the first burst, I started aiming. My aim was good. Nearer . . . nearer . . . now within a hundred feet I, confidently, opened fire with both guns! A measly spit or two . . . my intended victim turned, streaking it for Germany and although I hurriedly tried to clear the guns it was useless. They were hopelessly jammed. The Hun plane disappeared. Cursing my bad luck I turned away, sadly. A perfect opportunity was lost. But—how he ran!

.   .   .   .   .

Walter Avery was assigned to the 95th. As a member of the Paris defense patrol, whose duty it was to protect that city from enemy aircraft, he had flown a great deal and was an excellent, cool, level-headed pilot. Anxious to fly over the lines he now joined a pursuit squadron at the Front.

July 25th, he went on his first patrol.

Various and sundry are the stories of first patrols. No two are alike. Woodard was attacked by three Fokkers. Our patrol of three had met seven Fokkers. Others were killed. But it remained for Avery to get and give the greatest thrill of all.

With four others he reached the lines and was flying in an apparently clear sky when, without warning, a formation of Fokkers dove on them from the rear. One, singling out Avery for his special prize, poured a stream of bullets at his plane. They did not take effect. The German, realizing he had been unsuccessful, pulled up over Avery's plane, throttled his motor and, thinking his foe would again appear in view, waited for another opportunity. Avery thought fast.

A glance at the German plane above, then he, too, throttled his motor, keeping directly beneath his antagonist. Both planes, with barely enough speed to keep on even keel, fluttered. Both planes, groggy, were gradually losing altitude. Two clever pilots. Two master flyers. Each, hanging in the air, waited for the other to make the first move.

A wrong move meant death.

Outmanœuvred for a moment, but intent on getting his man, the German acted first. Pulling his motor wide open he banked up sharply to the right in an attempt to get on Avery's tail. A wily Hun . . . but again, Avery was too quick for him. He zoomed, pointed his plane at the Boche and, at the same instant, fired. Down went the Fokker. Down . . . in a spiral. Down . . . crashing into woods below.

Avery's motor stopped.

A bullet, from the first burst of the German's guns, punctured the oil line and, although for a time it ran without proper lubrication, now it was frozen. Helpless, he must descend.

French soldiers, who had watched this extraordinary duel, were already at the woods. Avery, landing on an adjoining field, saw them taking the German aviator, uninjured, but now an Allied prisoner, to a nearby automobile. Erect, the captured Hun walked between his captors. His boots were highly polished; his uniform, spotlessly clean, was well tailored; his tunic breast shone with many medals, some of highest order. One, Germany's most coveted decoration, given only for outstanding meritorious work, hung from a ribbon around his neck. Every detail was that of an important personage. A rare prize—an Ace of German Aces.

Avery had hit a vital spot in the Boche plane. This cunning Hun knew the fatality of attempting to glide away with a dead motor so, in a spiral to deceive his pursuer, he purposely crashed into the woods below and thereby saved his life.

A French officer invited Avery to ride with them. The Frenchman, the German prisoner and Avery sat in the rear seat of the automobile. No one spoke. Not a sound but crunching wheels on the dirt road.

The German, erect, sat stiffly. His indignant profile twitched as repressed fury battled with indomitable pride. A proud German officer, indeed. A Prussian who appreciated, fully, his own great importance. His attitude was one of splendid condescension for he understood, of course, the prize he was. Who could better appreciate, naturally, his opponent's splendid achievement.

"I am Captain Menckhoff!"

The words rang as if the universe should tremble.

"Captain Menckhoff" he repeated, "of the German Imperial Army!" And, as if soothed by the sound of his illustrious name, he continued, "Which aviator, which great French Ace, crippled me?" intimating even, he might congratulate his victor.

The great Menckhoff! One of Germany's foremost Aces. Menckhoff, with thirty-four Allied planes to his credit! No wonder he thought only an Ace could "cripple" him.

The French officer smiled.

"It was not an Ace who shot you down. It was not a Frenchman. But, a young American on his first trip over the lines. He sits, at this moment, beside you."

Menckhoff was nonplussed.

For a second he betrayed his utter astonishment and chagrin. Then, after a swift dissecting glance at Avery, he stared straight ahead. He did *not* congratulate "the great Aviator who had shot him down" but, with a head held high, remained silent.

Avery's conquest was telephoned to the squadron and returning later in the day he was showered with praise and plied with questions.

"Why didn't you take his medals as souvenirs?"

"Sure, why didn't you? The great Menckhoff's medals . . . Imagine!"

"His medals?" said Avery. "Why, I wouldn't take his medals; they mean a lot to him."

.   .   .   .   .

July 26th.

Early in the morning, despite unfavorable weather, mist and light rain, a patrol flew north from Château Thierry to Oulchy le Château. Five planes started but before the lines were reached two, with motor trouble, dropped out.

Northwest of Château Thierry a German observation plane was sighted. The three Spads, circling, dove and fired at it in turn. The rear guns of the enemy plane were silenced. The observer had been shot. The pilot, without his gunner, was helpless and diving to the ground landed in an open field. The Spads circled lower. The German pilot dragged his gunner's body from the rear cockpit, threw him on his shoulder and stumbled to an old barn.

Open country below but, during the days of the Allied drive to clear up the salient, each inch of ground was so stubbornly fought for that the exact location of the line was hard to distinguish.

George Puryear, with Avery's victory before him, saw an opportunity to take the Germans prisoners and thinking he was on our side of the lines, glided down.

He did not return.

When, without a word, another day passed we feared he was a prisoner. What would be his fate? Undoubtedly enemy troops had seen the fight and were enraged at our three Spads following and firing at their observation plane as it dove for a landing. If captured he was on bitterly contested fighting ground. The mood of fighting enemy soldiers is anything but amiable and they might, in retaliation, shoot him.

When, a few days later, we learned definitely he was taken prisoner we were relieved for, at least he had not been shot. The spot where he landed was, an hour before, Allied territory. When he arrived it was German. A half hour later it had been retaken by the Allies. Such was his luck!

"Well . . . Puryear's alive."

"Alive! hell! I'd rather be dead than a prisoner."

All felt the same.

Life—death—luck—fate—we faced them all and, in good grace, accepted what they gave. But to be a prisoner was our direst dread.

.   .   .   .   .

Captain Peterson loaned Avery his automobile for a trip to the Front where he shot down Menckhoff. Avery invited three of us to go with him.

We stopped at Château Thierry. The Germans had evacuated but a short while before. In their retreat they had completely sacked the town. Everything in sight was demolished. The destruction in the larger houses was deplorable. Priceless tapestries cut to pieces. Rare paintings slit from corner to corner. Silken brocades and embossed velvet coverings ripped from their frames. Marble and ivory statues hideously dismembered. Mirrors were smashed; china and glass flung at them, lay in colored heaps. Legs were torn from tables, chairs and settees. Irreplaceable marquetry and delicate examples of past centuries' craftsmanship were in piles. A valuable collection of old books, their bindings ripped away, were torn to bits.

We walked into a nursery.

A play-house, toppling and askew, was surrounded by smashed and eyeless faces of dolls; tiny legs and arms poked through a maze of creamy lace and pastel ribbons. The dainty contents of gaping cupboard drawers were ripped, burned or otherwise besmirched. Was this the salvage of war or the work of battle-crazed lunatics?

Leaving Château Thierry we bumped and twisted over roads torn by artillery fire. All was desolation.

At the spot of Avery's victory we met some French soldiers. They told of the recent capture of the great German Ace—Menckhoff. An American colonel, they said, who saw the entire fight, had parts of the wrecked Boche plane.

In an old shack, his newly acquired quarters, we found the Colonel.

"Ah! Aviators!" he greeted us cordially and invited us inside.

In one corner of the room, mounted on two wooden blocks, was an aeroplane motor. We inquired about its make and where he got it.

"That!" he said in the manner of one who knows a thrilling tale, "that! gentlemen, is the motor from the plane of the great German Ace Menckhoff."

He told us in flourishing detail of the fight, the skill, and the dramatic finish.

"That boy in the Spad; what a marvellous flyer!"

We all smiled.

Sensing his story was not entirely new to us, he asked, "Do you happen to know him? He's a wonder!"

We introduced him to Avery, who, smiling, extended his hand. Jumping up the Colonel warmly grabbed him.

"I've seen a great many air fights," he said, "but never, never, a more skilful one than yours. Accept my deepest congratulations."

Proudly he showed us the motor and said he had had it running. Two machine guns, the propeller and other parts of the wrecked Fokker were in a corner. Waving his hand at the pile he told Avery to take whatever he wanted. With the propeller and one of the machine guns in the car we were ready to leave.

"Well, boys, shoo over some more Huns when you're up this way again," he called.

Assuring him that our next victim would be none less than the Kaiser himself, we went away.

As we were near the front lines we decided to take a sight-seeing trip.

"Which is the way to the Front?" we inquired from an M.P. stationed at a cross road.

"There." He pointed ahead. "But you better not go, they're shelling that road."

We waited for a few moments but, seeing no shells explode, thought this fellow was overly cautious; so, disregarding his advice, we went along.

A few hundred feet further the road was blocked. The bodies of two dead Germans made it impossible to pass. We dragged them to one side and were getting back into the car when a shell burst almost at our feet. Up the road another burst. Turning the car around we started back. Another shell in front of us and still another burst near the cross road. The guard, as we sped past him, was nowhere to be seen. What happened? Was he struck?

We wanted to see Belleau Woods where the troops of the second division, against terrific odds and with tremendous loss of life, won undying glory for the Americans.

Arriving at the Bois de Belleau we left the car and walked. The ground was flat. Between the road and the edge of the woods a few bayoneted rifles, butts topped with helmets to mark the place where a soldier had been hastily buried, were thrust into the ground. We examined different objects. Casually, I lifted a helmet off a rifle butt. Inside, decomposed and full of maggots, was part of a human head . . .

We entered the woods.

The ground, damp, soggy and slimy, sloped at an angle which made it difficult to walk. Small trees were shot to pieces. Others, remains of terrific machine gun fire or broken by larger shells, were naked stumps. Cartons of biscuits and blankets were strewn everywhere. German machine guns, ammunition, partly filled boxes of hand grenades and other boxes, unopened, lay behind piles of rock and larger trees. The Germans, defending these woods, had not lacked for ammunition.

Sodden earth. Depressions, where Germans, flat on their bellies, sprayed the advancing Americans with machine gun fire. Rifles, slipped from the hands of dying Americans, lay rusting. Not a dead German did we see. The woods were full, full of reminders of our own soldiers who met death in this hellhole.

We came to a trench.

Ten feet long, four feet wide and four feet deep. Our boys dug it. They dug it in an attempt to hold the ground they had won at such a cost. Five rifles—with bayonets fixed and pointing up the hill, lay on its edge. Five Americans—covered with a sprinkle of earth and wet blankets lay, crumpled, together. They had dug their own graves.

Another body, stiff and discolored, lay on its back. The glassy, hopeless eyes stared into the blue sky. A postal card protruded from the breast pocket of its uniform:

DEAR JOHN:

I have not heard from you for two or three weeks, and am worried. Keep yourself dry and don't catch cold. Write to me soon.

Your loving

MOTHER.

God in heaven, what these chaps went through! We, even then, walked with difficulty. How, through a tempest of exploding hand grenades and machine gun bullets, human beings ever advanced up that wooded hill and forced the Germans from their hidden entrenchments is beyond comprehension. The price they paid is well known. Americans did it!

Emerging from the other side of the woods we came to a large field. Here was a different story. Bodies of dead Germans and horses were in a reeking mass. Bellies, swollen like balloons, hissed and made rumbling noises. Rifles, portable telephones, helmets and whole packs of personal equipment lay where the Germans left them as they fled from the fighting Yanks.

No dead Americans here—they had fought in the open.

A light breeze blew towards us. The stench was sickening. Holding our noses we skirted the woods, returned to our car and drove back to the aerodrome.

Dry quarters. Good food. A clean place to sleep. The day's work ahead, yes, but in the soft, pure heavens where death, when it came, was usually swift and life not dragged out in a filthy trench.

My admiration for those who had "gone over the top" was stronger than ever.

CHAPTER XI

REGULAR patrols of two flights a day.

Each lasted from one and a half to two hours. To survive, once across the lines, every sense must be alert. Good air sight meant life. Tiny black specks, almost indistinguishable, were deadly unless avoided. To insure a return to the aerodrome, surrounding country and landmarks had to be lodged in the memory; anti-aircraft dodged; the skies, in every direction, continually searched. A sixth sense must be awake, for at any instant a swift darting plane might slip down the sun's rays for a surprise attack. Formations must be kept tight. If separated, for a moment, one became easy prey for a lurking, prying, astute enemy.

Each flight was an unsolved problem.

New sensations; new surprises. Not until each phase had been met, encountered and surpassed, not once, but many times, did a pilot become a "veteran." Flying was automatic; shooting, second nature. To see the enemy first and outguess him was our problem. So tense a nervous strain, for even an hour, was tiring and we returned fagged out.

High patrols were not so exhausting. Reaching the cloud strata, the formation, to avoid collisions, would spread out. Then, through dense vapor, we climbed. On several occasions I was first to emerge.   Blue, blue sky above; clouds below, waves of yellow light, basking in a fluffy sun-cotton sea.   One by one my comrades would poke their noses through.   A point, purple, then sailing silhouettes, dark, clear-cut and beautiful against the whiteness.

New inhabitants in a new world. Far from earthly things. Unseen by pompous anti-aircraft, we assumed formation, headed for the lines and flew along, trailing our shadows.

.   .   .   .   .

The last day of July.

Since we parted on the road, the day of arrival, I had not seen Beauchamp.   Each day I half expected him; each evening planned to go over.   Only four hundred feet apart, yet every hour was crowded with work and my own squadron affiliations.

Days so filled with excitement made the time pass all too quickly.   With every atom of intelligence concentrated on the business at hand, it seemed impossible to get away.

We lived, seriously but joyously, with one thing in mind. To shoot down the enemy—to get our man.   All else was forgotten.

But, I missed Beauchamp.

I would wait no longer.   Would take time to see him —tonight.   After dinner I walked towards the billets of the 27th.

Leaning against a fence, in the midst of a group, was a pilot.   His companions listened in rapt attention.   When, in the high spot of some anecdote, he paused to laugh they, too, laughed, uproariously.   Beauchamp—it must be Beauchamp . . . Yes! . . . it was he.   I could see him now. The conversation stopped.   Straightening up he looked in my direction and, squinting, yelled . . .

"Archie! . . . Hey, Archie! . . . You big stiff, are you still alive?"

The old, familiar smile lit up his face. He chuckled. Introducing me to members of his squadron he said, "Here he is! Archie . . . you know . . ."

They knew? So—Beauchamp had talked of me—then, he had not forgotten—

"Come on," he said, "I'll show you my billet."

Through a gate, along a narrow path and we entered the door of a small house. A dingy hall and to the right was Beauchamp's room. A lamp, unlighted, stood on a center table, a cot was on either side, a cracked mirror, reflecting a bowl and pitcher of white china patterned with huge, red roses, hung above the washstand and a pair of flying boots stood up in one corner.

"Well, Archie," Beauchamp grinned, "shot down any planes yet?"

He flopped on one cot, hands above his head, and I sat on the edge of the other. We lit cigarettes.

"Gosh, it's good to see you, you old bum," he smiled.

"Ditto," and watching him, apparently the same impulsive madcap, I wondered if, way underneath, Beauchamp had changed any. For surely, with death all around us, he could not be the same reckless, carefree Beauchamp. Surely he must ponder, a little, about life up here and give serious thought to this sudden death staring us smack in the face.

"Well, what do you think of the Front?" It would be nice, I thought, to hash everything over with Beauchamp. Talk it all out, right from the shoulder. Have him tell me, confidentially, that after all war in the skies was no picnic. That, just between us, it did take the starch out of one's pants.

"Think?" his eyes flooded with laughter, "it's an error to think," he joked, "and besides it requires the usage of one's grey matter which is tiresome, you old rowdy, most tiresome . . ."

Beauchamp then told me about a fellow we had known at Issoudun. Raring to go, he was, and would he shoot Hell out of the Germans! Just wait till he got to the Front!

"Remember him?"

"Sure!"

"Well," Beauchamp sat up and lit another cigarette, "he's here in the 27th. A bunch of red-nosed Fokkers got on his tail the other day" . . . he poked a finger slowly through a smoke ring . . . "came back here with his ship looking like a moth-eaten blanket" . . . and he chuckled . . . "plumb full of holes. He's a great flyer, but not so anxious . . . doesn't talk so much about what he'll do; they sure have tamed that bird all right."

His amusement was infectious. As always, he made me laugh. Instead of thinking about another narrow escape I heard myself expounding. "Bet his plane looked like a cabbage leaf full of rose-bug holes . . ." and, as of old, we howled with laughter.

"Yes, siree, they sure have tamed that bird," he repeated.

It was getting dark. Beauchamp lit the lamp and snapping the chimney back in place, sat down beside me.

"They'll tame you too" . . . but the conviction now that nothing would ever tame Beauchamp was deep inside me even as I spoke the words. They might "get him"—in time. But, even so, it would never be shooting down a tamed bird. And it would take a mighty good shot, even with odds against him, to bag a wild hawk like Beauchamp, at that.

"Not me, Archie." He started pacing up and down the room. "No, not me! And I'll tell you a secret, you old dumb-bell, I'll be an Ace when this war's over! I'll go home with ribbons, boy, and" . . . sticking out his lower lip he drew a finger across his chest . . . "and medals on my breast."

Beauchamp was in his glory.

Life at the Front, with its excitement, dangers and activity satisfied his tempestuous nature. Here, his restless energy had an outlet. Fighting the enemy, chasing them from the sky, shooting, eluding them . . . or crippled and barely able to crawl home, he found a steady stimulant which the overspilling health of his youth craved. An excellent pilot, confident, ever eager and "at home" in the air, he was happy.

This was genuine. This was no pose. Beauchamp wore no mask. I was convinced he would go home an Ace, all right. I could just see him, arriving in Princess Anne, tall and straight in a new uniform with a decoration or two. I'd like to be there and see it all, watch him smile and poohpooh at any praise. It seemed so easy for him. And what confidence he inspired! Perhaps I was becoming overcautious. But, I'd watch my step and be damned canny just the same. And—not let Beauchamp think I was serious, either.

"Going to get married?" I knew that Beauchamp, of all people, would never want to be a demigod for personal selfsatisfaction.

"Ah-ha! detective Archibald," he jumped up and gesticulated, *"cherchez la femme?"*

Then I was right. He wanted to go home and get married. In a few years, with a home and wife and kids of his own, he would almost forget there had been a war. Funny, looking ahead like that. Years upon years and then, some day, we would be two old men. Veterans of the war. Old, old men who had been aviators. Real flyers who had flown in combat at the Front in the World War. Seemed incredible.

"Seen the orders for tomorrow?"

"No, have you?"

"Yes, I'm to fly a high patrol but you, Lieutenant Archibald of the 95th, will strafe the trenches at six A.M."

Never had I done such a thing nor seen nor heard of such an order. It meant flying low, diving lengthwise over the German trenches and sweeping them with machine gun fire.

"You'll catch Hell tomorrow," he said with a wicked twinkle in his eyes, "better watch your step!"

It was getting late and thinking he was serious I started to leave. "If I'm going to strafe the trenches at six I'm going to get some sleep and not talk to you all night." I tried to be casual but this trench strafing was, to me, a serious business.

How he laughed!

"No, no, Archie, I'm joking. Stay awhile . . ."

"Well, what are the orders?"

"You're on a high patrol at nine o'clock and I'm on an intermediate. That's all."

The lamp was burning low. Beauchamp turned up the wick. Stifling a yawn he lit a cigarette and flopped again on his cot. Then—he began to sing, " 'Three Musketeers In Iron Boots'—come on Archie, let's have a duet. Ready?"

"Shoot!"

Oh three musketeers in iron boots

He kicked his feet in the air.

Guarded old Paris town.

His burning cigarette was a baton,

The shrapnel fell; so they did too

Behind his hands he hid his face

And painted the city brown.

He jumped up. "That was some evening, Archie! Good fun, that air raid, eh?"

"You bet," and we giggled. He was a card, Beauchamp was.

A friendship rare, deep-seated and sincere expressed itself in hilarity and silly nonsense. That is the way with young men.

It was after midnight.

"Good-night, Beauchamp."

"Good-night, Archie."

"Don't worry about being shot down tomorrow. I'll be above you—you'll have wonderful protection. If any Huns get on your tail just waggle your wings; I'll chase them off."

"Oh Hell! Waggle your own wings. I've got a Spad now—they can't get me."

True, the 27th had received their Spads. The Nieuports were "washed out."

We stood by the door.

"Good-bye, Beauchamp—get some sleep."

"*Au revoir* . . . never good-bye, Archie. Good luck to you."

Walking away I looked back. His tall figure, bathed in yellow light from the room, stood in the doorway.

"Good-night!" I called.

"Good-night . . . glad you came, Archie . . . Good-night."

A black streak moved—up and down—up and down—he was waving. The yellow block of light thinned, to a crack. The door was shut. All was dark. Briskly, I walked away, whistling. What an evening it had been! How we had laughed! Beauchamp—he had a Spad!

.   .   .   .   .

The next morning. August 1st. Nine o'clock.

Eighteen thousand feet over the lines on a high patrol.

I remembered Beauchamp was flying intermediate and kept looking below for American planes. Not one in sight.

Back for luncheon. Scheduled for another flight early that afternoon, I ate and strolled to the aerodrome. Just before the patrol Captain Peterson called us together. Something had disturbed him. He was plainly irritated. What could have happened?

"Watch yourselves today," he said curtly. "A lot of Boche up there."

Never before had he warned us. Never before had he even admitted of dangers beyond the lines. His attitude, which always inspired us with confidence, was, like ours, ever offensive. Why did he talk of dangers now? We saw no reason.

"Any special trouble, Captain?"

"Trouble!" he snapped. "Seven planes started from the 27th this morning and . . . two returned."

Five planes shot down from one formation! Incredible! The greatest defeat the First Pursuit Group had ever known.

We adored Captain Peterson. His word was law. Our obedience was love. Daring, experienced and an Ace himself yet, as our Commander, he felt his responsibility. Like a mother with her trusting children he could not, without a warning, let us innocently fly into the very jaws of death. He could not be silent. From a human and fearful heart came his gruff words of caution—*"Watch yourselves!"*

The 27th? Did he say 27th? What? Beauchamp! My God! Beauchamp was in that patrol . . . Who was shot down? . . . What names? . . . Who? . . . Oh! Two missing . . . missing . . . Two . . . then Beauchamp was missing—of course. Missing . . . that was nothing. He would return. Beauchamp would. Sure! He always did. He'd come limping back somehow . . . they couldn't get

Beauchamp and, believing what I wanted to believe, I climbed into my plane and flew away to the afternoon's job.

Over the lines.

WOOF! WOOF! WOOF! "Oh, shut up and go to Hell."

My throat stuck . . . thirsty . . . wish I had a drink of water. Beauchamp will probably be back by the time we get there. Lagging . . . this is a crazy formation . . . God damn you, turn over . . . what's the matter with this motor anyway? Huns! . . . Look! . . . Go after those specks! Where in Hell's the leader think he's going . . . turning . . . all right, turn and be damned, who cares? Maybe he's home by now. Sure. There . . . that's better . . . now, if he finds any we'll go after them, eh?

The flight was hazy—I know we came back.

"Any more news?" . . . casually lighting a cigarette.

"Your friend, Beauchamp—"

"What . . . back already?"

"No . . ."

"Missing?"

"No . . ."

No—No—No. The fool, why didn't he say something? Not back . . . not missing . . . then! . . . God Almighty! . . . but it couldn't be . . . not Beauchamp . . . of all men . . . not Beauchamp. Why stay and talk to an idiot? Go over to the 27th where they know something . . .

I started across the field.

There was the hangar; just the same. Everything was just the same. But, it was quiet. No one around. Awfully quiet. The little operations tent; just the same . . . someone walking out.

"Hello there!"

Maybe he didn't hear me.

"Hey! . . . wait a second, will you?" I called.

"Oh, it's you, Archibald. Glad to see you."

His hand was cold . . . wet. His eyes, like sunken, burning coals glowed in a face lined, haggard and stony grey. I did not know this person, whose colorless lips opened, spread, twitched. Was he trying to smile?

"Your formation this morning . . . we heard that five were . . ."

"Yes . . . I . . . was . . . in it . . ."

So that was it. The terrific fight had unstrung him. He was exhausted and needed rest. I would not bother him. Would find someone else who . . . but no . . . this poor devil thought he had deceived me. He imagined his grotesque smile had concealed his feelings. Let him think so. He must never know that his brave but miserable attempt to hold himself together was horribly pathetic.

"You were? . . . well, what happened?"

"God! . . . it was terrible. A flock of Fokkers . . . twelve I think . . . attacked us. Just suddenly, from nowhere. We were surprised . . . everybody got mixed up . . . talk about a mess . . . no formation . . . nothing . . . a regular dog fight . . . every man for himself and then . . ."

"Beauchamp?"

"They got him!"

Then it was true. They got him! They got him . . . Beauchamp . . . after all. How? But what matter . . . I would hear no more. I would go home. Hell! . . . my knees hurt . . . where could we sit down . . . I would make him tell me every damned bit of it . . . funny, that ache in my knees.

"Yes, they got him, all right. Two of them. I saw it. They were on his tail, firing at long range. One turned and dove away but the other kept after him . . . firing and firing and Beauchamp . . . well . . . he zoomed straight up, turned over on his back and started down."

Thank God he was through . . . that was enough . . . anyway my knees . . .

"Killed instantly, I guess, the way he fell on his back . . ."

Stop talking . . . stop . . . stop . . .

"Think his body jammed the controls the way the plane whipped as it turned over and over." He paused. Now . . . to get away.

"Well, I'd better be going," I said. "See you again . . . good luck . . ."

"Thanks . . . same to you . . ."

We both turned. We both knew.

One-two-three-four . . . my knees were stiff; my legs were sticks. Five-six-seven-eight . . . I'll count the steps to the mess tent. Nine-ten-eleven-twelve . . . Christ! They got him! Beauchamp, in his little Spad . . . he said they couldn't . . . but they did. Thirteen—Dead . . . Fourteen—Dead . . . Fifteen—Dead. He's dead, I tell you . . . no sense thinking that . . . what good if you did . . . Beauchamp is dead; dead as a door nail . . . nothing can change it now . . . Nothing. He's gone . . . and that's that.

"Archie, been looking for you. Want a little bridge before supper?"

"Bridge . . . yes . . . splendid . . ."

"For the love of Pete . . . why trump it? . . . my ten was good . . ."

"Sorry . . ."

Hearts-Spades-Kings-Diamonds. Clubs-Queens-Knaves-

Colors. Red-Colors-Black-Colors-Trumps-Aces-Colors-Colors—

"That's thirty below the line and . . ."

"Come on, keep the score . . . We'll finish the rubber after mess."

Food. Plates. Knives, forks, spoons, food . . . jabber —jabber—jabber. "What . . . Hell no, I've had enough. Deep apple pie, my foot. A deep apple pie is *deep*, that's the difference." Rattle . . . rattle . . . chewing . . . water. "Did you say Mistinguette?" . . . "Grab that cheese before it walks away." . . . "She's fifty, they say, but her legs never grew old." "Ha-Ha-Ha . . . who brought that brandy . . . God . . . give me aqua pura, promised my mother I wouldn't drink . . ."

Alone . . . at last.

Letters to write—got away. The feather bed, my turn. God—what peace. The light, forgot to turn out the light. Well . . . get up and turn it out. Dark. Quiet. Sleep will come in a minute. Lord! It's hot. This damned pillow's too high. There, that's better, makes you sleep. Pillows are bad, they say. Too many covers, bad too. Now . . . that's the way to sleep. That light . . . is the moon shining? Yes, the moon is shining. Well, shut your eyes—

The moon is shining. Into my room, on the squadron tents, on the earth—the earth—earth—Oh! My God, Beauchamp is lying on the earth; he hates the light on his face; used to pull down the curtains. Beauchamp . . . Beauchamp . . . never mind the moon—Dear Jesus, let me go to sleep. To sleep-asleep-asleep on watch. Beauchamp—sound asleep on watch. I woke him . . . then. Issoudun—remember?—you and I bunking together. Fun!

Always laughing, but sometimes you were serious. Oh yes you were . . . when you read me letters from your mother and talked about that girl—I knew. The channel . . . hanging to that damned smokestack. Say, we nearly got drowned. Better under the moon, old fellow, than under that deep, black water. Your first solo . . . Gosh! you were thrilled that day, and at the Combat Field . . . why, every one said it was the greatest flying they ever saw. That was true, Beauchamp, honest you were marvelous. Cazeaux . . . your crash . . . talk about a narrow escape! It's a miracle you weren't killed right there. Then, when orders came for the Front. You sure were in a hurry. Hurry! Hurry! Hurry! that's all you said. And Paris, Beauchamp, Paris! . . . remember the air raid? . . . Three Musketeers in iron boots . . . damn it, what was the rest? . . . you sang it, you know. Then the train to the Front. Always remember you got to the Front, Beauchamp, lots didn't, you know—think of all those we left in Field Nine, and around. They didn't cheat you out of that, Beauchamp . . . that's something. And last night . . . or was it . . . we had a great talk, didn't we? "Good-bye," I said, but you said, "No, au revoir." That was funny. I was right, you see, it was—Good-bye. Lord I'm glad I went over—aren't you? You were in great form, Beauchamp. God, you were wonderful! and happy . . . why you just radiated happiness . . . you were in heaven . . . heaven . . . *Heaven!*—why you're probably in . . . Jesus! Am I losing my mind—talking to a dead man—Sensible now. All over, Calm—that's the way to be. Must write to his mother, in Princess Anne. Tomorrow. Beauchamp died for his country—think of the glory. Glory! but—God damn it—she doesn't want glory . . . why, he was her baby once, still is . . . that's the way with mothers . . . she wants *him*. Babies—men—wars—

the end. God damned nonsense . . . wars. Love of country—Patriotism . . . Sure. But babies do not choose their
countries, and grown men fight for the land they know.
Take the Germans. They love their country . . . babies
once, with mothers, too. Hell! Fighting—killing—sorrow
—love—all the same—everywhere. Some old fiddlediddles
scratch their beards and decide to have a war. But do they
fight? Not they! Do they have to kill each other? . . .
not on your life! But they killed Beauchamp, all right
. . . they killed him. War—war—war—what's it all about,
anyway? Say, Beauchamp—do you know—yet? I'll go
on . . . I'll go on . . . I've got to. If I don't get them,
they'll get me. That's the game. Fight for your country.
Kill—kill—kill—if this keeps up there won't be anybody
left. The moon's gone under a cloud. Rest, Beauchamp—
rest—the moon can't bother you now. Three Musketeers
in iron boots . . . sing, Beauchamp—sing! . . . and help
me . . . stay by. I can't fight this God damned war alone.
No moon. Dark. Sleep, Beauchamp—sleep. Don't forget
me, ever, will you . . . and . . . I won't forget you . . .
either.

CHAPTER XII

FATALISTS now, if not before.

Death was omnipresent in this game; only its time of arrival was unheralded. Quickly, it struck, and without warning. When a comrade was killed we never discussed it. No time had we, nor strength, to spend in grieving. We went along and tried to forget. Steady nerves and confidence were our only salvation. To falter was suicide.

A two-seated Salmson observation plane was scheduled for a photographic reconnaissance of enemy territory in the region of Fère-en-Tardenois. Our squadron received a request for protection, and information about the time, place and altitude at which to meet. As enemy airmen were especially active at this date seven Spads were chosen for the escort. We met at two thousand feet. The observation took the lead. Buckley and I, above and to the left and right, flew immediate protection while above, and in turn to protect us, hovered the other five.

Eight in all we started.

Just before reaching the lines the five Spads above rapidly climbed and headed north-east. Where were they going? High in the distance against the blue, sinister black specks of enemy planes. So!—that was it. They were climbing to ward off an attack. Good—but did the observation pilot know that only we two were behind him? The five Spads climbing in the distant sky grew fainter and fainter. They were gone. So, settling down to our job at hand we scanned the heavens and flew along. The Salmson crossed the lines. Buckley and I followed. Straight into Germany we flew. At an altitude of nine thousand feet, in front and about two thousand feet above—eight Fokkers. What a find, for them! A clumsy observation plane with only two Spads, throttled, flying protection.

They dove at us! The situation was desperate! A sorry plight. We were outnumbered and they even had altitude advantage. Our Salmson, quickly turning, started towards the lines while Buckley and I, flying close, saw the Fokkers fly back into Germany, climb towards their former altitude and circle. Evidently, as Boche pursuits rarely fought over the lines, they awaited our return. We were aggressors, yes, and our air battles were always over their territory, but even so, did they imagine for one second that in this helpless condition we would be fools enough to return? As I mentally complimented the Salmson pilot on his common sense he again started over enemy ground. What now? What was he thinking of?

Certain he would never be idiotic or unethical enough to force a losing fight I decided he was teasing them a bit. That was it! When they start for us he'll swing back . . . he's just annoying them. But—he kept going. Buckley, in desperation, dove in front and angrily waggled his wings. The leader, paying no heed but defying us as well as the Fokkers, held his course. My God! Had he lost his reason?

Eight Fokkers. To go under them was plain suicide. His false confidence in pursuit pilots and their Spads, a combination he thought capable of the impossible, led him on and outweighed his knowledge of the clever Boche who, biding their time, lurked above waiting for the kill.

Why follow and protect a madman? But, we did. When well over enemy territory, and not until then, the Huns swooped towards us. Eight Fokkers, in a solid unit, rushed in our faces!—Turn now, you fool; even now there's a chance—But no, he, who was sent to take pictures, was forcing us into a hopeless combat.

Furious and wrathful at the whole preposterous affair we had to think clearly; clearly and damned quickly. One Fokker will dive on the Salmson—then I'll dive on him and—but, simultaneously climbing to get all altitude possible before the fireworks began, I could plan no further. They were closer now; closer; all eight together, with their ugly noses pointing directly at us.

Nearer, nearer, about two hundred feet away . . . Rat-tat-tat-tat-tat-tat. They opened fire! The whole damned eight—all firing. One, below me, aimed at the Salmson whose observer standing up and leaning backwards wildly fired his guns. Tracer bullets filled the air. Swerving to the right I dove on the Fokker, opened both guns and, firing, roared down almost vertically. Streams of smoke filtered through his rigging. "I'll get you"—he pulled up over the observation plane and made a sharp left turn. "Oh! is that so . . . but I'll get you yet" . . . and I too pulled up, swerved and nearly crashed into Buckley as, broadside, he flashed across my path. Tangled confusion. A potpourri of swerving, twisting planes; smoke; bullets and the deathly rat-tat-tat-tat-tat of machine guns.

Phwit . . . my plane was hit.

Phwit—phwit—two more.

"Damn you!" . . . and as I frantically looked for the source a Fokker, streaking past, dove on the observation plane. No time to pick and choose so, diving on him I pulled both triggers. Speeding by the Salmson he continued diving so I, with both guns spitting lead into his plane, followed.

Rat-tat-tat-tat-tat . . . tracer bullets passed me on both sides.

Phwit—phwit—Who's chasing me now?

Phwit—phwit—phwit—"You're a good shot . . . but you haven't got me yet."

Phwit—phwit—phwit—"God damn you." I looked back. Fokkers—three of them—were diving on me.

Three! Good Lord! The bullets came thick and fast, grazing, hitting, missing. No wonder . . . with three of them. The plane ahead had disappeared but those behind were pouring lead at me.

"Three to one are you? Think you'll get me do you? Try it!" and I pushed on the stick . . .

My plane dropped. Plunging forward, completely out of the seat, I thought I was thrown out, but the straps held and my ship fell—like a rock. Down, down, the wind screeched through the rigging. "Come on now! Come on!" . . . Could any plane stand this terrific strain? "We'll see this out together, shall we? . . . we'll outdive them, eh?"—and down I went until the altimeter indicated three thousand feet. I had dropped five thousand so pulled up and looked around. Not a plane in sight. The air was clear and the Fokkers far behind. Momentarily lost, I headed in the general direction of home.

CRACK! CRACK! Anti-aircraft warned me that the lines were very near, but it seemed so mild in comparison that I held a straight course.

The Marne! What a wonderful sight, threading its paleness through familiar landmarks.

The mechanics rushed over and ran alongside my moving plane.

"Is Buckley back?" I asked.

"Yes, Lieutenant . . . yes, he's back. We've heard all about your fight but we knew you'd come home all right," and almost tenderly they touched the plane and steadied it up to the hangar. Instinctively knowing that I did not want to talk they busied themselves with the plane, counting the bullet holes and whispering, excitedly, together.

Buckley was waiting in the operations tent.

"Well, what did you think of that mess?" I asked.

Before Château Thierry, Buckley had fought on the Toul sector and was a skilful pilot with several enemy victories to his credit.

"Thought it was my last fight," he said. "It's a wonder we both got back alive. Where's the observation plane?"

"Search me. I passed it when diving on a Fokker."

The telephone rang.   . .

"It's a message from the observation squadron," whispered the operator and we listened to his one-sided conversation.

"Yes . . . yes, all back. Oh, is that so? What! you would have . . . yes, yes, all right."

Swinging around he said, "Their rudder was badly damaged and the observer shot through the arm. Wanted to know if you both got back. Said they saw one Spad diving straight down with three Fokkers on its tail."

Further reports were that the Salmson pilot boasted he would have gone back except for a disabled rudder.

"He'll go alone next time," snapped Captain Peterson, who knew no pictures had been taken and the entire flight was a hideous travesty.

Commandant Gerard of the VI Armée sent the following telegram:

> The Commandant of the VI Armée Aeronautique addresses his thanks and his congratulations to the First Pursuit Group for the efficiency of the protection given about II H 00 on the photographic mission of the Second G.A. He asks the commander of the First Pursuit Group to let him know if all planes which were

in the combat in the region of Fère-en-Tardenois have returned.

Later we heard, to our satisfaction I must admit, that the pilot of the Salmson was not only severely criticized for the maniacal combat he forced us into but was never again allowed to fly at the Front.

. . . . .

Orders were posted for a patrol over the region Serge-Cierges. The front line was moving steadily north and Fère-en-Tardenois, twelve miles northwest of Château Thierry had just been captured by the Allies.

Our formation of five planes had patrolled for nearly two hours when the leader signaled to start for home. My motor was skipping and despite constant efforts at readjustment became worse and suddenly stopped. Although over the lines my altimeter registered fifteen thousand feet so I had plenty of time to decide on a landing spot.

The instant I picqued a second Spad left the formation and, in a wide circle, was gliding down. Hurriedly scanning the sky for Huns, then for a place to land, I saw a small field. Although pitted with shell holes it was the only feasible spot. Below was Fère-en-Tardenois, the field was west; without a doubt it was Allied territory. I landed and almost simultaneously, abreast and about fifty feet away, the other Spad came to a stop. There, grinning, sat Buckley.

"What's your trouble?"

"Same as yours, I guess," he answered. "Motor stopped just as we started for home."

He suggested we go to Fère-en-Tardenois and send word to the squadron for mechanics. We climbed out. Two large shell holes, approximately ten feet across and four feet deep, were just in front of our wheels.

"We sure picked a pretty place . . ."

"Yes . . . so safe!"

Shell holes blanketed the field. Had either plane gone a few feet further it would have crashed. Marveling at our luck we took a road to the town.

Fère-en-Tardenois was but a name. Piles of twisted masonry, waste and desolation proved the demolishing accuracy of our artillery fire. Not a building was left intact, not a spot undefiled. We picked our way through the wreckage.

A piano. Soft notes . . . clear notes . . . sweet. We listened. *Pelléas* and *Mélisande* sang of their love, not in a cool, green garden but here in a dead, grey city. The music stopped. Should we go on? Would he sing and play again?

The debris crunched under our boots . . . there . . . wait . . . familiar notes filled the air. The voice began . . .

> *Quand Madelon vient nous servir à boire*
> *Sous la-tonnelle on frôle son jupon*
> . . . .
> . . . .
> *Elle rit c'est tout l'mal qu'ell' sait faire*
> *MADELON — MADELON — MADELON.*

Climbing over a pile of stone and brick we saw him. A lone French soldier—playing. A dilapidated piano—atilt —was perched precariously where a shell had blown it. The soldier's left leg was gone and his crutch, stuck into the refuse, trembled as he fervidly played and sang. So concentrated were his efforts that he did not hear us. Undisturbed, we left him, singing lustily of love and patriotism in an atmosphere of hate and destruction.

A place to sleep and word to the squadron were our next

concern. An American, on a motorcycle, told us of a Field Hospital near by and offered us a ride. We squeezed into the side car and in a few moments stopped on a flat field dotted with tents. Medical officers, standing near, were most cordial and, before we asked, invited us to spend the night. We sent word to our squadron and sat down to dinner.

Their interest in aviation was unbounded. During the meal and for two hours after, they talked solely of flying. Countless questions, sensible and inconsistent, all concerned flights over the lines. They told us of watching air battles, of their admiration for men who flew and said they saw Buckley and me circle and land. They seemed thrilled to have with them, in the flesh, aviators they had seen in the air. But, to talk flying with those who knew little about it was difficult. To be treated as heroes was embarrassing.

"How high were you when you left the others?" asked one.

"About fifteen thousand feet," Buckley answered.

A doctor shook his head. "Maybe you kids like it, but that's too high for me. That's a long way to fall . . . how about you, Collins?"

Collins, a southerner, lazily looked at Buckley, then at me and drawled, "You all must carry God right in your vest pocket."

Later.

An ambulance train of gassed cases is coming.

The night is starlit. The doctors prepare for new arrivals.

Two headlights, dimly glowing, shine over a low hill. Two more. Two more. Two more, until a dotted line of light, like a mile-long ochre serpent, winds, twists, creeps, slowly but steadily, towards us. A solemn procession, it plies its way in and around the curving road with a cargo of suffering humans. American youths, once vigorous, healthy and spirited, now but waste material sent to be reclaimed and, if possible, to be sent back to fill the holes constantly rent in a living wall of defense blocking the enemy's advance through France.

Empty tents, with open flaps. The train stops. Four stretchers, a motionless figure on each, are pulled from racks in the rear of the ambulance, placed on the ground, quickly picked up by orderlies and carried into a tent. Nurses and doctors, ready to give immediate aid, stand by. One tent is full. The ambulances move to the next, the next and the next until all of the half-dead mortals are discharged. The hospital staff, without conversation, systematically and quickly performs its duties.

A doctor motions to us. Following we enter a tent. Foul, nauseating, pungent odors fill our nostrils. The stench makes breathing difficult. Gassed men, lying on cots which rest on the bare earth, are a carpet of misery. Conscious, half-conscious, dying, they moan and screech in agony. One, crazed with pain, jumps up. Doctors and nurses grab him. Fighting to free himself he yells, "For Christ's sake, let me go. Let me go I say . . . they can't kill my buddy and get away with it. You damned dirty Boche . . . I'll get you . . . you . . ." He collapses. Limp, his thin body sinks into the doctor's arms.

Uniforms are replaced by soft, flannel coats and pants. A tag around each man's neck gives his name and outfit. The nurses can work only by spells. The terrible odor is so vitiating that, to regain strength, they must go into the fresh air every few minutes.

"What causes this awful odor?" I asked the doctor.

"Mustard gas." He shakes his head hopelessly.

The agony seems beyond human endurance. Saturated with mustard gas, their stinking bodies are a dirty yellow.

"Is there nothing you can do to relieve them?"

"Very little."

But there must be something, some way to help. Maybe I could think. Must we, well and strong, stand by and allow this torture? The smell, we can stand no more. Buckley and I walk out and are shown a tent for the night. The horrible sounds. The moans of suffering. I want to get up and run away. And these doctors think we are wonderful because we fly. They are crazy. God! that shriek, maybe he's dying; better perhaps if he does.

Another noise, different, the familiar drone of a Gotha. It comes nearer, others follow and four are distinctly counted as they fly directly over. Boche on a bombing raid! Heading for Paris. The hum of their motors becomes softer, fainter and finally hushed.

An hour later something rouses me. Buckley is talking.

"Why in Hell aren't you asleep?" I grumble.

"I'm waiting for those damned Boche to go home; they ought to be back by now; they've had time to bomb all France."

To stay awake and check their return never occurred to me but now I, too, lay listening.

Presently, the purring whirr of aeroplanes. The raid is over. The Boche are returning. The powerful droning increases. One ship passes. A second. A third and then a fourth roars directly overhead. Our count is complete. The sound of smooth running motors dies gradually as the ships sail for their base.

"Everything all right now?" I ridicule.

Buckley does not answer. Deep breathing tells me he is asleep.

Morning. Eight o'clock. Breakfast.

We thank the officers and ride in an ambulance to our planes in Fère-en-Tardenois. Two squadron mechanics

have the motors repaired and running. Over the shell holes
we build a temporary runway. There is an element of
chance in taking off from this short, narrow strip as the least
variation will result in a crash.

I go first, speed down the slim track, pull back the stick
and breathe a sigh of relief as my plane rises into the
air. Safe. Circling the field, anxiously watching Buckley,
I hold my breath as he starts. Will he, too, be lucky? He
rises, gracefully, climbs towards me and, our troubles over,
we wave congratulations to each other, laugh and head
southwest for home.

.   .   .   .   .

By August 6th the Germans had been driven from the
Château Thierry salient. The line now stretched from
Soissons along the Vesle river to Reims, and Fismes,
twenty-three miles northwest of Château Thierry, was in
possession of the Allies. During this major American offensive we flew daily over this stubbornly fought territory.
A panoramic view of the battle-grounds lay beneath.
Smoke and flames from burning stores as ammunition depots were fired. Roads choked with wagons, gun carriages
and troops as the enemy, in chaotic disorder, fled from the
onslaught of advancing Americans.

We would swoop down and spray the retreaters with
machine gun fire. The moving figures, as if touched by a
magician's wand, instantly melted into either side of the
road. Hundreds of soldiers, hugging the earth, formed a
dark, motionless border to a highway, swept clean by our
bullets.

A pair of horses, harnessed to an old farm wagon, frightened, terror stricken, made a dash, leaped from the road
and ran, full speed, across a large field. The driver, jumping from his seat, lay flat in the waving grass. Circling, we

dove, fired at the galloping horses and pulled up. As we headed for home the animals still ran wildly.

The Germans were evacuating Fismes.

Returning from a patrol we passed over the town and, looking down, saw a long column of smoke suddenly shoot straight up. Cone-shaped and tapering to a point it reached into the heavens for over a thousand feet. A terrific explosion. An ammunition dump blew up. Another explosion. Fismes was in flames.

Patrols over, we did as we pleased.

A near-by creek was our bathtub. Naked, we swam in the cool water, refreshing our bodies. We played bridge, wrote letters and some carved canes from propellers of wrecked planes. One, whittled from Menckhoff's propeller, was presented to Avery.

"If I sent this home," he laughed, "my father would certainly strut around the club."

Gravatt worked endlessly. His finished stick, covered with delicately carved and brightly tinted beetles, lady bugs, flies and similar ornamentation, was a work of art.

We took long walks on the dusty roads. Aimlessly strolling at random we tried to forget flying, to yield to the charms of the quiet countryside. We pulled long blades of grass and chewed at their tender ends. We touched the tree branches as we passed and drew patterns with our feet in the dust. The air was soft and, except for the vibrant whirr of an occasional plane, high above and near the Front, was very still.

A stone entrance was overgrown with weeds.

"We'll take a look in here."

We followed a path through bordering poplars. A stone bridge spanned a slender stream bubbling along with faint gurgles. It was a hot day. We lay flat and drank the

cool water. Then ambled along. The path, winding beneath the shade of full-leaved foliage, led into a green
lawn. Flowers were blooming. A robin's breast was flame
against the grass, and evergreens, dignified with age, flat-
tered the pure beauty of an imposing Château.

We saw some soldiers on crutches. Others, with band-
aged heads, sat on the lawn. Men were asleep on cots, too,
sound asleep in the warm fresh air. This, then, was a con-
valescent camp.

The Frenchmen smiled at us. They touched the wings
on our tunics, pointed to the sky and nodded their heads,
knowingly. They knew we were at the Front. They saw
us fly right over.

We did not stay long.

Well, we would never be shot up like these poor devils,
maimed and suffering. We'd get it clean. Clean and
quick—when it did come. *"Au revoir," "Bonne Chance,"*
they said as we walked away. The blind boys, their chairs
beneath a weeping willow, sat silent.

We flew around the clouds. One day Heinricks and I
flew over a lake and shot at the water. Countless times we
swooped down, shot, turned and dove. Good practice.
Heinricks went home. This was fun, I would practice some
more. Skimming down closer to the water and about to
fire I was amazed to see a man huddled in the bottom of
a small rowboat. A wonder we hadn't killed him.

A complaint came to the squadron. We were called together.

"Who shot at that man fishing in the lake?"

No one knew. An order was posted.

SHOOTING ON THE LAKE IS PROHIBITED.

Some pilots helped to condition their planes but this was
unnecessary as the mechanics knew more than we. They

felt close to their pilots, were as faithful as they were skilful, for they knew a faulty ship meant death and a perfect
one might bring success. They worked hard. Night after
night, long after we had turned in, they changed wires,
checked rigging and in general put the plane in perfect
condition for the following day's patrol. They pasted
patches over bullet holes, painted iron crosses on them and
figured to the fraction of an inch their pilot's narrow escapes. Among themselves they loyally boasted of our
ability and argued about our accomplishments.

We started a fund. Contributing* causes were many.
Poor landings, good landings, failures or victories, all cost
us something and the greater the accomplishment the
greater the sum. When the coffer was bursting Captain
Peterson gave us a party.

The *Hôtel de France et d'Angleterre* at Fontainebleau
was our favorite haunt. The day's work over, the planes at
rest, another night before the morning's job and we would
motor down. The ride, the change of scenery, the smile of
the elderly proprietress whose sons were at the Front and a
room unto ourselves beside a garden.

Then, to order dinner. First something hot, a little soup
—*"Oui, oui, soupe à l'oignon, Messieurs. Soupe à l'oignon
ce soir—"* Then an omelet, just plain. . . . *"Non, non,
Messieurs, une omelette aux fines herbes—."* And chicken,
of course—*"Oui, oui, oui, le poulet avec des pommes de
terre, une salade avec un peu d'ail et du fromage, Messieurs
—de la confiture et du fromage—delicieux et après
çà——."* We let him finish and then all hollered *"OUI."*

Expensive, yes it was expensive, but what was money
for? Besides, one more patrol and, well, one never knew.
A little champagne while we waited, why not, and then to
look at the pictures which lined the walls and stairways.
Prints, etchings, grey ones, colored ones, historical figures

yellow with age and how we laughed at those in the *"Cabinet pour Messieurs."*

Is dinner ready yet? *"Un moment, Monsieur, un moment."* We look across the street to the Palais de Fontainebleau; so silent, so many windows. A man in khaki walks up the stairs, down again and goes to watch the greedy carp.

"Le dîner est servi!" We eat and eat; we drink and drink, red wine, white wine, champagne and more champagne, then coffee and a brandy. We talk and talk, and smoke and smoke, tell silly jokes and laugh and laugh in blatant, harmless nonsense to forget the grind of war.

It's getting late. How clear the night; how bright the moon; good flying weather tomorrow, soon we must be going. Another brandy, sure, why not, to sip before we start and so we order brandy—real Napoleon brandy—and sip and sip and sip. Napoleon brandy!—The Palace—La Grille d'Honneur—La Cour des Adieux—We live in other days, in other wars, and so forget our own. *"Encore du brandy,* Napoleon brandy!" . . . for now we feel that Napoleon might stroll over for a brandy. Ha! Ha! Ha! . . . *"Encore du cognac!* . . . Napoleon cognac!" . . . Ha! Ha! Ha! Ha! . . . the waiters yawn, but we order more brandy for, if Napoleon should bring Josephine, Haw! Haw! Haw!—we want to have enough . . .

"Bonsoir, Messieurs—Merci Messieurs—Bonne Chance!"
"Bonsoir!—Good Night!—*Bonsoir!"*

We snooze while driving home . . . the utter relaxation, the let-down from the grinding strain, the sheer fun and the foolishness were exactly what we needed, for the next day we were rested, refreshed, alert, calmly eager for battle, over-anxious to chase Huns and more sure of our ability and subsequent victory.

CHAPTER XIII

DEATH was greedy.

A gate, a little brown gate with a rusty latch, was an early evening meeting place. It opened into a narrow path which led to our mess hall and here, waiting for the cook to appear in the doorway, wipe her brow and announce, *"Les messieurs sont servis,"* we assembled.

In a language of our own, explicit and concise, we learned or told of those missing or shot down. "Lieutenant —— was bumped off this morning," or "Lieutenant —— went West," was all. No details, no further remarks; we understood each other.

The meal begun, we talked of other things, remote from war and of a happy world apart. Gruesome news was seemingly forgotten and, to strengthen each other, we appeared light-hearted.

A Y.M.C.A. girl, in a shack down the lane, opened a store where we could buy cigarettes and chocolate. She often dined at our mess. Joining us by the gate she heard our curt remarks about a dead comrade who perhaps had been with us the previous evening. As men I believe she thought us plucky and brave but as human beings cold-blooded and cruel. To be one of us she copied our veneer of casualness.

Little did she realize that our attitude of stoical acceptance was a mask which covered hearts torn by grief when
death struck our squadron.

August 10th Lieutenant Curry and I were in a patrol of
five. My motor missed and forced to return I waited for
the others. Three planes landed; Curry was missing. The
leader reported a fight with no victories or casualties and we
were convinced that Curry with motor trouble had had a
forced landing. Later in the day we were deeply shocked
to hear that the body of Lieutenant Irby B. Curry had been
found close by the bank of the Marne.

A Medical Officer reported that a Spad, flying low and
evidently headed for the aerodrome, crossed the river, went
into a spin and crashed. Safe on our side—so near home—
what unusual accident had occurred? A control wire, shattered by a bullet during the fight, might have snapped or,
wounded and suffering from loss of blood, he may have
fainted.

At all odds . . . he was gone. One of the most lovable
and popular members of the 95th, his death was a stiff blow.
That night, by the open gate, we did not speak. Our deep
emotions were plain. We would not discuss Curry! We
would not talk at all.

Impatient, waiting for dinner to be announced, we stood
in the early twilight of a grey day and longed to be seated
at the table where a routine of rattling dishes, food and the
ever talkative perspiring cook, demanded a sham conversation of cheeriness.

The Y.M.C.A. girl ran up. "Well, Lieutenant Curry
was bumped off today," she said crisply in the excited offhand manner of one who delights in telling news.

Her remark struck like lightning! An icy stillness! She
stood there amongst us but ungreeted, unanswered, un-
noticed and . . . alone.

She had dared!   The cruelty—to open a half-healed wound with her flippancy!   The insolence—to tread with hobnailed boots upon the sacred ground of our dead.   Our own expression, yes, but from an outsider it cut like a two-edged sword.

Embarrassed—she waited for a reply; for just a word Several pilots walked away; others ignored her.

"Mademoiselle et messieurs, le dîner est servi."

Silently we filed in and, as the cook, a jovial soul, began her usual chatter, sat down.

"Du bouillon, ce soir—du bouillon très chaud."   She stopped.

No jocose replies . . . no laughter . . . no praise for her bouillon—her nice hot bouillon.   Something terrible had happened.   Her young men, they were sad tonight!   Indeed yes, she could tell and with disappointed understanding she shuffled from place to place serving her tempting dishes.

We ate our dinner; not a single word was spoken.

The girl scanned each face for a sign of forgiveness or understanding.   She knew, now, that in trying to be one of us, to appear calloused and untouched by death, she had made a grave mistake.   She also knew what Curry's death, really, meant to us.   She knew—too late.   Toying with the food her searching eyes mutely cried for help.   She tried to swallow, choked, rose from the table and, half-crying, ran from the room.   Filled with pity I rushed out to find her, trembling and half-hysterical, by a clump of summer flowers which hung on the gate.

She burst into tears.   "I will never forgive myself," she sobbed.   "Never . . . never . . . Oh, I know now—and I can never come back."

Clumsily, I tried to console her, to help her understand, to assure her it would soon be forgotten but she refused my sympathy and, still sobbing, walked down the road into the dusk and out of sight.

She did not dine with us again. She never came back. I never saw her after that. If, perchance, she should read this will she please believe I understood; that all, later, realized her remark was not intended to hurt; and that we truly missed her when, night after night, she did not return to the 95th for dinner.

Mere flying was commonplace.

Any hazard, except in combat, was never thought of.

A pilot delivered a new Spad. I recognized a friend of training days.

"Hello, Milham. How are you?"

"Fine! I hear quite a few have been bumped off up here. How's everything going?"

Images passed before me, shadows of friends, memories, but I replied carelessly, "Oh, all right. Going back to Orly?"

"Yes, ferrying back a discarded Nieuport."

A moment's conversation, a message to a friend, and he walked away. I watched him climb into the Nieuport, wave a Good-bye and roar across the field. His ship rose, zoomed, fluttered and plunged to the ground. "Milham!" I dashed over. He lay, motionless, in the tangled wreckage. His head was crushed. Thick blood oozed from a hole where the machine gun's rear sight had drilled through one eyeball. Dead.

Yes, Milham, they're still being bumped off up here.

We were about to leave for a patrol.

The wind, which usually blew across the field, blew towards the hangar. Therefore the field's entire length was available for a take-off, a rare but satisfactory situation.

At the far end of the aerodrome tall poplars formed a natural barrier. Ready to go I pushed on the stick, opened the motor and, with the total length of the field ahead, purposely held the plane on the ground for a long, steady run, as, planning to zoom over the trees, I wanted all the speed possible. Three-quarters of the way down the field, going at full tilt, I eased up on the stick to take off. But it did not come back. Another slight pull. It was caught. A quick glance into the cockpit. Wires to the machine gun were wrapped around the stick. They held it in a vise and, taut, prevented it from coming back sufficiently to take off.

The trees were ahead. If the motor were "cut" I'd crash into them; if the stick were pushed forward to release the wires I'd nose over; I could not pull it back. A Hell of a fix, but something must be done. Taking my left hand from the motor controls I frantically grabbed the wires, yanked them terrifically and at the same instant jerked the stick. The plane shot straight up. Both guns went off. A lurch. The landing gear grazed the tops of the trees, the plane fluttered but, as I pushed on the stick it dove, gained speed and leveled out. *Whew!* My pulse slowed. Circling, to assure myself that everything was all right, I left the field.

My motor stopped.

The oil line had broken. Hot castor oil poured into the cockpit. Nosing over, barbed wire entanglement in front; oil in the cockpit at least three inches deep; and gliding over the wire with the plane held in a flat glide, I tried to get back to the field. Speed was lost. The ship fluttered. "Careful, don't break your neck the way Milham did," an inner voice whispered. "Land!—right now." So, pushing on the stick, at a good rate of speed I attempted to "pancake" on the wire entanglement. The landing gear caught; the plane whirled and, ducking into the cockpit—I waited.

Terrific jerks. Then as the plane settled on its back, hot castor oil poured over me. As I crawled out, face, head and clothes were covered with the dirty lubricant. My plane was a total wreck.

"*Mon Dieu!*" . . . cried a high, shrill voice. "*Mon Dieu! Mon Dieu!*" A young girl, with black hair flying and her little petticoat flouncing behind, ran towards me. Arriving quite out of breath she waved her slender arms, gasping, "*Mon Dieu!* You . . . you *Monsieur l'aviateur* . . . . you will keel yourself."

It was hard to convince this highly strung little one of my wholeness. With hesitancy she believed me and then, with large brown eyes looking solemnly into mine, unclasped a fine gold chain from around her neck.

"*Voilà!*" she said, proudly holding up her little hand. "*Voilà!*"

In her palm was the replica of a lady bug, exquisitely made of cloisonné. Before I could remark about her tiny treasure she grabbed my hand and found my identification bracelet. After examining, with the puckered brow of a connoisseur, an ivory elephant, a monkey and other good luck charms, she added her precious trinket. Then, abashed and spinning on one heel, she announced, "You, *Monsieur l'aviateur American* will never have the hurt when you wear theese." I thanked her and started to leave when up she jumped, wound her arms around my neck, kissed me and scampered off.

At the aerodrome Captain Peterson met me with a smile.

"Well, Archibald, did you do a good job of cracking up?"

"Perfect, sir! A complete washout!"

"Fine! We need some spare parts," was his only comment.

"Lieutenant, that was some take-off," said my mechanic hinting for an explanation. None was offered for my Spad —my little Spad—was a complete wreck. I had fought in it, had faith in it, knew its every characteristic, and felt it never, never could be replaced, but the next day when Captain Peterson assigned to me a brand new ship, my spirits rose a bit.

August 11th, the day after, with Bill Russel flying rear position on the right, I flew rear position on the left, and a formation of five planes again sallied forth on its daily search for Fokkers.

Two days previous, flying the same position, we were well over Germany when the leader, banking left, headed back towards the lines. In such a manœuvre the pilot flying rear right must speed up his motor and turn quickly in order to keep his close position. Should he turn gradually he becomes separated, lags in the rear and is easy prey for Boche planes hidden by clouds or sun.

Bill lagged.

Far in the rear and above I saw him. The chances he took were useless for ever watchful enemy planes could easily shoot him down before we would have the slightest chance of flying to his aid.

Each moment I expected a group of Fokkers—they appeared and disappeared like magic—to swoop down on this single, isolated ship which hung alone in that death infested space. A fearful anxiety gripped me until Bill finally resumed his correct position.

Landing, the leader cautioned, "Don't take such risks, Bill. Don't lag on the turns. If Huns are around they'll single you out and you won't have a chance. Keep a tight formation."

Bill laughed. "All right," he said.

Utter nonsense, he thought. Bill had a positive contempt

for enemy tactics. He liked to be separated. To sit alone, above and where he could view the formation was his sheer delight.

This day we flew about four miles into Germany, were fifteen thousand feet up and with the identical movements of the previous day the leader swung left and started towards the lines.

Bill lagged.

I glanced back. There he sat, approximately five hundred feet behind and a relative distance above. With a strange premonition of danger I dove in front of the leader as a signal to turn and pick up Bill but, simultaneously, two Fokkers dove and poured streams of lead in Bill's direction. Trailing smoke. We all turned. The enemy planes pulled up, swerved and flying back to their hiding place behind a cloud were out of sight.

We were too late.

Bill's plane shot straight up. At the peak of a perpendicular ascent it slopped over and, dizzily whirling, dropped towards the earth. ,

"Pull up, Bill! . . . Pull up! . . . they're gone."

It was still possible that, in an attempt to draw his attackers beneath us, he was spinning purposely.

"Pull up, Bill! For God's sake, pull up!" and hoping against hope I strained my eyes to see him straighten out. Down—at a terrific rate—spinning—dropping—

"Bill!—surely he isn't hit. Bill!—he'll come out," but he fell in a terrible whirl. Down . . . down . . . down . . . for thousands of feet I watched his plane until, below the horizon, the tiny speck of him melted into nothingness.

Bill was gone.

Instinctively we four functioned as one. With a sacred determination to avenge his death we cruised around looking for the Fokkers. They had vanished.

Flying back to the aerodrome—in the rear and on the left—I tagged along. Bill! To my right, where his little Spad should be, was a hazy, bluish space—white flecked and empty.

A few days later a report confirmed what we already knew. The advancing Infantry had found a wrecked plane and the body of Lieutenant William M. Russel.

.   .   .   .   .

Sunrise patrols.

A gentle hand. A soft, almost reverent voice, "It's time to get up, Lieutenant . . ." Night. Black. A candle is held by the window; a face is pressed to the pane. "Clear weather, Lieutenant—clear weather . . ." Clear—then the patrol will go, and wide awake one reaches for his boots. Movements under blankets; a stifled yawn; the candles sputter and hurriedly dressing we watch huge, fantastic shadows of ourselves upon the wall.

The morning is chill. We wait for the truck, shiver and slap our sluggish bodies. Huddled together we are driven to the aerodrome where the smooth purr of motors and the hustling attendance of mechanics make us forget the tardy dawn.

"Which way is the wind blowing?"

"Will those clouds blow over?"

"Yes, Lieutenant, the day will be clear."

A few muffled sentences. The sky is cool steel. Rustling poplars are sentinels in the grey dawn. A paled morning moon floats lazily in the sky.

"Everything's all right, Lieutenant."

Satisfied we climb into our ships, roar across the field, circle, assume formation and head for the lines.

The clouds dissolve; the air is clear and the sky turns robin's egg blue. It is amazingly beautiful.

We are alive! We glow with adventure. Flying Launce-
lots in gilded planes.

The sun peeks over the horizon, blazing. The illusion is
gone. Aroused, we realize this shower of light is not for
fanciful dreams but for grim realities. We do not fly alone
—to romance. We fly together—to kill. Death in unseen
planes rides too and hordes of men prepare to fight on earth.

WOOF! CRACK! WOOF!

Anti-aircraft fills the air.

WOOF! CRACK! WOOF!

Alert, we climb, zig-zag, and dodge the bursting shells.

WOOF! CRACK! WOOF!

The enemy knows that we have come—on our early
morning's call.

The fight is on!

We attend to our job and, if intact after the battle, fly
home together. If not we fly alone and wonder who will
return. I hold the stick between my knees, take off my
goggles and helmet, stretch my arms wide and let the rush
of wind force them back. Luck again. Hungry, and after
a hot breakfast, I ask when the next flight will be. This
afternoon? Fine! Just another day and it is summer time
in France.

.   .   .   .   .

Voluntary patrols.

Scheduled flights for the day are completed. It is dusk.
It is still. Bored, inactive, nervous, we suggest a voluntary
patrol. Pilots respond with renewed enthusiasm, flip a coin
and three planes sail off in the twilight. Their primary object is a German observation balloon.

Theoretical plans for its destruction are simple. They
will sight the balloon. The leader, as he signals for attack,
will dive and spray the ground with machine gun fire to
demoralize and scatter the enemy crew manning the defense

guns. The second plane will dive on the balloon and set it on fire. The third, hovering protection until the attack is successful, will then dive and shoot the observer as he floats in a parachute away from the burning balloon.

Easy—quick—effective. A perfect idea. But simple theories prove difficult realities.

The leader sprays the ground but the guarding Boche gunners do not disperse. As the second plane dives to attack the air is filled with flaming onions, machine gun fire, explosive shells, whirling white hot chains and glowing metals of all sizes and colors which churn protection around the balloon like a Fourth of July celebration. Our plane, entrapped in a withering wall of fire, swerves away from the sausage and is forced to fly back through this seemingly impenetrable barrage of whirling missiles.

Never once did I see the third plane shoot at the little parachute. It was a thing we did not do. If the balloon was destroyed we enjoyed sufficient victory; if not we flew away allowing the drifting human target to float unmolested to the ground.

     .   .   .   .   .

Letters from home were disconcerting. "Take care of yourself"—my mother wrote. "Be careful my son." My God! How little they knew. This was a great place to take care of oneself. But, it must be hell just sitting and waiting. "Write us all the news," they said. That would be dandy, simply dandy to tell them our losses were so heavy that, although still alive, I would probably be dead by the time they got the letter. For, death crouched closer. I felt living on borrowed time. Everytime I returned from a flight the thought—your turn next . . . your turn next— hung over me. I expected it, yet I didn't want to die. I was facing it, though. Not that I didn't mind. I did. But, this luck could not continue.   Beauchamp, Bill Russel, Curry and so many from the group were gone.   Dead. Hard to believe it too.   Your turn next—your turn next— better write my mother a letter and tell them how I felt. Might ease the shock a little if tomorrow—and sharpening a red pencil, I took some paper over to a corner table.

My dearest Mother;

As you know I am "somewhere in France."   But, my thoughts tonight are with you, at home.   I can see you there, so plainly, in the living room or on the verandah.   I can even see the pictures on the wall of the home where we four were so cheerful and carefree although we may not—I know I did not—have known the happiness we were enjoying.

Little did I imagine say two years ago, that I would be an officer in the Army, flying a small Chasse plane at the front, in this great war.   Little did you think that you would be the mother of an aviator, doing his utmost for the cause in which he came to France.

I often thought, when at home, what a worthless, meaningless life I was living, and wondered if I would ever amount to anything.   Now I feel as if I had compensated for the years in which I accomplished nothing.   It is thrilling to feel that I am one of those upon whom the world depends for a victorious ending to this frightful war.   At last I am doing something worth while.

I do not want you to worry or think of me continually.   A pleasant thought each night that you had a son with health enough to be here, and then go quietly to sleep.   Surely, if you had your choice, you would have me no other place than here.   Surely, down in your heart, you would rather have me killed than not to have left home at all.

I often wondered how true and big my courage was; what I would do in face of death.   Was I the real man you would have me be or a faking coward? I am proud that, having gone through the supreme test, I find I face death with understanding. I have become more and more a fatalist. What is to be will be and, whether now or twenty years hence, it is much better that my life be ended here in this way than just dwindle away.

If I could only transmit my feelings and viewpoint on the value of a human life as I now see it! I only hope and pray that you gather enough from what I write to get the trend of my thoughts. Death, here, is so commonly portrayed. So, should this everyday occurrence happen to me, your son, do not grieve and think you have lost something dear to you but try to feel proud that you were able to contribute to this cause. Then, you will see it entirely differently.

My love to Father and Hazel.

Jim.

American troops had made tremendous advances. The Front had receded to the north. With our aerodrome now between thirty and forty miles behind the lines effective work was impossible. Consequently a refilling station and advanced field, from which patrols and alerts were dispatched, was established at Coincy, nine miles north and slightly east of Château Thierry.

August 17th.

We were to patrol over Courcelles—Fismes—Magneux at a high altitude. At Coincy we learned that pilots from other squadrons of the First Pursuit Group were included. Bruce and Smythe of the 94th, three from the 27th and Gravatt and myself from the 95th completed a formation of seven Spads.

An infantry sergeant, at the Front during the big drive, had seen many thrilling air combats. He came to Coincy to look at the flyers he had watched in high patrols above the battlefields.

Familiar, a face—a chum of his childhood. "Hello, Gravatt! How's the boy?" Firm hands cling. Brief greetings. Rapid questions about each other's lives. Both across for several months, they met, for the first time in many years, on the flying field. A hardened doughboy who journeyed simply to gaze at aviators found a friend who had become a flyer.

Gravatt, ready to leave, climbed into his ship.

"Hey! do some stunts when you get up there. I want to see how good you are." The doughboy laughed contentedly.

Gravatt nodded, took off, climbed to two thousand feet, flew over the field, tumbled, flopped, turned upside down and hung on his back.

"Je's, right there is where you could let me out," exclaimed the soldier, "none of that for me. He's a great boy, you bet, but I'll take the ground for mine and go over the top from a trench."

A calloused doughboy, a survivor of bloodstained battles with not the slightest desire to fly was thankful to be in the Infantry with his feet on the ground.

How different our viewpoints. Climbing into my plane I thought, "When I go over the top it will be twenty thousand feet over," and content with my lot rose into the air to fly rear left in a group of five with Bruce and Smythe, the sixth and seventh planes, back and above.

Crossing the lines a few clearly defined white clouds hung just above our level. The formation was tight. Continual manoeuvring and *manette* adjustments were necessary to maintain proper positions. At eighteen thousand feet my constant glances showed Bruce and Smythe hovering close by.

Tac-tac-tac-tac-tac . . . the grim message of enemy guns spitting destruction.

TAC-TAC-TAC-TAC-TAC. . . . Twisting my neck I glanced back.

Two Fokkers were rushing upon us. Streams of smoke streaked towards our formation. Bruce and Smythe were in the direct path of this deadly lead shower. Simultaneously and with the same instinctive movements they dove to swoop down under our group of five and draw the attacking Fokkers beneath us. A sickly thud! Horror of horrors! They had collided! Diving, to help us, they smashed—into each other.

We turned and, firing, raked the air behind the fleeing Fokkers. Scooting away, black crows in the distance, they flew in hiding behind the clouds.

The planes of Bruce and Smythe hung in the air. Quivering, they tried piteously to maintain their lofty positions in the thin element. As living things, reluctant to give up a losing battle and plunge through the vast space, they fought for life. The earth, her round bosom a fatal boundary, waited.

Gravity tugged at them—victoriously.

One, its nose straight down, dropped like a plummet. The other, fluttering like a wounded bird, struggled in vain to grip the elusive air. Down . . . down . . . down . . . they went. I watched. One ship, a speck diving vertically, was lost to view. The other seemed, for a moment, successful in regaining control and in a tight spiral made a few turns but fell off again and, tumbling . . . tumbling . . . tumbling . . . dissolved into the black-green wall of a forest far below.

This was the cruelest deal of all. Comrades; friends; pilots in the same squadron, they went forth side by side to fight the enemy and ended by killing each other.

Did the Germans know our planes had collided? Did they realize the result of their attack? I hoped not. Confirmation of the deaths of Bruce and Smythe were received. Bruce crashed into a forest of tall trees and Smythe, his companion in the air, lay close by—his companion in death.

PART TWO

CHAPTER XIV

THE Château Thierry show was over.

The final curtain down; each act completed; the scenery shifted and trappings sent to a new location.

On August 31st, through verbal and telegraphic instructions, we received orders relieving us from duty with the French.

The first day of September.

Truck trains left with the squadron's equipment and pilots' baggage. September 2nd we flew our ships to a new field at Rembercourt, about three miles northwest of Bar-le-Duc on the St.-Mihiel sector.

While our Infantry, in the great Marne offensive, drove back the Huns, we of the First Pursuit Group were pitted against the most experienced and skilful squadrons of Germany's vigorous Pursuit. Offensive, at all times, we maintained a steady barrage over the sector.

Heavy indeed were our losses. Many of our best pilots, the most daring, courageous and proficient in the art of aerial combat, met death. Others—equally courageous but novices in a tricky game—crossed the lines in a daze of glorious excitement and never knew what happened. An eager face, a deadly shot, a body crumpled in the cockpit, dead hands tight on the stick and a plunge—into eternity.

Still others, although skilful flyers, were fair prey for matured enemy Aces and, out-manœuvred in combat, were killed. Some had plain bad luck. A chance shot, fired at random by a Boche, hit its mark and took its toll.

But—our victories more than equalled our defeats.

During these two months we lost thirty-six pilots, scored thirty-eight official victories and many more, although not tabulated, were in truth real conquests.

The French would not confirm an aerial victory unless, without the slightest doubt, they themselves knew that the German plane (after combat with the pilot who claimed it) had hit the ground. To fight, to get our opponent, to see him descend in a fatal spin, did not mean a credited victory unless someone else, also, had actually seen the crash. This was often impossible. Practically all our air duels were fought far back over the lines. How could French officials get information from an eye witness? Who would be that witness? A German, perhaps, yes, but would he give credit to an opponent who had killed one of his own? Who else would be on German territory calmly sitting on a raging battlefield to notice who fell, and where, and how?

Therefore many victories were not confirmed. This had anything but an encouraging effect on us. On August 15th our squadron had six combats and claimed four hostile planes but none were ever officially credited.

It is safe to assume that although we had thirty-eight official victories at least seventy-six enemy planes were shot down by the squadrons of the First Pursuit Group.

Confirmations, therefore, were officially obtained as follows:

1. An enemy plane will be considered as destroyed when it is brought down in flames, falls in pieces in the air or is seen to crash.
2. An enemy aircraft will be considered as brought down

out of control when it continues as long as seen to descend in an abnormal manner but is not seen to crash.

3. In order to get information of an enemy aircraft it will be necessary to obtain besides the testimony of the pilot concerned one or more written confirmations given by any one of the following:

    a. Of witnesses of the combat.

    b. When in our lines of witnesses of the wreck of an enemy aircraft in the approximate locality and of the same type (aeroplane, balloon, zeppelin) claimed to have been destroyed.

    c. In special cases testimony of captured aviators.

Through the stern realities of death combats in the air I had, somehow, survived. Chance, Luck, Fate—one or all had ridden with me and now, unscathed and graduated from a school unmerciful, relentless and severe, I felt immune.

.   .   .   .   .

Now we were part of the First American Army A.E.F. September 3rd our first patrol flew over the new sector, St.-Mihiel-Châtillon-sous-les-Côtes and actual operations began.

The Allies, preparing for a big drive on the St.-Mihiel Sector, were transporting vast quantities of supplies and concentrating thousands of troops in the vicinity. Numerous enemy observation balloons were active and one, near St.-Mihiel, was so situated that it could watch these stupendous movements.

The first pilot to shoot down an enemy balloon would be given five days' leave. Never, since joining the squadron, had I known of any pilot who took leave. As for myself, so exciting was each hour, so thrilling each flight over the lines, so exacting each combat, so interesting the work, that such

a thing as leave never occurred to me.   But now to get a
balloon and in turn a few days' rest before the resumption
of daily patrols was my aim.   We possessed but two balloon
guns and two older pilots already had them mounted.

"Will incendiary bullets in one Vickers gun give me a
chance to get a balloon?" I asked Captain Peterson.

"Why, yes," he answered.   "Mix some incendiary ammunition in with the ordinary tracer bullets.   That will do
it."

The mechanics were working on my plane.   "Put incendiary bullets in the right-hand gun," I said, "but only tracers
in the left.   From now on we will prepare to get a balloon."

A French bulletin was translated for the interest of all
concerned:—

> A captured aviator of the III Army was afraid of
> being shot because he carried incendiary bullets in his
> machine gun and did not have with him a special order
> to carry such ammunition, in principle reserved to the
> attack of balloons.   He also declared that English and
> French aviators fallen in enemy lines have been shot
> for carrying incendiary bullets and not having a writ-
> ten order to attack balloons.   All German pilots made
> prisoners have with them an order stating that all in-
> cendiary ammunition must be used only to attack bal-
> loons and must not be used in attacking other planes.

Consequently the following order was issued:—

> The English give also a similar order to pilots carry-
> ing Buckingham bullets.   Although it has not been
> verified that English or French pilots have been shot
> for having incendiary bullets without special orders it
> is necessary hereafter to give an order similar to model
> (in operation order #38) to all pilots with missions
> to attack balloons.

Operations order #38 read:—

1. Incendiary ammunition must not be used except for attacking captive or dirigible balloons.
2. Its employment is forbidden in aerial combat between aeroplanes. Consequently aviators must not carry incendiary ammunition except when they receive orders to attack captive or dirigible balloons.

Operations order #39.

1. Squadron commanders will see that all pilots carry with them when going on missions over the lines the following orders:
   a. One copy of "Operations order #38."
   b. A squadron order made out daily in the form given below.
      Lt. .... is ordered to attack captive or dirigible balloons.

Why such care about the use of incendiary bullets? Troops on the ground used hand grenades, flame throwers, poisonous gases, knives, bayonets, large shells and every imaginable weapon designed to spread death. The Germans fired long range guns into the non-fighting population of Paris and bombs filled with TNT, released from great heights, destroyed peaceful out-of-the-war villages and killed civilians. Yet we, pursuit pilots supposed to clear the skies of enemy aircraft, must fight according to air etiquette and politely obey a certain code. To get our man we must use regulation bullets and, if an occasion demanded incendiary bullets, carry an order authorizing their use. To break this law of aerial propriety was punishable by death.

The regulation seemed absurd. Such a far-fetched, precautionary measure was taken with a grain of salt. What pilot, flying and fighting daily, would stop each morning to get a signed, dated piece of paper in case a complicated incident, one remote chance in thousands, might occur? Why carry this order? Why bother about a slip of paper, useless unless a miraculous combination of miraculous events happened? Namely: to attack a balloon; to be crippled by your opponent; to fall on German territory; to be taken prisoner; to keep alive until you could flourish your paper order. Then who would pay attention to it? We were at war! The whole business was so ridiculously illogical that rarely—if ever—was the order carried.

My first flight on this new sector was made over the region of Montsec-Vigneulles and that same afternoon volunteers were called for a balloon-strafing expedition. They attacked a balloon without results.

September 4th our squadron flew a high patrol over Watronville-St.-Mihiel. That same day and every day thereafter we flew permanent hourly patrols at eighteen thousand feet over the field from six A. M. until dark to prevent the enemy from photographing our aerodrome.

Two balloons were attacked on September 6th and another on September 7th but all attacks were without results. Failure was due probably to two reasons: lack of balloon guns and not enough incendiary ammunition in the bursts.

Mitchell, Avery and I wanted to get a balloon.

Mitchell led, Avery flew right, I flew left, we sighted an enemy sausage and manœuvred for attack. Mitchell dove first, poured a stream of bullets into the balloon and swerved away through wisps of dirty smoke. We waited. Instead of bursting into flames it floated lazily, defiantly, and as if inviting attack. Avery hovered protection and as I swooped down, firing into the large, round surface, the German ground crew set off their flower-pots. A split second and I was caught in a flaming tower of fire studded with burning missiles. Could I get out? Must get out! Taking a deep breath I gouged into an orange sea where ugly reptiles, straddling red-capped waves, stuck out their forked metal tongues—and came out! Whee! Made it! Now to see the burning balloon! Fat, sleek, secure, it was floating like a swollen porpoise. Mortified and unable to find Avery or Mitchell I flew home.

"That was a swell expedition!" said Avery as we walked to dinner.

"What are their damned sausages made of—asbestos? I certainly fired."

"Now, Archie," laughed Avery, "you must go close when you fire. You opened up too far away."

"Far away, Hell! I was almost inside her."

.   .   .   .   .

Certain personal flights at this sector are vivid. I remember distinctly flying between our aerodrome and the lines, over St.-Mihiel, the Meuse river and other adjacent Front landmarks to familiarize myself with new territory. Also I remember high patrols, the balloon expedition and flights over German territory for combat work. Hazy or clear they are before me. But one flight remains a mystery.

I do not remember leaving the aerodrome. I do not know in what kind of a flight, under what orders, or where I was bound for. I have no recollection whatsoever of where or when I crashed or where I tried to land. All that is a complete blank. Whatever happened so stunned me that it wiped from my conscious mind everything relative to the uncanny experience itself and even robbed my memory of days previous. Horrible to me then, it is even more horrible now, for to rack your brain for years, to comb your very soul for an elusive something that will not be prodded out, to think, think, think without results, until your brain cells hurt and then admit to yourself that you have been so shocked you can never recover what is your own, is dis-

tracting and, at times, harrowing. I can tell only what little
I know.

As one who suddenly awakens from a nightmare, trembling, but unable to recall his frightening dreams . . . I
awoke. Night. Pitch black. Groping my way through a
narrow, twisting street I stumbled and fell. My head
buzzed; my legs ached; my back hurt and rolling over I
got up, shaking. Where was I? Why was I here?

My eyes burned; I had stumbled. My God! was it really
night or was I blind? Turned to stone, I stood . . . thinking. Outlines . . . faint . . . small houses took shape
. . . I could see. Houses? Then this is a town—but, what
town? My thoughts swirled but would not take form.
Swirling, swirling, they chased round and round in my head
as, mightily, I tried to think, to remember, to catch something in this chaos of nothing. What was the matter with
me? Something strange had happened, very strange. I
would not have it—I would remember. Somehow, I must
think. Some way I would make sense. Like a wild man I
pounded my fists into my throbbing temples.

Now—I would start from the very, very beginning. Well;
I am Jim Archibald. My address is 1206 Marion Street,
Seattle, Washington, and that's . . . right. Go on—what
else? . . . Oh God, I can't . . . go on. I can't remember
. . . anything else. Yes you can, think! Why did you
leave Seattle? Why? . . . Why? . . . Oh! the war. *My
plane—my squadron—must get back to the squadron!* The
patrol . . . when was the patrol? Today? Yesterday?
What patrol? What day is today? What day was yesterday? Have I crashed and lost my senses? Nonsense, the
rest will come . . . by and by. But must get back to the
squadron; maybe they need me for a patrol. Must find
. . . someone . . . and, aimlessly, I plodded over cobblestones.

Not a light. Not a sound. Is it evening, midnight, or just before dawn? A curve; a mass; something blocked the road and, edging around, I saw before me stark, naked ruins. Deserted houses in deserted streets. One-eyed windows glared at me; empty doorways stared at me; disheveled gardens watched me pass and the streets, vacant, crooked, black, called not for strange company. Same old story, this place has been shelled. I'm near the Front.

One little stone house stood intact, alone, dark and with shutters tightly drawn. Someone might possibly be in there, and walking up three steps I rapped on the door. No one came. Chilly . . . my head was cold . . . where in Hell was my cap? Suddenly nauseated, I sat down on the top step. What was that? . . . someone in the house? Getting up I pounded with my fists, pounded, pounded—then again, exhausted, sat down. A crack of light. The door opened . . . stealthily.

"*C'est moi!*" I cried.

"*C'est vous?*" came a voice.

"*Oui, oui, un aviateur Américain, et je pense . . . je crois que je suis égaré.*"

"*Ah, un moment.*"

The crack widened and an old Frenchman, in long woolen drawers and a white undershirt, stood in the doorway holding a kerosene lamp above his grey tousled head.

"*Aviateur Américain?*" he questioned with suspicion, so standing up I pointed to the wings on my tunic.

"*Égaré oui!*" he nodded, "*mais vous êtes très malade aussi, n'est-ce pas?*"

"*Non, non. Pas malade, Monsieur, mais il faut que je rentre . . .*" and the whole of me was slipping . . . slipping . . . slipping into warm space.

Wind—Wind!—it slapped against my face. Revived and wrapped in a strange coat, I sat in—something which was

speeding close to the ground.   What kind of a contraption is
this?   My brain churned.   Chug-Chug-Whir-r-r-r.   A
dot of yellow light ahead jiggled as it hit the earth and now
and then a bit of green.   Chug-Chug-Chug-Whir-r-r-r.
A motorcycle is chasing me! Turning, to look behind, I saw
a man close beside me.   His body was bent over handle bars;
his face intent on the road—I was in the side car of a motorcycle!

Now—what has happened? Who is driving me?   Where
in the devil is he taking me?   I'll ask him.   We hit a bump.
Sharp pains shot through my body and I could not speak.
"Sacrebleu!" Cursing under his breath, he slowed down.
So—a Frenchman is driving me and, feeling secure and
protected, I thought of the old man and his lamp.   He told
me I was sick. *"Malade,"* he said. *"Vous êtes malade."* But
then what? . . . that was the last I remembered.   Probably
he was right.   I did feel sort of queer and drowsy and,
patching this and that together, decided I must have
fainted; the kindly old man had taken care of me, read my
identification tag and found someone, a soldier no doubt, to
return me to my squadron.   But . . . what filled in the
interim?   Unconscious, until a moment ago . . . did this
happen tonight . . . an hour ago . . . last night . . . or
had I been ill somewhere for weeks?   Fainted?   Merely
my own idea, and even so, would they bundle up a limp
body and immediately stuff it into a side car?   Maybe, unable to revive me, they were sending me to a hospital!
Doubtful, wary and fearful of my destination, in this jumble
of conjectures, I questioned. *"Où est-ce que nous allons?—
il faut que je——"*

"Comment?"   He slowed up.   "I speak the English."

"Where are we going?" I yelled.   "I've got to get back
to——"

"Oui, oui, I take you to the aerodrome.   That is very

excellent, *n'est-ce pas? Restez tranquille*—be good—we hurry now, *voilà!*" and speeding up his engine we bumped along.

He is taking me to my squadron! He is taking me back to the aerodrome! Happy to the point of delirium I wanted to scream; to shout; to tell the trees, the bobbing light; the black sky and the one far away star: *I am going back to my squadron.*"

Along . . . along . . . is it far from here? How long have we been riding? Bolt upright I sat to watch the road. How well I felt! What a glorious ride! What people, these French, what kindness and understanding! I would remember this man; send him a present some day; yes and the old one too. Never would I forget them . . . never.

Light inside the tent. A radiant welcome for it meant that other pilots were awake. Glowing with the pleasure of a belated homecoming; eager to see my comrades and hear the news; I quickened my steps. There they were . . . talking . . . undressing . . . arranging their cots for the night. The joy that flowed through my veins! Taking a deep breath, I walked in. The indescribable happiness!

"Hello!" I said—beaming.

"Archie! Look! It's Archie!"

"God Almighty! It is—Why, Archie!"

"Well, I'll be damned! And where have you been, Rip Van Winkle?"

Their words hurt. The curt, half-finished ejaculations and would-be humorous sentences curdled my blood.

Were these my friends; these men who stared at me with vacant faces? Was this my longed-for greeting? No one rushed up. No one whacked me on the back. No one grasped my hand or asked a question. Like a stranger, unexpected and unwanted, I walked stiffly down the tent aisle.

My cot was gone.

My blankets and flying equipment were missing.

My trunk, open, was stripped bare. All my clothes had disappeared and not a vestige of a personal belonging was in sight.

I stood, hollow.

No one spoke. Wheeling around, flushed and angry, I shouted, "Where's my cot? . . . who opened my trunk? . . . who in Hell took my clothes? Bring them back, I tell you! . . . bring them back this minute."

One of the pilots walked over. "Now listen, Archie!" he said tenderly, "don't get excited. Listen to me for a moment, I'll tell you where everything is."

"Well, go ahead," I agreed, softened by the tone of his voice and humiliated at my outburst but, as he started to explain, I noticed that he was wearing my sweatshirt, my only sweatshirt, which was stretched, soiled and had a tear, right in the front. His lips were moving, he was talking, I tried to hear but could not and choking with anger I roared at him, "Take off my sweatshirt! Take it off! Go on, take it off or I'll tear it off."

He stood still.

"God damn it . . . take it off!! . . . do you hear me?" and like a madman I rushed around demanding my things.

My blankets, on different cots, I tore off and threw into a pile on the floor. Someone or everyone followed me, trying to talk.

"Shut up!" I said, brushing them aside. "Shut up! Talking's no good. Give me my things! That's all . . . *give me my things*."

"Archie, your cot's in the other tent, I'll get it."

"Oh, no you won't," I sneered. "You don't need to help me, I'll get it myself," and rushed out, found my cot, dragged it in and set it up.

The pilots, one by one, brought different articles of my

wearing apparel and piece by piece each personal possession was returned. Glumly, I accepted them and disorder became order as, without comment, they were put in their proper places.

"Here's a toothbrush, Archie . . . a brand new one."

Paying no attention I made up my bed and poisoned from the madness which had gripped me sat down—exhausted. A hand touched my shoulder.

"Will you stay quiet now for just a moment?" The voice was behind me. "I'm sorry, Archie! . . . we all are. You see, we thought you were dead and, well, you know how it is. We were sure you would never come back so we divided up your things. Then when you just strolled in that way, well, it was a surprise and I suppose we did act like a lot of ninnies. But we're glad you're back, Archie, you know that, don't you? We just couldn't believe our eyes and that's a fact. That's why things went the way they did. You understand . . . don't you?"

"Yes . . . tell me some more."

"Well, two planes were seen to go down out of control. We heard that one pilot was killed. We waited and waited and when you didn't show up we thought it was you and so—"

"How long did you wait?"

"Why, Archie! . . . surely you know when . . ."

"Yes, yes . . . of course . . . sure I know . . . what a silly question . . ." and with an empty laugh: "Let me tell you something. If ever two planes are missing and I'm one of them, just depend on me; I'll come back."

"But where have you been? How did you get back?" He was insistent.

"Oh, it's a long story," feigning a yawn, "tell you some other time; tomorrow; dead tired now," and I started to unbutton my blouse.

He looked at me and shook his head. "Of course you are," he said. "Have a good sleep. Good-night."

"Good-night."

Dreading further questions I hurriedly undressed and got into bed. Lights were out—sounds of heavy sleeping—wind flapping against the tent.

I had acted like a lunatic, a wild lunatic. They thought I was killed; no fault of theirs; look how I raved and tore around. Of course they divided my things—always did—what of it? If dead I would want them to use everything. An extra blanket was a luxury and as for my flying clothes who had a better right? How could I have so misunderstood? Upset, I guess and a little excited. My nice new toothbrush . . . that was damned decent . . . course they got a shock . . . but—"Where have you been and how did you get back?"—tormented me. Imagine not asking the motorcycle driver where he had picked me up. Of all the stupidity! Such a nice fellow . . . careful over the bumps and . . . thinking of the ride I came to a stone wall. With the exception of sitting in the side car and the scene in the tent every incident of my return was completely gone. We neared the aerodrome . . . of course . . . which direction? . . . where did we stop? . . . did I climb out? . . . where? . . . the coat . . . did I take it off . . . or did he? Good Lord! . . . maybe my mind was going . . . how did one know? Surely, surely I thanked him . . . said good-bye . . . something . . . terrible to forget that. I was on fire! Maybe going crazy, slowly, who could tell? Cold. Wet. Hot. Freezing. Better get my coat . . . put it over me . . .

"Archie!"

"Yes?"

"Everything all right—want anything?"

"No—I'm fine, thanks," and slipping deep into my bedding roll decided to forget the whole damned business. Alive—home—in my own cot. Better count my blessings and be grateful instead of worrying. Questions . . . could avoid them . . . they need never know . . . what did it matter anyway? . . . soon I would be flying again over the lines.

But, Hell No! . . . it did matter! No sense fooling myself. Might as well face it. Must find out, somehow, how long I'd been gone. Could not just go on and on and never know. Must get the whole story! Would ask questions myself in a day or so, just in an offhand way, about who else was on the patrol—where we were going—how far over the lines—what position I was flying . . . and every damned thing about it . . .

* * * * *

The next morning. September 8th. Sunday.
A glorious sunny day and, up early, I went first to the operations tent, then to the hangar.

"We're going on a patrol at eight-thirty," I told my mechanics.

"Lieutenant! . . . Say! . . . Gosh, it's good to see you." They grinned and bustled around a plane.

"Put a full belt of incendiary ammunition in the right hand gun," I instructed them.

Hungry and needing a shave I planned to have a snack of breakfast and clean up before we left but was so happy preparing for a flight, talking shop and examining the ship that time passed swiftly and, before I realized, it was nearly half-past eight.

The planes were wheeled out, the motors were started, whirred in the sunshine and, oblivious of everything but flying, I climbed into my ship.

"Everything all right?"

"Yes, Lieutenant. Good luck! and . . . be sure to come back."

"I'll be back all right," and thrilled with the day, the flight and unsolved problems ahead I took off with four others for a patrol over Watronville-St.-Mihiel.

Two planes, with motor trouble, dropped out, leaving Avery, Heinricks and myself, who climbed and headed for the Front. The fever of flying suffused me and, in my element again, joy tingled to my very finger tips as we approached the lines at about six thousand feet altitude northwest of Watronville.

My motor, although running smoothly, was not turning up the required number of revolutions, so my ship did not climb as rapidly as usual and was gradually dropping behind and below Heinricks and Avery. But, thinking it would function normally as soon as it warmed up—I followed along. We continued into Germany about a mile, turned right and flew parallel to the front lines in the direction of St.-Mihiel.

The air was still and, except for a speck of an observation plane at great altitude, too far away to attack, was void of enemy planes. We continued our course. By now—decidedly lagging—I was a considerable and dangerous distance in the rear and beneath the other two, but, confident that when the motor warmed up more I could catch up . . . trailed merrily along.

Avery and Heinricks leveled out, increased their speed and, flying swiftly far ahead, were rapidly disappearing. Gone. I was alone.

Crack! Crack! Crack! Ear-splitting explosions rent the air and puffs of black smoke, almost within reach, encircled my plane. Bewildered by the intense barrage, its suddenness and the accurate aim of German anti-aircraft I could not believe I was trapped in a terrific bombardment.

Crack! Crack! Crack! Instinct told me to dive but a split-second thought warned me that at low altitude, over the lines and harnessed with a weak motor I might be forced to land on enemy territory. Anything but that! *Anything but that!* Crack! Crack! Crack! Crack! Never had I witnessed such violent anti-aircraft; never such aim; never so close. What could I do? A light cloud bank above me. What a haven of refuge! I could climb— Crack! Crack!—hide in it and be safe from the Boche ground gunners.

I started up. Crack! Crack! Crack! Deafening explosions in rapid succession. Would I make it? Seconds seemed hours. Crack! Crack! Crack! Crack! Holding up the nose of the sluggish plane I tried to climb, but either the cloud was further away than I had reckoned or my plane was climbing unbelievably slowly. "One of those shells will break right under my seat in a minute," I thought. "That will be the end of me," but immediately assured myself with the contradiction, "Anti-aircraft has never hit me yet, they're damned close but they won't hit me now," so climbing toward the haze, but imbued with the latter thought, I felt secure from threatening destruction.

Crack! Crack! Crack! The smoke puffs were so close —could grab one if I wished; or two, or three, if I wanted, and let them sift through my fingers. Black, curling, thick gobs which hung, spread, and spiralled into grey. They fascinated me! They seemed to hypnotize and hold me! Making no effort to turn or dive out of the menacing mass I watched them, still pointing the ship's nose up, and struggled to reach the clouds of safety.

C-R-A-C-K! A thunderous explosion. My plane was tossed up.

C-R-A-C-K! A piece of aluminum cowling on the nose flew into space.

My motor stopped and I pushed on the stick.

W-H-A-M! Another shell burst and my plane, hurtled to the right, flopped over and started down in a side slip. The right wing was low. Trying to right the ship I pushed the stick to the left but the control was useless, the plane did not respond and, still on my side, I continued to fall.

Luck had left me!

Shrapnel had struck my motor and hit my plane. Putting the stick to the right I pulled it back and in this position my Spad, answering the controls, started to spiral. Frantic —I held my plane in this precarious tight turn, swiftly losing altitude. The anti-aircraft died away; no more shells exploded. What now? Were the gunners satisfied that they had fatally crippled me or was I falling too rapidly for them to aim their guns? Whatever reason the bombardment stopped.

I was dropping—fast. In a last vain attempt to right the plane I cautiously and slowly moved the stick toward the center but, falling down again in a perilous side slip, quickly pulled back into another spiral, the only possible position in which the ship could be even partially controlled. A quick glance: a large hole torn in the upper right wing. This or an aileron, broken by shrapnel, was causing the trouble. Tossing . . . tumbling . . . feverishly endeavoring to control the shattered plane . . . I lost my bearings. A crash was inevitable.

Dreading the result and dropping rapidly I cautiously kept in a tight spiral fearful of losing completely my threadlike hold on the doomed ship. Around and down . . . fighting Fate; down and around . . . combating Destiny. Confident and optimistic of the outcome I desperately looked below, praying to see a forest, for trees would break a dire collision with the earth. Trees, trees to lessen the certain and terrible blow, but in lieu of the longed-for blackish-green I saw, to my terror, a barren field, white as chalk and gutted with shell holes.

I was in the lap of the Gods. In a minute—it would happen. In a second—it would be over. Every flying instinct was alive, and gripping the stick I held it well over and back to the right as down and around I dropped . . . dropped; down and around I spiralled . . . spiralled and—clinging to life—prepared to crash. "Judge your distance carefully," I admonished a stranger. "Kick the rudder just before you hit." The ground—rushing towards me. "Keep your head!" The earth . . . there it was . . . "Now or never!" and with a terrific blow I kicked right rudder . . .

CHAPTER XV

DAZED—I was sitting on the ground. Stunned—I could not see. Bewildered—I reached for my goggles. Groggy—I took them off and the non-breakable lenses were blurred with a thousand cracks of white frosting. About fifty feet away my plane lay on its back; a sorry sight. My leg hurt. Holding it, tight, between my hands I limped to the ship. It was a complete wreck, with the cockpit but a few inches from the ground. How did I get out? Was it possible to crawl through that small opening? If so, does one crawl when unconscious? Perhaps the safety belt, struck when the plane crashed, opened and I was thrown out. Odd—but why figure? There was one certainty—I was still alive. That did surprise me!

And, as if one miracle should be followed by another, I reasoned that during my descent the plane might have floated back across the lines. Vain hope, alas, for in my soul I knew this must be German soil.

To catch fire and fall in flames or to be shot down and killed were two ways I often thought might end my flying career but this . . . *this* was an undreamed-of predicament.

In the hollow of a broad field, hidden from view by rolling hills, I stood beside my Spad . . . wondering. Forms appeared on the hill-top; figures of men which stopped, hunched together and started down the slope. Frenchmen? . . . straining my eyes . . . maybe they are! . . . maybe—anything is possible. Then, with the tell-tale skull caps and grey uniforms, my last hope seeped away for German soldiers! . . . Germans! were coming to get me!

Nervous and excited I watched men who until now had been strange people of another world. German soldiers!— in the flesh—were coming for me. Over the hill; down the slope; rifles in their hands; they were running and hollering. Quickly counting, I totaled twenty-five. There I stood, numbed, ransacking my brain for a way out. There was none. Caught. Disgusted, I cursed aloud—blasphemous words—aloud and to myself. Then, momentarily resigned to unalterable circumstances, the nervous tension left me and calmly I waited, marveling at my composure. The Huns, about three hundred feet away, formed an arc which, as they came closer, shouting and with rifles pointed, converged towards me.

Gruesome stories, of the fiendish treatment Allied soldiers had received when taken prisoners, flashed through my mind. Wonder what's in store for me? Closing in—yelling, yelling, about two hundred feet away—like a pack of hounds barking joy at a tired fox. At this range, I thought, they'll probably take a shot to try their marksmanship. Dominated by the law of self-preservation I squatted behind my plane; crawled in close to the motor; summoned a veneer of bravado and, assuming a philosophical attitude of indifference—waited.

Nearer . . . nearer . . . nearer . . . I could hear them now and, peeking through the wreckage, was amused at the procedure. Stoically, seriously, and uttering guttural sounds they encircled my plane. Rifled and unafraid— they pointed their guns. Aggressive and daring—they

peered from under their silly round caps. Brave and courageous—they squinted for a glimpse of their ensnared victim. Funny!—it was unaccountably funny for I, helpless,
unarmed, and crouching beneath a demolished little plane,
was the reason for this dramatic ceremony. Smiling at
their false respect for my power and feeling foolishly the-
atrical I giggled.

They heard me.

.."*Ach! Was ist das?*" One German—bolder than the
rest—slowly, cautiously, and with mincing steps approached
while the others, soldiers staunch and true, stiffly stood
guard. The aggressor, peering into the wreckage, spied me.

We looked straight into each other's eyes.

"*Deutscher Gefangener! Heraus!*" he yelled, shaking
his rifle and warning me to surrender. I came out. More
commanding gestures and, obeying, I held up my hands.
Twenty-five Huns surrounded me—twenty-five rifles
pointed at me—twenty-five pair of eyes stared at me. The
atmosphere was one of tense solemnity but, standing there
with arms upstretched, I felt silly as a clown.

The first soldier, after thoroughly searching me, called to
his cohorts. With lowered rifles and scowling faces they
surged around. One, younger than the rest, shook his fist
in my face, threateningly, but the searcher, shoving him
away, plainly showed his authority. I was *his* prisoner; he
would take charge of me; no interference was wanted.
That suited me, perfectly.

He grabbed my arm and we led a parade across the
field. The other soldiers, exultantly loquacious, followed,
eyeing me with keen interest.

"*Amerikanischer Flieger! Ja! ja Heruntergeschossen!*"
was all I could glean from the conglomeration of words in
a language once studied but now a hated tongue, stale
to my ears. Drawing out a package of cigarettes I offered

it to my escort. Indignant, he snorted refusal. I had no
matches, could not think of the German word for match
so in English, translated by gestures, asked for a light.
He hesitated; looked; coughed; then acquiesced.

Further along, across a dirt road and back from the street,
was a wooden house surrounded by a picket fence. He
opened a gate and firmly piloted me through. The others,
left outside, were still staring. Three steps led to a porch.
He stamped up, took me through an open door, walked
down a narrow hall, knocked on another door and turned
the handle.

We entered.

In a tall-backed red leather chair, behind a flat-top desk,
sat a German of high rank. My guard, at rigid attention,
saluted, spoke a few words, walked stiffly to a corner and
stood watch. No notice was given me. A chair was
near by so, reaching for another cigarette, I prepared to
sit down. A hornet's nest of action. The officer, whirling
in his chair, jumped up, rushed over and with eyes flashing
yelled, *"Sind Sie nicht imstande, sich vor einem Vorge-
setzten anständig zu benehmen?"* I understood perfectly,
but, German might be of use now, must not give myself
away, so I looked at him—blankly. His tirade continued
until, in disgust at my seeming stupidity, he strode back
to his desk and, in a lordly manner, seated himself.

His hair was close cropped, medals were pinned on his
tunic, his manner was overbearing, insolent, and in fact
he was the exact replica of what I imagined a Prussian
would be. Tapping on the desk until his fury abated he
turned to me, and, in labored English but with great dignity, questioned. "Where is your aerodrome?"

I did not answer.

"How long have you been at the Front?"

Again, without answering, I looked at him, blandly.

"What mission were you on this morning?"

I acted puzzled.

Motioning me to come to his desk he took a map from a drawer, unfolded it with care and, pointing to different places in France, asked such simple, direct questions that I dared not refuse to answer or pretend to misunderstand. His attitude was ferocious. He placed the map before me and I felt that my future was at stake.

"Where is your aerodrome?" he asked again.

I put my finger on a spot southwest of Château Thierry, nearly ninety-five miles from our aerodrome at Rembercourt.

"What course do you take to the Front?" he continued.

I pointed to Château Thierry and the region north. The drive at Château Thierry was over and I knew my answers gave no information.

"How—how, then, did you get here?" He tapped violently at the map, evidently pointing to where I had just crashed. His finger was on a spot near Etain which meant I had fallen between one and two miles over the lines. Quickly checking the distance I knew that, according to what I had told him, our usual course would have to be fully a hundred miles away.

At all costs the secret presence of the First Pursuit Group on its new Front must not be disclosed so I said, "I must have been lost. I've never been up here before . . ."

He launched questions at me swiftly, cleverly and with such rapidity that fearful of consequences I lied and lied until, confused, my story did not hang together.

"YOU LIE!"

His voice was thunderous and knowing it would be futile to offer any explanation I did not speak.

"YOU LIE!" His lip curled, sarcastically. "All Americans do that," and, with precision, he folded the map.

The interview was ended. "Stand at attention!" he bellowed and with premonition of evil I watched his face, trying to analyze his thoughts, but not one change of expression altered his steel-like countenance.

A soldier entered, saluted the officer, said *"Sprengstoff!"* and produced two bullets. "Explosive! Explosive!" yelled the officer glowering at me.

Incendiary bullets. They were, unquestionably, from my right hand machine gun.

A second soldier entered. He, too, had some bullets. *"Sprengstoff! Sprengstoff!"* he expostulated and glaring at me snarled, *"Schweinehund!"*

A short interval followed in which the officer telephoned, held several short conversations, pawed over papers and paid little attention to a lieutenant and two more soldiers who burst into the room with more bullets and the same words, "Explosive! Explosive! Explosive!"

With no alibi but in an effort to avert utter condemnation I said, "No. Not explosive . . . Incendiary."

The others grumbled. The officer, shrugging his shoulders, smiled, "The difference please . . . the difference?"

Explosive! Incendiary! "The difference please," and his wry smile. Why all this display of bullets, this snarling, this general hubbub? . . . Letters! . . . they jiggled together . . . formed words . . . sentences, and in the same plain print, but much larger, I saw our squadron bulletin. One section stood out:

THAT ENGLISH AND FRENCH AVIATORS FALLEN IN ENEMY LINES HAVE BEEN SHOT FOR CARRYING INCENDIARY BULLETS.

Good God! That was it! Death. That was the penalty unless one carried a written and dated order.
I had none.

Still, no bullets had been fired; my belt was full. Would this help or condemn me? But—my plane had been looted; some bullets might be kept as souvenirs; I could never prove anything . . .

"Schweinehund! Schweinehund!" they hissed.

"Sprengstoff! Ja, Ja, Sprengstoff!"

No doubt what they thought of me—a pig, a dirty pig who had committed a heinous offense.

The officer, commanding them to be quiet, addressed me. "Rest yourself," he said benignly offering a cigarette and a match. "Take off your coat." His smile was enigmatical.

Relaxing from attention, rigid since my entrance a full two hours before, I removed my flying coat, folded it, put my helmet and goggles on top and, placing them on the floor, sat down.

Through the opposite window the road could be seen and crowds of German soldiers, massed together, were talking and looking towards the house. In the distance, an observation balloon floated high in the air. There's one of the damned things, I thought. Wonder when it went up, didn't see it before, the haze would have hidden it anyway; wish I'd had a shot at it, won't get another chance; and, without speaking or being spoken to, I sat there . . . thinking.

"This is, for you, a bad Sunday," the officer, in a tone of commiseration, interrupted my reverie.

"What do you mean—a *bad* Sunday?" I parleyed.

"It is a bad Sunday," he repeated.

His manner of curbed sympathy, his urbanity and unexpected politeness bothered me. Defiant, I arose.

"Yes," I said, trying to be calm, "a damned bad Sunday . . . cooped up here with you Germans."

He took no exception to the remark. Why this gracious

deviation from former animosity? He was *too* nice and
surging with indignation in the oily atmosphere of com-
placence I inadvertently examined my goggles and glanced
out of the window. Eight soldiers, in double file, were
marching toward the cumulative mob. Each man carried
something which, as they halted by the gate, I discovered
was a musical instrument.

They started to play. Slow notes; low notes; chords,
wailing and plaintive, ruptured the quiet air and hushed
the jabbering crowd.

Dum — Dum-de — Dum — Dum — Dum — Dum-de—
Dum—

The musicians puffed and blew with swelling cheeks;
blew and puffed with deflated jowls, in unsynchronized
measures of tuneless misery.

Dum — Dum-de — Dum — Dum — Dum — Dum-de
—Dum—

Was this their idea of music, this heavy, wearisome
moan? If they must blow, and it seemed they must, why
agonize over such a diabolical conglomeration of Dum-
Dums? Why not *Hansel and Gretel,* a Strauss waltz perhaps, or the march from *Lohengrin?*

They had no music; knew it by heart . . . most of
them.

Dum — Dum-de — Dum — Dum — Dum — Dum-de
—Dum—

That rhythm, familiar, what the devil was it and humming to myself my blood froze. God Almighty! That
funeral march! I looked at the officer. He looked at me.

"What are they playing?" I asked.

He did not answer.

"Why are they playing . . . *THAT?*"

"You know *that, that* march?" he quizzed.

But I did not answer.

Together now, blowing away, the woeful dirge of death pierced my soul. Am I to pay the penalty for having incendiary bullets? Cold sweat on my forehead. Surely not; didn't use any, but for what reason would a band play here, outside this window, where soldiers are gathered to catch a glimpse of a prisoner? A squad of six soldiers, shouldering rifles, goose-stepped toward the gate, stopped and stood at attention.

The firing squad!

They have come! This is the beginning of the end, and the band played on. The officer's eyes, slits of crinkled parchment which hid the rims of blue glass beads, studied me beneath scowling brows.

"A cigarette?" he offered.

"Thank you." I took one, and his lids, widening, framed eyes of velvet, soft with pity.

Lighting the cigarette, I leaned back looking at this man, this citadel of human understanding barricaded and almost smothered by years stern with the discipline of Prussian militarism. Why, if leniency had touched him, did he not say something; do something; explain? His eyes had betrayed him. Why, then, did he not save me? He had power. Was it merely the ostentatious authority of a chief automaton who, directed by a main lever, must start the machinery which ground out life? You could just as well hold me prisoner, I thought, you'll gain nothing by shooting me and, fathoming for a way out, I saw a touring car, its natural aluminum body marked by hard usage, stop before the gate.

Two officers, walking briskly, came up the path. Steps echoed in the hall, a knock, the door opened and they entered. Both wore long overcoats; each had an iron cross pinned on his breast and they saluted with extreme formality. The superior officer rose, and, to my utter astonishment, introduced me.

"Gentlemen, this is an American aviator."

They bowed, shook my hand and said, "We are aviators, too," then glancing at me with cool unconcern nonchalantly brought forth more bullets and indifferently showed them to the officer, who, nodding acknowledgment, put them on the desk.

These German Aviators were cleanly shaven, had close cropped hair, hands conspicuously cared for and were immaculately dressed.

"You are going to take a ride with these two gentlemen."

As the officer spoke the flyers, quickly, stood on either side of me.

Wrathful, I thought, "they have come to carry out final orders; plans for my execution have been made." Bitter and helpless I felt they were taking advantage of me. They could just as well keep me prisoner.

My body seemed to swell.

I was growing. From the tips of my toes to the crown of my head new blood was flowing; new muscles thickening; new bones hardening. Bloated—arrogant—I experienced the stature of a giant and possessed the strength of twenty men.

The contempt I had for them! The hatred! I'm going to be shot; positively; not a hope left.

I saw my mother, my father and my sister. Would they know what had happened to me? I pictured myself before a firing squad, a white handkerchief in my hand and six men aiming rifles. I'll wait until the last moment, then ask permission to write a note home, and—planning for my last moment on earth—was vainly conscious of the great form on my account, the pompous etiquette on my behalf and felt an exotic pride in the attention.

Strange as it may sound, I was neither afraid nor nervous; neither timid nor cowed. Scorn, odious scorn for my captors was paramount. Damning them for their cowardly actions, which, because of a ridiculous air code, gave them the unexpected chance to kill a helpless prisoner, my indignation and resentment were stronger than fear.

This was not courage; not bravery; not gallantry nor defiance of danger. Far from it. An ordinary young man, caught in a trap. I was unexcited by a deep-seated excitement; unafraid from a deep-rooted fright; calm because of my own importance and the dramatic events which had gradually led to a tragic climax.

Momentarily not my normal self, Fear had inoculated me against Fear. An army instructor once said, "When a man goes into battle and says he is not afraid he is either a liar or a damn fool." Not afraid—I was a damn fool.

A bang! The door flew open. A short, stocky officer burst into the room. Perspiring and trembling with excitement he quickly saluted, bowed, panted, waved his arms and, in gulped eloquence, announced that he had news of great importance. A balloon insignia was on his uniform. The officers, without interruption, gave undivided attention to his oration. Words, fast and furious, poured forth and, staring vacantly out of the window, but straining my ears to translate what he said, I was astounded at the grandiloquence of his fabrications.

In terms of stirrring elocution, with high lights of descriptive intonation, he explained that I had attacked his balloon. The liar! He told, in fiery detail, how my many bullets had grazed his sausage. He explained, sparing no particulars of his own great skill, how his ground crew opened up with intense anti-aircraft and—after a terrific battle—shot me down.

I was spellbound; so was his audience. I felt the world

had lost a great actor; the others seemed proud of a gallant hero.   Closing my ears to the further burning description I decided two things: First, he is proving he was on the job. A hostile plane appeared; he efficiently discharged his duties.   Second, he is claiming credit for shooting me down. He wants recognition for getting an Allied Chasse pilot . . . an iron cross perhaps.   The dirty dog!   I wanted to yell that he was a damned liar.   Then . . . DEATH!— UNLESS ATTACKING A BALLOON . . . the words floated, burning, before me.

My God!   Here was a way out!   Believe him!   Believe him!   He's a rotten liar but believe him, that will save me.

Silence.

He's through.   Do not move; not a sign that you have understood; not a flicker; your leg is shaking, pinch it! Here's your chance.   Talking, all talking; do not listen; look out of the window; pay no attention.

The officer, spinning on his heel, was beside me.   "Was that balloon shooting at you?" he fired the question, pointing to the distant balloon.

"Yes."

"You did not say so—*before*."

"You did not ask me—*before*."

Walking to his desk he picked up the telephone, impatiently banged for a connection and talked with unmistakable authority.   I caught this much.   "They are leaving, yes, yes, right away.   What?   The American aviator, yes, yes."   Then turning to me he said, "You will go now."

The officer held open the door.   I walked through.   The two aviators followed.   So did the spectacular liar.   Down the path, out the gate and to the automobile.   The band stopped.   The performers stood at attention but their eyes, trying to get a glimpse of me, nearly rolled from their sockets.   The rifle squad of six stood by.   Other soldiers, gaping and whispering, moved across the street. The officer joined us. Why had he come out? He was unquestionably nervous; his hands trembled; his face betrayed tense emotion and he said a few words, low and indistinct, to the aviators, who, motioning to the chauffeur, told me to get into the car. The officer looked at me. I looked at him and sat down in the back seat.

The balloon hero smiled, saying, *"Auf Wiedersehen!"* and strutted away. The aviators, seated on either side of me, ordered a rifled guard to sit beside the driver and gave orders to proceed. The band began playing. The engine started, and we drove off.

The music bothered me.

"Why is that band playing?"

"They were called on duty . . ."

This answer, in perfect English, was unsatisfactory, but I thought it wiser not to question further.

We drove a short distance up the road.

The car stopped.

A clump of trees. The place of execution? Probably. I felt sick. That lying, self-glorifying nincompoop of a balloonist; surely they believed him. Yet, how could they? Still, why not? The aviators got out; so did the driver; the guard, shouldering his rifle, stood attention by the door; the other three, walking out of hearing, talked seriously as if making a decision.

Faint wails. The band was still working. Some consolation not to have to die before those puffing idiots. The guard stared at me insolently, and looking through him I plotted, "If you get me out of this car you'll have to drag me out." Would I go, voluntarily? Never! Let them drag and haul me to death; no heroic acquiescence on my part. The conversation was brief . . . they were nearing the car . . . *"Ja, Ja, das ist gut."* The stolid guard was left on the roadside, one aviator sat with me, the other beside the driver and we drove along.

"These are explosive bullets you carry," my escort carelessly held them before me.

Hesitating, I thought, "What of it; so do you," but without comment reached to take the shells. Swiftly, he pulled his hand away and put them in his pocket.

"I suppose you are a sportsman?" he queried. "All German aviators are sportsmen; I am a tennis player . . ."

He waited but I did not speak.

"I have played with Norris Williams, your champion," he continued, and told of different places he had been in America. "I have visited in Long Island, New York," he appeared to be pleasantly talking of happier days, "and there I met a man named Ted Curtis."

Ted Curtis!

I could not believe my ears. Curtis was in my own squadron.

Dumbfounded, but on my guard, I wondered what hidden motive was behind this casual mention of a name in the 95th. How much did he know? Could these Germans find out everything, or was it merely an uncanny coincidence?

"Do you happen to know if he is an aviator?" His tone was cajoling.

"No. Never heard of him." Agog with curiosity, but suspicious to a fault and afraid of complications, I lied.

"There are Americans over there," he pointed towards the lines. "In a few days they will start a big drive but they will get nothing."

Knowing the drive was scheduled for September 12th my answer was: "Is that so?" but thinking, "they'll run you out of here, old Krauthead," I said nothing further.

The rest of the ride we sat in silence.

CHAPTER XVI

A SMALL village. We were bumping over cobblestones.

"Where are we?"

"Conflans."

The car stopped. We got out, entered a building, went into a rear room and stood before two German officers seated behind a desk. Ordered to stand with my arms outstretched I was searched. All papers were taken and carefully perused; all personal belongings were minutely examined. In an envelope, with a letter from my sister, was a hundred and fifty francs but this money, much to my surprise, was promptly returned.

The incendiary bullets, always termed explosive, were briefly discussed and questions verifying my name, age, military rank and so on were asked, although all this information was on a card which every pilot carried.

"One more question . . ."

"Yes?"

"Whom shall we notify in case of death?"

For a second, under the circumstances, I hesitated.

"*Who*, in case you die?" one of the officers demanded gruffly. "Quick! We have not time to waste."

"Captain David McK. Peterson, 95th Aero Squadron, First Pursuit Group, A.E.F., France." Yes, in case of death, he, my commander, would attend to everything and send the news home.

That was all. The aviators saluted, bowed and, each taking me by an arm, we walked out, stepped into the automobile, drove through the main thoroughfare and stopped before another building.

German soldiers came out; others went in; all were shouldering rifles and I deduced it was the guard house. The chauffeur opened the door; we in the rear got out. *"Eine Minute,"* said my companion to the aviator in front. Walking in the door we entered a hall, where, at a small table, sat a sergeant, tall, of heavy build, ugly and sullen.

Handing him an official paper the flyer turned to me, bowed, saluted and with taunting sarcasm said, "Well, war is war, good-bye," and smiling ironically, left.

The Sergeant called a guard, issued curt commands, and as I was led down a long hall an open doorway at the end gave view of a garden. Abloom with flowers, shrubs and vegetables, it was divided down the center by a stone foot-path leading to an outhouse. A tall, boarded fence surrounded the inclosure, and guards with fixed bayonets paced back and forth. Three bent figures sawed wood in a corner. One was an American in khaki; two were in faded French blue.

Upstairs, down a corridor and into a dingy space. The guard, snapping about, shut a door, locked it and a heavy bolt clicked. Alone—I was in a room. Shutters, closed and padlocked over two small windows, kept out the sunshine, and in a mousy light, streaked with sallow yellow, particles of dust cavorted in foul air.

A square table. A low bed. Wooden slats for a mattress and two blankets, cotton, grimy and reeking with antiseptic, were the furnishings. The one other tangible object was a pamphlet which, gingerly, I picked up and translated.

> You are born with the blood of your parents. You possess and are able to give but one life in this world. It is most glorious and courageous to give that life in time of war. Death comes to everyone, but he who sacrifices his life for love of country is forever covered with glory and honor.

Why this bit of religious philosophy? Did they expect prisoners to die, or was it put here for me? Over and over I read it, to assure myself of correctly deciphering the meaning and when not a doubt remained, the words held but one significance—Solace. They were making preparations for my execution. I was locked up until official red tape was unwound and formal orders issued.

What time was it? Walking . . . walking . . . walking . . . up and down the room. What could I do? Pacing . . . pacing . . . pacing . . . back and forth. Told the mechanics I'd be back. Look where I am! Striding . . . striding . . . striding . . . a dead stop. Sounds. A clang or a tinkle was pregnant with meaning. A clatter or a hush was alive with information. Uproarious or still they were all absorbing, each separate cadence vibrating with news. Walking men. Horses' hoofs. Iron-tired wheels. Wagons on the cobblestones. Noises, common noises from the village street. Rapid conversation below, the guards were gabbling. Rhythmic beats of tramping men . . . tramping by . . . tramping by . . . columns of German soldiers, weary, marching to the Front.

Ears, wide open and atune, received and transmitted to my brain the significance of variant intonations which meant Life or Death.

Listening—interested. Listening—curious. Listening—frightened. Listening—subconsciously waiting for the end.

An automobile stops; brief commands; heavy footsteps; a guard is climbing the stairs. God! . . . they're coming for me!

I stand . . . frozen.

The guard descends the stairway; footsteps thud out; the automobile whizzes away; I slump on the cot . . . melted.

My stomach groans. Pains in my belly, rumbling disturbances. When did I eat last? No breakfast this morning, wish I had, and the unaccountable days before, no wonder the groans. What time is it? The light, a bilious, greenish-grey, makes me dizzy. The sun is dethroned by a sick twilight. Dimmer; pacing the floor; listening; listening and even the sounds, at least distracting, grow fainter.

Voices—far away. Steps—strolling and unhurried. The light laughter of a child and the shrill bark of a puppy. Darker. The table and bed are stark pieces of thick dusk shrouded in mauve and grey. The four walls press in . . . darker . . . darker. The ceiling is gone. Walls are smutted out and everything, obliterated in a dreary purple, fading into ink-blue . . . vanishes. Black.

My eyes see nothing . . . my ears hear little . . . the smell . . . the smell . . . suffocating. Antiseptic, that's all, then other odors, foul, nauseating, stuff my nostrils. The place is stinking. Gulping, dreading to breathe, my insides are racked with noises and no longer able to control the upheavings I run to a corner holding my head, tight, to ease the wrench of vomiting. Nothing comes.

Reeling, I stumble to the cot and lie down. The lassitude, the weariness. Morning will bring the light . . . nothing can be done. Morning will bring—Death perhaps . . . but nothing can be done . . .

.   .   .   .   .

My neck is stiff, my hip bones sore, my spine cramped and, awake, I stagger up, claw at the shutters and try to pull them open. God! for a breath of air. My clothes, reeking with antiseptic, stick to my body. Sweat. Cannot stand it; must have air; a noise will bring a guard; if he opens the door, warning me to be quiet, some air will get in. I bang on the walls—kick over the table—pound on the shutters and wait. Not a sound. Not one. You fool, you're a prisoner, no attention will be paid to you. You're locked up, tight as a drum, better get that into your head.

A prisoner in Germany! The actual truth dawns on me. *I*—am a prisoner in Germany! Befogged . . . cannot believe it. Sick . . . cannot digest it. For the first time the verity of my dilemma overpowers me. The unbelievable thing has happened; it honestly and truly has, and to me. Must, must, must get out—somehow. Men escape from prisons, all the time. Why did I stay there like an ass and let them take me? Should have run, somewhere, run like Hell and hidden. The stench! Germs galore must be running around in my lungs; enough to poison one. A prisoner in Germany! God Almighty! why did this have to happen to *me?* How did it—anyway? My motor was not turning up . . . should have gone back . . . lagging behind . . . tagging along . . . what a fool . . . what a God damned fool! Scared to death of missing a flight; crazy to get a balloon; strange plane; and just back from a smash-up or whatever it was. Should have rested for a day. Sitting there . . . watching the anti-aircraft . . . unable to climb . . . why didn't I dive out? What was the matter with me? What in the devil was I thinking of?

Mortification at my own stupidity mocked me. Bitterness at my own foolhardiness tortured me. Regret for my every action since beginning the flight crucified me, and saddened to a point of distraction with visions of acts which could never be rectified, mistakes which could never be corrected and flights—flights over the lines—never to be flown again . . . I thought I should go mad. Pacing, pacing, up and down; back and forth; around in a circle, then in a square, dragging my finger along the wall. Must not take it so hard, men have been prisoners of war, all through the ages. Some—went crazy! Weakling! Anyone can go crazy, easy way out, if you allow it. But, some —died of starvation! Food, certainly need food. Hungry, but that's a Hell of a long way from starving. Borrowing trouble, that's what you're doing, borrowing trouble and destructive thoughts will set you crazy. A healthy mind means a healthy body and constructive thoughts mean sanity. First, keep your sanity. Second, care for your body. And methodically taking deep breaths of the pungent, sticky air I put myself through every known exercise until, spent, I flung my body on the cot, pulled up the filthy blankets and relaxed. Some time elapsed; maybe I slept. Springing up—terrified. Why all this scare, no doubt you'll be shot in the morning! Exercises. Breathing. Exercises. Breathing. Well—they won't shoot a blithering idiot! "Yes, had to kill him . . . explosives you know . . . poor little devil went all to pieces . . . lost his wits." How they would glory in it! An Allied flyer could not stand the strain! The smug satisfaction! An aviator, an American aviator, went under. Well—they may not shoot a brave man but—boast they fired at a sapheaded dotard—Never!

Footsteps. Someone climbing the stairs. Listening. They came down the hall slowly, quietly and stopped outside my door. Welcome—anyone would be welcome; anything for a change from this solitary confinement and isolation from the world outside. A grating sound. A piece of light, about two by six inches, hung like a tiny picture against the black. Bright at first, then murky grey with an eye, a human eye, in the middle, rolling from side to side. A peekhole, of course, and I yelled, "Come in."

The eye stopped, peered at me as if unseeing and, going closer, I saw it was looking through dirty glass.

"Kommen Sie herein!" But the peeper, close to the pane, stared until satisfied it was safe to approach a dangerous character. A key turned; the bolt was pushed back; the door opened; a sergeant, ordering a guard to stand by the door, entered, carrying a bowl in one hand, a pail in the other and a loaf of black bread stuck under his armpit. He put the bowl and bread on the table, the pail by the cot, and started out.

"Hey! wait a second!"

He stopped.

"Have you got any cigarettes?"

He did not answer so I continued. "Here, I've got money," flourishing the French francs, "get me some cigarettes and tooth paste; I'll pay you for them."

Still he did not speak.

"Will you do it?"

He was walking away.

"Will you—will you—will you get them?" insistent and following him.

"All right, all right," in broken English, plainly anxious to get out, which he did, locking the door.

Food! Something to eat at last! Brown liquid in the bowl, coffee, how splendid and, swallowing a mouthful, I spit it up. Lukewarm, bitter as gall; was it coffee or sour soup? The bread, like a clod of dirt, was spotted with mold and smelled. My appetite was gone. Unable to drink the slop or touch the bread I thought, I'm not hungry after all, that's fine! The food is terrible but if really not hungry you don't need food. People eat too much anyway, that's what doctors say, especially Americans, we dig our graves with our teeth, and, sincerely believing if not hungry it was unnecessary to eat, I said half aloud, "Will not eat one bite in Germany, not one bite; not hungry anyhow." The thought of cigarettes, promised by the Sergeant, was pleasant; he would be along any time now.

Hours passed. No cigarettes. Weary of pacing the room, indifferent to consequences and headstrong I stamped on the floor, jumped up and down, beat the door with my fist and created a wild racket.

"*Was ist los?*" The Sergeant, excited, came in.

"Where are those cigarettes?" I yelled. "Get me something to smoke, do you hear me?"

Subservience to a superior officer was so instilled in this poor man, his spirit was so cowed by German military system, that, although I was a prisoner, he felt inferior to me and listened as a subordinate. Sensing this I ranted, "Bring me some cigarettes! Immediately! Now get out!"

"Yes, yes, all right, *ja, ja, gut,*" his manner was placating and he shook his hand as a gentle caution against such disturbance.

Tap! A faint knock. Where was it, or was it? Tap! . . . Tap! . . . above or below; could not locate it. Someone has heard the furor, maybe it's a signal, probably another prisoner, and I tapped back.

"Cheerio!" . . . A feeble voice sounded across the hall.

Companionship! An Englishman is locked up here. I was thrilled and about to answer; the Sergeant bellowed for him to be quiet.

Time dragged. Faintest, yellowish slits through the shutters meant it was high noon or later and a glorious day. That imbecile has no idea of bringing me cigarettes, pretended he would to quiet me, and obsessed with but two ideas, a long breath of fresh air and a cigarette, I stamped, banged and yelled.

"Cheer-r-r-io!" . . . The soft, English voice was an

approving congratulation for my actions and again the Sergeant appeared.

"Where are my cigarettes?"

Meekly, he looked at me, so using the psychological advantage of an officer I stormed, "You did not bring them! Well, let me out for a walk instead," visioning a stroll in the clean garden.

His expression, dumb as it was, showed consternation at this demand but, turning to go, he questioned, "You vait a minoot, *ja*—be quiet, *ja?*"

Stopping him I glared into his eyes. "*Ja, Ja,* a minute, but if you stay away again I'll bang the house down. Smell this room, smell it, I want some fresh air, that's all. I cannot hurt anyone or get away, a little walk is all I want. Bring a guard with you and he can take me out."

The Sergeant's feet went clapping down the stairs.

"Cheerio!" came the call . . . "Cheer-r-r-rio."

A few minutes later the key clicked, the bolt slid, and, fully expecting an enraged officer to discipline me, in peeked the Sergeant.

"Come," he whispered.

Surprised at the results of my tirade, I followed him down the stairs and into the garden.

The sunshine was blinding. Standing, eyes shut, I breathed and breathed the glorious air, then, looking about, saw three guards, apparently advised of my visit, watching me suspiciously. The American and two Frenchmen were still sawing wood in the corner.

Air! What a luxury!—air! Could I ever get enough into my lungs? What beauty! Healthy vegetables and colorful, sweet-scented blossoms; even in this high walled prison garden, one could drink in the radiance which nature, with half a chance, will shower on the earth.

Rambling over to the woodpile I spoke to the men. The

three guards galloped up and fiercely remonstrated. The men sawed away.

Carrots, rows of them, feathered, green-topped above a bit of coral. A raw carrot to crunch, my mouth watered and, daring, I leaned over.

"*Halt! Halt! Halt!*" The three guards were on top of me brandishing bayonets and yelling about rules but, conveniently understanding no German, I looked askance, decided fresh air was more precious than a carrot, and submissively walked down the path.

A German Frau, buxom and rosy, emerged—with proper decorum—from the outhouse. She shook her skirts, patted her hair and, with serious business ahead, walked in my direction. Her shirtwaist, blue and tightly fitted, clung to her large breasts and a black tailored skirt, girdled with ribbon and a shining buckle, swished around her thick ankles. Competent, efficient, she was without doubt a good woman.

To be courteous, I stepped aside and, with the evil thought that such niceties might prolong my stay in the dear little garden, saluted. Mercy me! Stock still; her piercing eyes glared at me; her bosom heaved with indignation and, with a haughty toss of her head, she trotted on. Smiling, I sauntered over to a bush near the fence. Large and spilling with red berries, which sat on olive-green leaves and lay like piles of rubies on the ground, it hid me from view as, walking around, I examined its enchanting symmetry.

"*Wo ist der amerikanische Flieger?*" boomed the Sergeant's voice. So, as I judged, the sweet lady had reported my insolence which had so affronted her dignity. Indeed—she was a pure female.

Such commotion! The Sergeant, not seeing me, worriedly called the guards who scuttled about, peered, peeked, hunted and yelled. Fearing to anger them further, I left my innocent retreat.

"Bad, bad! *Kommen Sie mit!*" and rushing over the Sergeant grabbed my arm and marched me to my room.

.   .   .   .   .

Morning. The arrival of a second bowl of "coffee" gave opportunity for another request. "I want to talk to the American who was in the garden yesterday." At this bold suggestion the Sergeant's head rocked back and forth at my brazenness. "You're a good fellow," I argued. He liked that. "You're in charge of me, aren't you?" He nodded. "Well, you are not afraid, I know that, now be a good sport and bring him up." Gulping down the coffee, I heard him sidle out.

To my surprise he dutifully returned with an American soldier, not the man who sawed wood in the garden but an American, a countryman, a comrade to talk to. Enthusiastically I greeted him, shook his hand and, as the Sergeant, leaving the door ajar with a guard outside, left us alone, told him to sit on the bed.

He slunk into a corner, stared at me with a look of indescribable fear, but did not speak. On and on I rattled, asking how long he had been here, how he was treated and anything to coerce him into conversation. Like a hunted animal, frightened to the point of near insanity, he crouched against the wall pointing to the loaf of bread.

"Do you want that . . . Lieutenant?" It was a pathetic appeal.

"No, take it." I handed him the bread.

Clawing at the loaf like a wild thing, he hid it next to his body and started to go.

"Don't go," I urged. "Stay until they come for you." But laboring under stress of mental anguish his staring eyes filled with tears and he pleaded, "I better go, Lieutenant . . . I know . . . better go."

"See here!" shaking him. "Don't be a fool, stay as long as you can," and talking rapidly to divert him I shut the door.

His body was emaciated, his hair was matted, his finger nails were chewed off and physically, although still young, he was a pitiful wreck. Fear was eating at his heart; the soul within him was not his own; his mind, terrorized, was going. Was it too late to help him?

"What is the trouble?"

"I'm hungry," patting the hidden bread, "hungry all the time," he confided in a rasping whisper.

Food—his uppermost thought. Bread, black, sour bread crusted with mold—his greatest desire. When the Sergeant entered he turned pale as death and, slinking like a whipped dog, sneaked out the door.

God! What life in a German prison had done to this American doughboy. I wished he were locked up with me, that might help, and worrying about him brought misgivings as to my own future.

.　　.　　.　　.　　.

Seconds. Minutes. Hours. All the same in the dark, putrid room. It was well into the afternoon when a German officer about sixty years of age and two German aviators, all steeped in their own importance, arrived. The elder man, tall, stalwart, handsome, and with his wavy iron-grey hair a sharp contrast to the close cropped heads of the aviators, appeared—excepting his uniform with tunic decorations and an iron cross—more like an American. He bowed and saluted saying, "Well! We have come to call on you." His English was faultless, he shook my hand—most cordially—and a smile showed his even, white teeth. The aviators, in conspicuous elegance of smartest uniforms, pol-

ished boots and valorous decorations, stood like statues during the greeting and then, like well trained seals, bowed,
smiled too pleasantly and also humored me with firm hand-
clasps.

"Well, my good man, how are you?"

The unbearable condescension! Keenly embarrassed by
my unshaven face, unwashed hands, filthy and mussed uniform I foolishly apologized for my appearance.

"Have you had anything to eat?"

"Not a thing."

Surprised, tut, tut—he called a guard.

"Hole etwas Brot und Marmelade für diesen Offizier!"

"You poor fellow, I've ordered some nice hot food and
jam for you."

"Thank you." He had ordered only bread and jam.

Four chairs were brought in. We sat down. The older
officer, always the spokesman, told without a sign of animosity of his travels. He knew New York and other cities
in the United States, spoke of France, the attractions of
Paris, the Château country, had lived in South America
where he managed an export and import business and "just
happened to be in Germany on a business trip" when he was
drafted. He was not in sympathy with the war, not at all,
only came to his Fatherland once every four years and was
forced into service.

He inquired about my personal life. Was I the only son?
Yes. Well, well, well—and brothers and sisters? Just one
sister. Interesting, eh?—interesting. My parents—both
alive? Yes. Fortunate, eh?—fortunate. Then he asked
why the American government did not provide their "gallant aviators" with parachutes. It was a pity, such a pity,
and he told of a friend who, by jumping with a parachute,
had saved his life three times.

"Would you like to write a note to your commander?"

A favor! He would do me, a prisoner, a favor? What a

joke! Another ruse to get information and, smiling, I did not deign to reply.

"Would you?" He was insistent.

This suggestion was not for my benefit and, skeptical, I answered, "Thank you, I think not." He seemed astonished at my non-acceptance of his generous offer.

"If you care to write a note one of our aviators will drop it over the lines."

Why this inducement? What did he care whether I wrote a note or not? It never would be dropped over. My expression of disgust at this horse-play must have betrayed me for he questioned, "Do you Americans not do that?"

"Certainly!" angry now. "We do, but I do not believe you will."

Not a wince, not even a sign of mild displeasure, but in a cool tone he continued, "You write the note—it will be dropped over the lines," and handed me paper and a pencil.

No harm to write one and a refusal will be final. If they drop it, well and good; if not, nothing is lost. How—how to get information to my squadron? Scribbling, I started to tell where I was shot down, hoping that would indicate where the crack German anti-aircraft battery was located.

"Not a history!" he interrupted, watching me like a hawk. "A note . . . just a note. Say your motor stopped and you landed in Germany, that is sufficient."

They might drop it, they might! Anxious to inform my squadron I was alive, words took form under my hand.

> Capt. Peterson,
> 95th Aero Squadron,
> 1st Pursuit Group
> A.E.F.
> France.
> Motor quit. Landed in Germany.
> Not wounded. Kindly wire my parents.
> Norman S. Archibald.

He folded the paper and put it in his pocket. The aviators, who through the entire playlet sat like sphinxes, nodded—majestically. The officer, opening a brief case, took out a map and spread it on the table.

"Now let us see," he began, adjusting gold rimmed glasses. "Here is Paris, Ah! that wonderful city, and here is St.-Mihiel. The Americans will start a big drive here soon but it will amount to *that*," (a snap of his fingers), and with jocular remarks and senseless quips and quirks he pointed to various places.

"What did the Americans think of our troops annihilating the Second Division?" he asked without a change of manner or tone.

"Did they?" A look of inquiry.

"What?" he snapped. "You, an aviator, a gentleman, an educated man, never heard that the Second Division was wiped out?"

"You flatter me, sir, but I never heard it."

"You say you never heard it?" Threatening, domineering.

"No!"

My word, my word as a gentleman, had been questioned! Rude! Preposterous! But, of a fiery yet forgiving nature, I would deign to explain.

"In fact, I happened to hear that the Second Division won a great victory at Belleau Wood." Very politely.

Would the room hold him? His fury was scathing and walking around the table until the storm abated he changed his method of indirect questioning and blurted.

"Where is your aerodrome?"

The Jekyll had changed to Hyde. Not daring to insult his intelligence with a lie and fearing the consequences of a refusal I said, "Sir, I am sorry, but I cannot answer your question."

"What! . . . you . . . you dare . . ."

"I dare nothing. You want the truth, a lie would not deceive you, and any answer of mine would be a lie."

Angrily he rose, folded the map and, with the spick-span aviators, mum as oysters on a holiday, trailing behind, started away.

"Will the food and jam be sent up?"

Without noticing me he flicked imaginary specks off his coat and complaining about "the horrible ordeal in this filthy place" brushed past the guard.

The click of the bolt . . . alone again.

Four empty chairs, and, trying each one, a sense of satisfaction came over me. The afternoon had been interesting, almost pleasant, and a high officer of the German Intelligence Service had failed to get any information. Would I be punished for my attitude? And walking the floor I rehearsed word for word what had been said, contemplating the aftermath.

Pangs of hunger. Must be six o'clock or later. As I stamped on the floor, which always brought results, the soft call, "Cheerio, Cheerio," like a wind-blown song, drifted over. Wish I could meet that Englishman. . . .

"*Was ist hier los?*"

"An officer who was just here ordered food for me, where is it?"

"*Ja*, it comes now. *Ja, ja, bald* . . ."

Funny little Sergeant, almost liked him.

About fifteen minutes later in came a guard with black bread and a saucer of jam. The jam looked appetizing but, shoving some into my mouth with a finger, I found it was old, musty and made of carrots. Thankful, however, to get anything I tore the moldy bread into chunks, spread the sticky stuff over it, and ate my supper.

CHAPTER XVII

COUNTING the days. September 10th. Tramping men in the distance. Nearer, steadier, louder until their heavy boots, hitting the cobblestones, passed by. Hundreds upon hundreds, on and on; more soldiers marching to the Front for the drive of September 12. Another night. A long wait for dawn; a bowl of *ersatz* coffee; black bread (ravenously eaten) and a request to walk in the garden which was refused.

The morning was an eternity . . . arranging the bed, changing the table, placing a chair in a corner with the hope it might be overlooked, fiddling with the shutters, walking . . . walking . . . thinking and planning to escape. About noon. A clatter. People climbing the stairs raised my hopes. Callers! more Germans to question me; even a third degree would be welcome and, sure enough, they stopped outside. The door was unlocked. Lo and behold! there in the clouded opening stood two American aviators and a German guard.

We looked at each other . . . soberly. Words were not needed. Lest we be separated, our emotions must be concealed from the guard who, grunting, took out the chairs and bolted the door.

Three men. Three Americans. Three flyers. Three

prisoners of war were, for the nonce, ill at ease and abashed in a moment of strained pleasure.

"Have a cigarette," offered one who, beaming with delight and comprehension at my eager acceptance, introduced himself as Lawson, his comrade as Foster, and sitting on the bed, we told of our captures.

Both were observation pilots.

On September 7th Lawson and his observer, well over the lines and photographing enemy territory, were surprised by an attack of Fokker pursuit ships which dove on the tail of their lone plane. The observer, swinging his guns, fired at the swift enemy planes and then, wounded, slumped into the cockpit. Lawson, his rear guns silenced, was alone and helpless in a slow machine so, with no alternative, he dove. The Fokkers, pouring machine gun bullets, pursued him and by some miracle Lawson, unhurt, safely landed his bullet-riddled ship at Puxe, near Conflans. Dragging his half-conscious gunner from the cockpit, he laid him on the ground and, while he was trying to stop the flow of blood pouring from a leg torn to pieces by bullets, one of the Fokkers landed. The German pilot got out of his plane, left his motor running and watched Lawson as he worked feverishly over his wounded observer. "If I only had had a pistol I could have shot that Hun, put my observer in his plane and flown away." An officer with German soldiers arrived. One, examining the Allied plane, accidentally discharged the rear machine guns, severely wounding two onlookers. Fuming with rage, revengeful, they surged around Lawson and would have taken his life but for the stern intervention of their officer. The observer was growing weaker and as Lawson tried to bandage up his leg the Germans pulled him away. "Good-bye," he said, looking back. The wounded man, gurgling an answer, groaned and was still. "I never saw him again," said Lawson.

Foster, too, had been attacked by a formation of Fokkers. Another fight against hopeless odds. His observer, loosening his safety belt, stood up to man the rear guns. An enemy burst got him; he slipped into the cockpit . . . dead. Foster, frantically trying to shake off his wasp-like antagonists and escape the death spatterings on the wings, pulled up and kicked over on his back . . . "A dark thing flashed before my eyes—the body of my observer." His dead gunner, hurtled through space, fell into eternity and Foster, forced to land, was taken prisoner.

Two o'clock. The guard brought in three steaming bowls. Soup!—Hot soup! Greedily we ate to ease the gnawing of stomachs pinched with hunger. Brown, unsavory, sticky and thick, it was filled with small leaves, twigs and particles similar to, if not, sawdust. But it was hot and it was food, so gulping it down we talked of our future.

Three things were vital to our existence: food, sleep, air. Food, ill-tasting and unwholesome, must be eaten and we would eat all we could get. Sleep, on boards and in our uniforms, was difficult but sleep we must. Air, except for my delightful recess, was denied. This manner of living, we knew, could not be withstood for long.

When would the war end? We would reason logically. America was a big factor. Hundreds of thousands of troops and vast quantities of supplies were pouring into France. In the spring the Allies would, doubtless, start a drive which would end the war. But—spring was a long way off, a real offensive could not be expected before and a winter in Germany was unthinkable. What if Germany were not defeated?

"I've heard that after eighteen months prisoners are exchanged." Lawson, downhearted, grasped at a straw.

"Eighteen months? God! A year and a half in these

holes . . . we won't be here." And deciding that escape, our only salvation, was problematical but possible we plotted a get-away.

Escape! We must escape! No alternative; no other solution. Dreaming of freedom we whispered that if ever moved from here we must judge distances and watch for landmarks. While we were planning the sergeant came in announcing, "You are going now." Foster and Lawson got up. We shook hands. "Good-bye," I said, telling them how much their visit meant. The sergeant interrupted, "You going too."

"What?" doubting my ears.

"You going also."

"Me?"

"*Ja, ja, ja,*" pompously. "Dot's fine, *ja?*" Stolid, square-faced, nice little man, he felt my liking for him and was proud as Punch to bring the good news.

"Fine! You're right, it's fine, *ja, ja,*" and talking excitedly we started out.

"Cheerio . . . Cheerio . . ." The voice was faint, the good-bye but an echo. He may be sick . . . or dying . . .

"Fast, we go fast." The sergeant, under orders, was in a hurry. Leaving this filthy place, it was too good to be true, but following him down the hall, the great tide of joy backwatered and memory of the Englishman with his beautiful voice and game "Cheerio" was an undertow pulling, pulling me back.

"Keep your eyes open," we whispered to each other as, at the foot of the stairs, an officer and four guards took charge of us.

Grouped together, the guards around us in a square, the officer in front, we walked down the center of the village street. Passing some soldiers, the swipe of a cane knocked my flying cap high into the air, but catching it, I shoved it into my pocket and marched along.

We boarded a train. In a compartment with the guards in strategic seats in the four corners, Lawson, Foster, the officer and I sat down. Doors and windows were locked; revolvers were brought to light. "If you try to escape, we shoot you," one guard patted his gun. The train started.

Where were we going? What direction? Why the change? Long after dark the train jerked to a stop. We walked for several miles over fields and low rolling hills until we came to an enclosure. Two barbed wire fences, about ten feet high, six feet apart and turned over at the top, surrounded a low brick building and in the open, outside, was a wooden structure, presumably the guard house. Met by a German sergeant, we were led through gates cut in the double row of prickly meshing and into the brick building, which was but one room wide. Two beds, planks for mattresses, were built steamer fashion against the wall. Two others, boards nailed to posts, stood two feet from the floor. Inside. The door was shut. Four walls of solid brick and we were in total darkness but for a tiny window near the ceiling.

"This is a pretty little spot," Lawson tried to laugh.

"How do you know, you can't see it?" Foster aimed at cheerfulness.

"I can smell it, same old smell . . ."

But solitary confinement was a gruesome fear and, expecting darkness and smells, I was grateful for companionship.

The door swung. A guard, holding a kerosene lamp, threw something in and slammed out. We found torn pieces of heavy cloth and accepted them as bedding. Thick walls held us tight, but within thick walls we could talk freely. Plans for escape, new ones, crazy ones and a ray of hope

blasted against impossibilities.   Our talk went in circles.
Weak from lack of nourishing food and tired we agreed to
go to sleep.

Thunder!   A storm came up, rain fell in torrents and the
wind, howling and blowing a gale, screeched through the
barbed wire. Sheltered from the blustering weather, thankful to be warm and dry, sleep came quickly.

A boisterous racket.   Loud talking; swearing; scuffling of
feet; a fight and the guards, plainly distraught, pushed a
human figure into the room.   Accustomed to the dark I
could see him, sprawled on the floor, in a fur-lined flying
suit, holding his head in pain.   Stooping with a hand on his
groin he got up and for fully fifteen minutes stood motionless. We did not stir and at last, without removing his rain-
soaked flying suit, he crawled into an upper bunk.

Dawn—rain pattered, gently.   Daylight—sun shone
through the high window and a shaft of light, apricot
through the black, ripened into a golden spot on the floor.
When the guard, with bowls of coffee and a loaf of bread,
came in we called to the stranger.   Laboring with pain he
eased himself down but, sipping the coffee, was so depressed
he could not talk or eat.

"Well, what happened to you?"

Without answering he looked at us, sadly.

"Take off your flying suit, be comfortable," we suggested
to this man on the verge of melancholia.

After repeated questions he sniveled, "Ah! this is terrible! A prisoner in Germany! To be locked up; to fly
no more . . ." But, assured of our sympathy—were we not
all in the same boat?—he told his tale.

A Frenchman, a bombing pilot, he was on a raid over
Germany when caught in the storm and, forced to land, he
was taken prisoner.

"It's a wonder you weren't blown to pieces," we congratulated, "hitting the earth with a load of explosives. Where is your bomber, and why did you ever leave your aerodrome in France in such a raging storm?"

His grief was overwhelming. His answers, evasive, incoherent and always in unaccented English, meant nothing. Our suspicions were aroused. Would a Frenchman in such distress never revert to his mother tongue? What pilot could so disregard the safety of his observer? A few more leading questions, easily answerable by plain and honest truths and we knew this whimpering nincompoop was a German posing as a French aviator to get information.

He got it!

"I got by with . . . this!" Sweet was his childlike expression as he pulled out a pistol. That was the last straw. One thing the Germans did with great thoroughness was to search their captured enemies.

"So you did, you lucky scamp!"

"How wonderful!"

"Damned clever of you . . ."

We congratulated him with boyish, unstinted enthusiasm.

"Did you fellows get by with anything?" he went on. The cute rascal!

Admitting, shamefacedly, our lack of cunning, we again lauded his sapient nimble-wittedness until the impostor, employed to fool us by trickery and deceit, thought we believed him. Basking in our flattery, accepted as a Frenchman, a flyer and a comrade, his smile was smug and forgetting completely his ailments he coerced us "innocents" into conversation. What news he would hear! What knowledge he would glean! Content with his chicanery he saw a decoration, an iron cross, perhaps, as, confidentially, we told him—everything.

Of course he knew what enormous quantities of supplies

were coming from America? Yea, forsooth—all Frenchmen were aware of that. The millions of troops already in France?—just a starter; millions more were en route and millions frothing to come. As for the tremendous power of the Allies, well, it was inestimable, and food (he pricked up his ears) surely he had heard what delicacies—yum! yum!—smack!—were pouring into his beloved country?

Knowing that the mere mention of anything to eat would rack the very guts of a German we spun fantastic fairy tales about dainty edibles now available in France. He listened attentively, without comment, and switching to Germany, we glibly confided how the Americans, when thoroughly organized with their Allies, would crush "our mutual enemy." Poor Germany! Ha!—ha!! At the end of her rope. And the Great Imperial Army—what a joke—soon to be annihilated.

Noon. A guard with the pretense of transferring the prisoner to another camp, took him away. "Good Luck! Keep your spirits up," we encouraged. "It won't be long now." And with a last jab, "The *Vaterland* is doomed, do not worry," we said, *"au revoir."* The door clicked behind him. We rocked with laughter.

. . . . .

Two drab, uneventful, hungry days followed. The third morning we had a pleasant surprise and were allowed to walk between the brick walls of the prison and the inside barbed wire fence. Confined, in a strip of space, we enjoyed "Freedom." Penned in, with glum guards shouldering bayoneted rifles, we drank in the air. Escape, from here, was impossible and lingering looks towards France were tantalizing.

Forcing conversation with the sergeant commander we learned that this prison, about thirty miles from the Front, was on the outskirts of Montmédy. Taking mental notes of distances and directions for future escape, now hopeless, we were resigned to the present.

Next to food, cleanliness was foremost. Since our capture we had never taken off our clothes. Beards covered dirty faces; hair, uncombed and disheveled, was smeared with filth; our bodies, sticky with sweat and odorous, were objectionable. We complained to the guard. We demanded a way of sanitation. We coaxed and begged for a bath. We made him smell us. Then, by flattering, wheedling and bribing we got a bowl of water and a flour sack. Faces first, then our hands; sparing the "towel" as best we could. Still dirty, but refreshed, we gloated in the privilege and with the daily bowl of water came a lavation performed as seriously as a religious ritual.

Breakfast—*ersatz* coffee and black bread. Luncheon— soup. Supper—a cup of *ersatz*. The lack of food was reflected in our dispositions. Underfed, always hungry, we were irritable. Walks in the air meant an appetite and an appetite, without food, meant dizziness and pain. Languid and loath to admit our feelings we talked and talked. Were all German prisons like this? Was this a permanent camp? Would we be moved again? Four days. Four nights. Mental disintegration and physical weakening. Only four days, yet æons had passed.

"We're here till the end of the war—if we live." Our feelings surmounted any previous pretension and with the admission that escape from here was unachievable we openly despaired.

The fifth day. The sergeant, bringing the *ersatz* minus the bread, announced our removal. The news, once so wanted, left us unmoved. We were in Montmédy; but where were we going? The further into Germany, the less chance of escape. "We know where the lines are from here,

for God's sake, let's make a break at the" . . . In came a
lieutenant, and with four guards we plodded over the hills.

The officer was a caricature. He was short; he was
fat; and his apple-pink cheeks were dumplings which puffed
proximity to a little pug nose. Infantile, self-satisfied, his
face, excluding his shifty rat-like eyes, was effeminate and
blubbery. A toy-like soldier, filled with toy-like importance,
a toy-like pistol rested in a holster on his plump left breast.
In a burlesque he would be a riot. As an officer, he was one.
His carriage, his small red mouth pursed with deciding
nothing and his entire demeanor were those of an indis-
pensable personage. In fancy—he was a conqueror. In
truth—he was a dodo. This perhaps explained why, with
four guards to escort three defenseless prisoners, he could
flip-flap over hill and dale instead of fighting at the Front.

We had walked for about half an hour when yells of
"Halt! Halt!" came from behind and a guard, from the
prison, was running pell-mell to catch us. *"Halt!"* our
master's voice, and we waited as the dispatcher, between
puffs and blows, gasped out his grave message. An article—
could not catch the word—had been stolen. We, the Americans had taken something valuable. Thieves—we were—
common thieves; it must be returned at once. Burglars,
mean burglars, to run away with a precious thing we knew
did not belong to us. Give up the loot! Give it up! Who
was the culprit?

The officer, scornfully, looked us over and deciding that I
was the most desperate character suggested they search me
first. Innocent and wondering what any one could find to
take, I helped in the turning out of pockets and patting of
intimate places. *"Nichts!"* Nothing! Lawson was next.
Closest overhauling, and much to their annoyance they
found *"noch immer nichts!"* Foster was the felon. Foster,
of all people, had committed the crime. Under his shirt,

neatly tucked, was the booty, the plunder, the stolen goods —the soiled flour sack. The guard, happy with his contraband rag, started away. The officer, treating Foster as a contemptible thief, promised to punish him.

A train, alive with German troops, pulls into the station. Human beings, jammed together, bulge the cars. Squirming heads and shoulders, wedged in the windows, make the sides a mass of movement. The soldiers, a pack of war-crazed lunatics, whoop and yell. They notice us. Wrathful and jeering they point their fingers, shake their fists and, as the train slows to a stop, shout unspeakable oaths, scream vile threats and cry, *"Schweinehunde! Schweinehunde!"*

Our officer warns us to be quiet. He is worried. "Do not look up," he cautions, "pay no attention to their actions," and quickly opening the door of a compartment, he orders the soldiers out. They do not move. Another loud-voiced command, with a hand on his pistol. Insolently, taking time to stretch and mumble, they relinquish their seats. Close together, four guards tight around us, we near the door. The officer, again admonishing us, orders out one remaining occupant. Sitting in the far corner, wearing an Iron Cross and smoking a clay pipe, he does not budge. Fuming with rage the officer shouts angrily. The soldier, puffing away, holds his ground and yells defiance. Platform guards are ordered to drag him out. Rebellious, he fights, kicks and screams as his body is thumped down the steps. Pugnacious to the last, he shrieks and curses the officer as he is hauled away. This is the first disobedience we have seen. The remarkable discipline of the German troops is cracking. The strain of war is telling.

Pushed bodily into the compartment we sit down. The officer and guards follow. "Be silent, do not look out," we are warned. Crowds of soldiers, with hatred for an officer who had pushed out Germans and put Americans in their places, swarm beneath our open window. They grumble, threaten to mob us and are on the verge of rioting. A tense moment. The train starts. Worked up to a frenzy they run alongside, but soon, gaining momentum, we are speeding across open country. The window is shut and locked, the door is bolted and we are told to take off our shoes.

Knapsacks . . . rifles . . . four guards . . . an officer and three prisoners stuff the compartment to its capacity. Wedged in, stocking footed, we can barely move. Lawson wiggles his toes. Foster wiggles his toes. So I wiggle my toes and suspiciously they watch our monkeyshines.

"Try to escape and you will be shot!" Rifles are fixed for immediate use.

We laugh, all three of us.

"Stop laughing," we are reprimanded.

We stop. A carrot, a turnip, a chunk of bread and the guards begin their midday meal.

The officer, spreading a paper napkin across his knees, daintily opens his lunch box. Hungrily—we watch. Bread is brought out, liverwurst, and then a hard-boiled egg. Oh! . . . that hard-boiled egg! Smacking his lips he eats and eats, slowly, as if to tantalize us. My brain, my wicked brain, tells my empty stomach about that egg and the latter organ, jealous with resentment, belches—audibly.

"Where are we going?"

The young pretzel delights in secrecy but one guard, older, fifty perhaps, smiles at us broadly. We smile back. Later in the afternoon he shifts his position and, with one hand over a kneecap, yawns. We watch him. Taking a chance, he turns his hand and hidden in the palm is a scrap of paper scribbled with the word KARLSRUHE. Our faces show delight, for we know Karlsruhe is a large and permanent camp for Allied prisoners. We beam our thanks. He nods acknowledgment, smiles and yawns again. The good old soul.

Hustle, bustle, our shoes are returned and the train stops. "Metz," whispers Lawson.

We are less than twenty miles from the front lines. Surveillance is close, and as we walk from the station our slightest movements are scrutinized. A sign, KRONPRINZEN KANTINE, emblazons the entrance of a long narrow building and, entering an addition still under construction, we sit down on a pile of lumber. A droning babble—hundreds of voices like bees in a bottle—hums in our ears. A door blows open. German soldiers in a seething mass are milling around in the Kantine and we smell a strong odor of beer. The officer, jumping up, slams the door and this precautionary measure, after the Montmédy incident, has our hearty approval.

Two guards leave. They return with frankfurters, bread and pails of foaming beer. They all eat again. Weak, thirsty, hungry—we ask for something. Ha! Ha! . . . what a joke! They laugh heartily, and the officer points to a water spout. "Have a nice drink of water," he says.

Turning to me, his mouth dripping beer foam, he demands in slopping English, "Your name? Vat is your name?"

"Archibald," wanting to strangle him.

"Archibald . . . Ah!" drooling bits of chewed frankfurters, "Dot iss a German name. *Ja*, dot iss German."

"Oh, no," repressing my anger. "Archibald is English."

"Vat?—bald?—bald is German, denn Archi-BALD—dot iss German too." He is stating an unequivocal fact.

"It's English," my tone is dogged, "it's English!"

His definite assertions have been questioned; squinting his eyes, a plain challenge for me to answer again to the contrary, he loses his temper and yells, "Bald . . . bald

. . . bald . . . dot's German and Archi-BALD . . . dot's German."

It is all so damned ridiculous that I parrot, "Bald . . . bald . . . bald . . . dot's German and Archi-BALD . . . dot's German! Certainly! Hell yes, that's German." And with this false admission the argument ends. The younger guards look nonplussed but the elder one smiles.

My thoughts wander. We are near the lines . . . what results from the St.-Mihiel drive? Near the lines . . . near the squadron . . . my squadron, and I slip, slip, slip into the lumber. The aerodrome at Rembercourt . . . the pilots climb into their ships . . . everything all right? . . . yes, Lieutenant . . . we sail away on a patrol. Freedom! . . . the freedom and the old joy flow through me as I fly into the heavens and . . . W-H-A-M! God! I am a prisoner, under guard, going to Karlsruhe! Terror grips me afresh.

The guards, statues, look at each other. We listen. The whining roar of a shell—B-O-O-M! It hits and the earth trembles from a mighty explosion. The babble in the Kantine is hushed. Silence. The officer, pale and shaking, explains, "The Americans are shooting at you!" He is terrified. "The Americans, they shoot *you*." A sickly smile does not conceal his dread of shells, which he insists our own countrymen are aiming at us. The ass. W-H-A-M! nearer now. W-H-A-M! mighty explosions at close intervals. The Americans are getting the range! Great, keep at it, shoot away, boys, your aim is perfect; and watching the terror-stricken guards . . . especially the shrimp officer, we are so exhilarated that danger to ourselves is never thought of. W-H-A-M! Such overwhelming uproars are not from ordinary guns; must be the railway Naval guns belching destruction on the bridges and railroad yards at Metz.

B-A-N-G! A Titanic concussion! . . . close.

Hundreds of Fritzes, like scurrying ants, pour out of the Kantine and, running helter-skelter, knock each other down as they scuttle to underground shelters. In less than a minute, with the exception of our four guards, not a Boche is left. The KRONPRINZEN KANTINE, doors wide open, and beer running from overturned pails, is empty. The guards, daring not to leave us, grip their rifles with shaking hands and look paralyzed. Their officer, the darling, made a hasty, if not manly, get-away long ago.

Five, ten, about fifteen minutes pass and the explosions stop. No more shells come over. The Fritzes, emerging from their safety holes, return. The prattle of beer-drinking Germans resumes. The guards relax. But—where, oh where, has the little runt gone? Our champion, our leader, our master of ceremonies is nowhere to be seen. Ah! Look to the left, in struts Sir Galahad himself, proud, unafraid, cool as a red pepper and about to order more beer.

The day passes—we are hungry. Evening comes—we are weary. Night. A train whistles. Weak and tired we climb aboard. In a fourth class coach, filled with soldiers, our shoes removed, doors and windows closed and the air permeated with nauseous body odors, we rumble towards Karlsruhe. Stops. Delays. Vigilant guards and carousing of troops.

Midnight. Sick fatigue sets in. Our heads droop and we doze off. A rifle butt jabs our ribs. "Stay awake." The guards are watchful. We try, mightily, and spitting on our fingers rub them across burning lids, but our eyes will not stay open. It is torture. Again, involuntarily, we slip into stupor. Another jab, deeper this time; the guards revel in their proddings. Our exhausted bodies ache on the board seats. We cannot turn; we cannot stand; we cannot keep awake and we are sore from the thrusts.

Retaliation is impossible. The night is a night of torment
—a night in Hell. God! What an existence!

Morning. The train stops. Seven o'clock.

The soldiers file out, march away and we step onto a
deserted platform. The sun shines, the wind blows, the
air is fresh and excitement revives us.

This railroad station is immaculate, spotlessly clean and
a glaring contrast to rubbish-laden stations in France.
Lawson, Foster and I, with the four guards shouldering
rifles and the officer ahead, start toward the city. Sidewalks and paved streets are free from dirt; buildings glisten; Karlsruhe is clean, orderly and beautiful. Civilians,
going to work, glance at us. We trot along, quite happy,
for Hope trots with us. We are nearly there. Soon we
will be in a large, permanent, well-organized camp. There
will be a courtyard. We will walk in the air. The food
will be better and strength will come. Other Allied prisoners will talk to us and, with companionship and health,
we will be in a penned-up Paradise.

Along the street, parading the middle, a turn and on our
right is a large, imposing edifice. Beautiful, white, it has
the semblance of a fashionable European hostelry closed
after a gay season. The main door is shut. The officer
rings a bell.

"Pretty luxurious," Lawson smiles. "Suppose it's the
prison?"

"Never!" Foster and I agree the "Nabob" is stopping
for directions, but the door opens, he motions to the guards
and we are taken into a spacious front hall where stands
a German sergeant.

"Some style to . . ." But before he finishes, Lawson is
jerked away by a guard.

Foster and I look. We dare not speak and the guard,
returning, takes Foster away. Alone with the other four

guards, Chowderhead, and the sergeant commander of the building, I wonder what next when, taking my arm, the Sergeant starts with me.

"Vell, Archi-BALD," sneers the stuffed-bellied moron, "goot-bye, see you in de next var, Ja?"

Unheeding, wanting to kill him, I am pushed down a long hall.

"Go fast up the stairs!"

Climbing . . . climbing . . . climbing . . . One flight. Two flights. Three . . . my knees are crumpling.

"Hurry! fast up the stairs!"

Steps . . . steps . . . steps . . . will I make it?

Four flights.

A corridor. A door. The Sergeant unlocks it, gives me a shove and I trip . . . fall headlong . . . and land in a room.

CHAPTER XVIII

DARKNESS, again. Alone, again. The room, about ten feet square, has a table, a wooden-slatted bed and a tiny frosted window near the ceiling. Bewildered by this turn of events, raging at the uncalled-for treatment, I try to analyze this strange, foreboding exigency.

Pacing the floor! Infuriated by my fall! Anger melts into curiosity; curiosity travels to facts; facts bring fear and fear, unadulterated fear, crushes me. Iron hands . . . squeezing, squeezing, squeezing, I am a string.

This is Karlsruhe. Why am I separated from Lawson and Foster? This is Karlsruhe. Where are they? This is Karlsruhe; the permanent prison camp; yet, I am in solitary confinement. In solitary confinement . . . in Karlsruhe? Despair defeats me. Hope slips out, I feel it go, and misery stalks in. The frightful truth is clear, too clear.

Rage, anxiety and gruesome facts mingle. My analysis is correct. This is Karlsruhe. No more changes. This is permanent. Solitary confinement for the rest of the war. The thought freezes me. To live in solitary confinement is impossible. I am doomed.

Lawson and Foster . . . are they alone? Other prisoners . . . just caged animals waiting for the end? Food—

how do they feed them all? Separately? A lot of trouble carrying food to each cell. Must be a main room, easier for them, where all eat together. Over and over I tell myself, aloud, that midday will prove there is a central eating place. Bet Puryear will be there. Nine . . . ten—is it eleven o'clock yet? Why pace back and forth like a tiger, noon will come. Even the Germans cannot stay the tides.

A step. The lock. Twelve o'clock.

Here I go—sure as Heaven. Bet it's a large hall, everyone filing in, Lawson, Foster, Puryear, and— The door opens. A tall man with a black beard sidles in. Loose trousers hang from his hips and beneath a dirt-caked undershirt, gaping down the front, a hairy chest and belly stick out. He grins, foolishly. I grin back. He puts a bowl of soup and a cup of *ersatz* on the table and starts away.

"Wait a minute, listen . . ."

Turning, he shakes his head, sadly.

"Warten Sie einen Augenblick!"

Not understanding, he shakes his head, again.

"Russe?"

He nods, smiles, pulls up his trousers and his eyes burn fire as he speaks to me in Russian. I shake my head. A guard's step in the hall. The Russian cowers and hurries out.

Soup and coffee—nothing to chew. The soup is the worst; get it down and then the coffee. Thick, sour as swill but, determined to keep it down, I hold my nose, pour it in, throw the bowl on the bed and walk around fighting a rebellious stomach. The *ersatz*, after a rinsing swig, I sip, sip, sip to prolong the act of doing something.

The afternoon is harrowing. Obsessed with thoughts of solitary confinement I am nerve-racked. Tired, but too jumpy to rest; weary, but too awake to sleep. Undress—

that will take time. Slowly, I take off my clothes, count the garments, shake them and slowly put them on again. I haul the bed around, change the table and lying on the floor watch the white window frosting. The Russian will be along with supper. Kindly, how he wanted to talk! Why in Hell had I not studied Russian? *Durch—für— gegen*—even know *t*he German rules. *Aus—bei—mit— nach*—they govern the dative. Damned waste of time, that. Grey frosting. Twilight. Anticipating the return of the Russian and something to chew, a certain content- ment comes over me.

Black. The days are getting shorter. September is an autumn month. Summer is gone and the days are shorter. Leaves are turning to red and gold . . . somewhere—yel- low, red, and gold, blowing in the wind and spilling on the ground. How we used to tramp in the rain, pouring rain, around the lake and through the woods! Hazel, always kicking the leaves, and one day, just walking along, she made up a poem:

> *I walked me through an autumn wood*
> *The wind was blowing high*
> *And leaves of gold, of red and gold*
> *Came tumbling from the sky.*

"Soaking wet, you children are soaking wet." Tea be- fore the fire, stuffing, stuffing, toast and marmalade and ginger cookies. "No, not another bite, you will spoil your appetite for dinner."

A step down the hall. The Russian is coming with my supper! My breath jerks . . . I face the door. Plank, plank, plank, the steps go past my room. Odd, probably going to someone else. Breathless now, standing in the black. Plank, plank, plank, past again and the sound dies away. Must be the guard, days are shorter, not time for supper, yet. Too early, by and by, maybe a whole hour. Waiting, waiting, how the minutes drag. No idea of time when one is alone. Too early for supper, after a bit, maybe two hours—

He never came. No supper. I lay down on the wooden slats.

A rattle. Stupid from a deadening sleep my eyes, half opening, see a wall. My bones ache on the hard boards but the warm glory of slipping back into priceless oblivion enfolds me. A sound in the room, and startled I sit bolt upright. Beside my bed stands the Russian, solemnly. My head pounds, and doped with fatigue my body topples. Arms of iron catch me, sit me up and the Russian, grinning, points to *ersatz* and a lump of black bread on the table. So—it is morning.

Must eat. Coffee and bread. Must eat breakfast. Need food and, swaying, I start for the table. A tight band grips my waist; a bowl is held to my lips; words unknown are understood and, held in the strong arms of the Russian I open my lips and the coffee, trickling down, revives me. The bread is put into my hand and, leading me back to the bed, my benefactor leaves. Stimulated by the *ersatz* I munch at the sour bread and, with a dogged determination to be nourished, eat every crumb.

Nine o'clock. Ten. Eleven. Twelve. My head is splitting. Need food. Luncheon will be at noon. Pains, like steel arrows, shoot through my temples. Crazed with agony I stamp on the floor and kick at the door. A guard, rifled and with a long beard, enters to say angrily that such noises will not be tolerated. I explain in German my lack of luncheon but he pretends not to understand. In a tirade I insist on seeing someone who speaks English. About fifteen minutes later he returns with a man of slight build with blond hair and in civilian clothes.

"They have forgotten to bring luncheon," I complain.

"You get supper at four o'clock." He is contemptuous. "Two meals a day here."

"But I had no supper yesterday and . . ."

Motioning the guard to shut the door he goes out.

Holding my throbbing head I lie on the bed. The pain is excruciating. I try to walk but my legs are silly, and, dizzy, I lie down again. At four the good Samaritan appears with soup . . . only soup. Familiar and tasteless; I drink it down and chew the twigs.

Another sick stupor. Hours of blessed forgetfulness. Nature's holy restorative, rest without suffering, and another dawn.

At eight o'clock the Russian, entering softly, looks at me with pitying eyes. Gesticulating my gratitude and jumping about to assure him of new strength, I greedily start on the bread and coffee. A clumsy hand pats my shoulder; a smile, compassionate; he yanks up his trousers and slouches out.

The morning passes quickly. A clear head and the joy of false vigor makes me active with schemes of escape. Physical contrasts, from seeming health to utter lassitude, frighten me. To stay here means death. Pulling the bed below the window I put the table on it and climb on top. My eyes are just below the sill but by standing tip-toed and stretching my neck until the cords pull I can see. A small, clear spot in the frosting is my peephole and before it are the streets of Karlsruhe. People walking. Blue sky. Clear. What weather! What flying weather! Sunshine and a light breeze. What perfect flying weather!

Looking . . . looking . . . nose flat spread against the pane, hands tight on the narrow ledge. Straining . . . straining . . . one eye and then the other with toes trembling on the shaky table. Four stories up. Could I squeeze through some night and drop down? What was below? Pressing . . . pressing . . . my eyeballs touch the glass and the table topples over. Dangling . . . hanging by my finger tips I let go, slide down and my hand is ripped open on a protruding nail-head. Blood and telltale bits of skin on the wall. If seen, they might move me to another room. The peek-place is precious and tearing off a piece of my undershirt I spit on it, try to erase the marks and with another strip tie up my hand.

Afternoon. About two o'clock. Shrill, whistling notes shriek through the quiet. Sirens! Screeching blasts whine their warning and again I strain, stretch and peer out. An air raid on Karlsruhe! People scattering through the streets. The Allies are bombing Karlsruhe! Clutching, holding my balance, I am thrilled that bombing planes are spitting into a German city.

Men running, women hustling, toddling children crying and dogs howling as the distracted inhabitants hurry to safety. The streets are clear. The sirens are silent. Guns, anti-aircraft, blasts and whangs cause bedlam in the deserted city. Shrapnel rains on the pavements. Torrents of steel pour on the sidewalks. WHAM! The powerful explosion of a bomb! Allied planes are unloading their annihilating projectiles. German guns, hundreds of them, belch back defense destruction. BANG! A high explosive bomb drops . . . what a satisfaction! "Give them Hell!" I shout. Defense anti-aircraft retorts with a thunderous barrage. BANG! . . . another; the planes are flying directly over the city. BANG! BANG! . . . two in succession, still closer. The ships on their approach had flown beyond the city, turned and are unloading as they head for France. W-H-A-M! . . . a deafening explosion! A stupendous concussion! A direct hit. The building shakes, and hurled through the room I land on the floor. Confusion in the hall—running—loud talking—shattering glass. More glass breaks—the building must be hit! Lying in a heap I wait for, and fully expect, the prison to collapse.

Glass tinkles; the building, shivering, rights itself. A dull Woof: a bomb exploding in the distance. The planes, all their missiles released, are flying home. Arranging my tumbly tower I climb back. High in the sky, dark birds against the blue, two Allied bombing planes sail majestically towards France. "Good work, boys! Good work!" And as five Fokkers climb in pursuit I yell, "Too late, Heinies, too late; those boys are on their way."

Watching, watching, until the brown specks, smaller and smaller, dissolve into the blue. They are gone. The sky is clear. The air is still. The raid is over. Figures move in the streets.

Crawling down I wonder what aerodrome they were from, and sitting on the edge of my bed I can see them sailing for France—sailing for home. God! to be with them. What a day for flying! Thoughts of my squadron and the old flying days suffocate me. Unhappiness chokes me. Cooped up here, stagnant, inactive; wish the damned building had gone over. Might have run away . . . might have been killed . . . better that, even, than half dead in a filthy prison. Wonder who is left at the aerodrome? Which ones? Never to fly again over the lines; never to start in the cool dusk of dawn; never to sail for home in the twilight; never again to stroll into the hangar and smell the carbonized castor oil; never to fight quickly in the sun; but, slowly, to battle for life in the dark, to grow weaker, weaker and sit alone until the whole show is over. Never

again . . . never . . . never . . . never—a noise at the
door and tears are hastily wiped away.

The guard, flushed and excited, glances in. He sees
me, smirks guiltily, mumbles *"ja, ja,"* hurriedly locks the
door and clatters away. Supposedly on watch during the
raid he was in safe hiding and now, fearful, is full of duty
checking up the prisoners.

Four o'clock. The Russian grins. A bowl of soup. A
bug crawls up the wall. Utter darkness. Plans for escape
are illusive; dreams of flying are disturbing; a long, long
night ahead, the ache from the boards—guess I'll try the
floor for a change.

Early the next morning a bushy-faced individual, of uncertain nationality, crooked his finger and with an authoritative grunt beckoned me. I followed him down the hall;
we entered a room and there, in civilian clothes, sat my
blond visitor of two days before.

"Good morning," smiling and rubbing his white hands.
"Sit down." And he pulled a chair conveniently near him.
"Have a cigarette?" holding out a full package. I took
one. "Have some more," he urged, "certainly, take two or
three."

Thrusting four into my pocket I sat back, watching this
anæmic Hun and surmising the reason for his generous
hospitality.

With paper and pencil before him he started on the old
worn-out questions.

"I have answered all these questions," feeling too weak
to be goaded. "An intelligence officer questioned me when
I was captured."

"You will answer my questions!" His thin, pale face
screwed up. "You are a prisoner of war! You are under

the jurisdiction of the German Empire!   I know you understand this and will not cause unnecessary trouble.   These questions must be answered.   Your name?"

In rapid succession my name, age, rank, squadron and where captured were written down.   Then technical queries: the speed of a Spad, its climbing ability, manœuvring qualities, type and horsepower of its motor, etc.   The Germans had all this information but this pale-faced rake, I knew, had no knowledge of flying and my spontaneous answers were wide of the truth.

"Where is your aerodrome?"

"I cannot tell you."

"You refuse to answer?"

"I do."

"The penalty, do you know the penalty?" striding up and down the room.   "But I will give you one more chance, now where is your aerodrome?"

"I cannot tell you."

"You will suffer, you will pay," and yelling, "Take him away!" he waved his arm in dismissal.

Back in my room, counting the priceless cigarettes, I felt the joke was on the interpreter.

Time for luncheon.   No Russian.   No *ersatz* or bread.   The dirty pig, so that is his penalty.   All day long, hour after hour, tilted and strained I watch the city.

The light, in contrast to my four drab walls, is giddily beautiful.   Each ordinary movement of an ordinary town is fascinating.   Eyes surfeited with the dismal room are enchanted by commonplace activities; sights unworthy of notice are given meticulous attention; Karlsruhe, through the small circled vision, is a fantastic amphitheatre; remnants of the population are the actors.   A bent form in petticoats, a basket on her arm, waddles past.   Where is

she going?   A slip and, hunched on the table, I tumble
to the floor.   My neck aches, my legs pull, my eyes burn,
but the ever changing panorama is a siren's song and up I
climb.

Children, colorful and skipping, dance all too quickly into
the white border.   A larger space . . . could see a lot more
. . . and teetering, teetering, my finger nails scrape at
the frosting.   Damn!   A vain clutch at the sill and my
body bangs on the floor.   Obstinate, curious, with an un-
satisfied craving for the diversion I again peer at the ka-
leidoscopic performance.   Soldiers parade before a sky
curtain.   Civilians, exempt from service and disabled, are
a dreary background.   An automobile, a cart, a slow-gaited
horse and a playful puppy blend into the picturesque scene.
Drama, comedy, burlesque or a bit of opera, according to
the eye, the sound and the imagination.   Not until standing
on my toes becomes agony and stretching my neck is torture
do I, unwillingly, crawl down to rest.

Four o'clock.   No supper.   Soup—cautiously gaining the
peep-hole—time for soup.   Damn that interpreter.

Grey gauze covers the town; a figure, without limbs,
passes.   Soup . . . the devil take that putty-faced Boche!
Two soldiers, phantoms in a black veil, march . . . march
. . . march . . . and darkness drops her final curtain.

The middle of the night.   Thirsty.   Wish I had a drink
of water.   I pace the floor.   My lips are parched.   A tall
glass of cold water.   The saliva burns.   Clear, cool water
to drench my scorching mouth.   My tongue is thick.   Water,
a spoonful, to trickle down my hot throat.   Water!   I
kick at the door.   Not a sound.   Water!   I swallow, swallow and pound on the walls.   Quiet in the hall.   Not a stir.
Water! . . . water! . . . water! . . . just one drop . . .

CHAPTER XIX

MORNING. About seven now. Breakfast at eight. Famished I wait and wait but nothing comes. At eleven a guard enters and, holding fast to my arm, leads me along the hall, down four flights of stairs and into a courtyard.

The sun is blinding. Armed guards with spiked helmets pace back and forth on the rim of a medieval-looking wall. This stone wall, fully twelve feet high and four feet thick, surrounds a small enclosure where Frenchmen, Italians, Englishmen and Americans, in different groups, all talk at once.

"Archibald! By God! never thought I'd see you again." Lawson, pale and drawn, greets me. "Thought we were in solitary confinement for the rest of the war."

"So did I."

Joy at seeing him is spoiled by my weakness.

"Did that blondy in civilian clothes question you?" Foster, too, looks miserable.

Exchanging stories of our treatment Lawson interrupts. "That damn fool asked so many silly questions about my plane I said, 'It's in a field near Conflans, why not run over and get some first-hand information?' "

"What did he say to that?"

"Not much. No food for a day, but I'm used to fasting."
He smiles bravely.

We stroll around the courtyard.

Stooped figures. Emaciated bodies. Boys once exuberant and proud in bright colored uniforms are men, listless
and ashamed, in faded, ragged clothes. The enthusiasm of
youth is supplanted by apathetic old age. Sunken eyes
stare in bewilderment. Pale faces, ugly with scars and
burns, are repellent. Hollow cheeks, drawn by raw wounds,
are disfigured . . . *permanent decorations of valor*. Bandages, black with dirt, slip over still green sores. Waxen
lips tremble. Thin legs wabble. Fear, suffering, mental
anguish and hunger have left their marks . . . *indelible
medals of war*.

"CHEERIO!"

That voice! That inimitable voice! Same word . . .
same inflection . . . is it the mystery prisoner of Conflans? Where is he, where, where, and looking I call,
"Cheerio! . . . here, come over here."

A tall chap, about twenty, ambles over. Loose arms
swing, long legs stride, and sun glints in his light wavy
hair. A Blue-boy grown up. A Prince Charming comes
to life. Features, chiseled from Dresden china, are pinched
and drawn. His face, although haggard and lined, is delicately æsthetic. He smiles; deep blue eyes reflect the
undaunted spirit of an ardent optimist. Hope ever whispered a flattering tale to this young Englishman.

"I knew your voice." We shake hands. "You cheered
me up a lot calling across the hall and . . ."

"What a fuss you made! Ripping, simply ripping. And
demanding things. By Jove, it was jolly! That's the way,
at first, but"—indicating the others—"not after a real
taste of it."

An American limps over. His gaunt face, shriveled and

tender from severe burns, twitches. A finger, burned to the bone, is stiff and crooked. He smiles, painfully. A scorched uniform is full of burnt holes. Silver wings glisten on his breast! An aviator! Reserved, he modestly explains he was shot down in flames. Shot down in flames and still alive? Inconceivable! To fall, in a burning plane, down, down, down with the rush of wind fanning the licking fires and survive? Miraculous!

"What squadron?" We are spellbound.

"The 95th," he answers proudly.

"What! The 95th? That's *my* squadron." I grab him. "The 95th! Good God, are you McKeown?"

"Yes." He seems embarrassed.

The sad story of McKeown was well known. A wonderful fellow, they told me, shot down in flames . . . dead.

McKeown is ill but his first thought is of the squadron and he asks eagerly, "Did Thompson ever return? He was missing for two days before they got me."

"He was captured on July 5th," I tell him. "No details but he is a prisoner somewhere."

"What about the rest of the bunch?" His fears are plain.

"Vann, Russel, Roosevelt, Curry and Blodgett are dead."

He winces.

"Dusty Rhodes was captured July 7th, the same day you were shot down. Puryear was taken prisoner July 26th; heard anything about him?"

He does not answer.

"Montague was captured on July 31st. Did you know Casgrain, too, was a prisoner?"

"Yes." His voice is far away. "They sent him to Northern Prussia for punishment."

Longing looks toward France. He mentally counts the

casualties of the 95th, saying, "With you and me that makes twelve. Wonder how many more?" He is sad.

"But I have good news for you," wanting to brace him up. "The Group received thirty-eight officially confirmed victories at Château Thierry and only lost thirty-six pilots."

His pathetic face brightens. "One more chance at the Huns! One more and I'd be satisfied . . . just one more," he says.

He is bitter. His only ambition is another crack at the Huns. He wants to escape. It is an obsession. He talks of nothing else; he has received despicable treatment and is unforgiving. Just once more, to fly just once more, that would balance the scales. He has an account to settle. Why so relentless? Why so revengeful?

He tells us.

On July 7th, patrolling over the Château Thierry Front, three Fokkers dove on McKeown. Machine gun bullets, tailed by smoke-wisps, poured at him. McKeown, turning, accepted combat and fired. A dog fight. Three to one. The trio of Fokkers, swerving, diving, zooming and spitting deadly fire; the one American fighting, tenaciously, for his life. A death combat. The odds were too great. A game, single-handed fight was lost. Explosive bullets struck his gas tank and McKeown's plane burst into flames. Fire! He was caught in a flaming death trap and the Fokkers, satisfied, flew away.

Death by fire! Fire! . . . the airman's most feared enemy. At five thousand feet a swift downward plunge, to extinguish the flames, only added fuel to the seething furnace. Fire!—devouring his ship. Flames!—licking his face and hands. His clothes were burning. Down, down, down—plunging, he was burning to death. The intense heat was overpowering. He was burning alive.

"I didn't want to die—but the fabric was burned from

the wings . . . knew what that meant so, holding back the stick, tried to glide to Allied ground. Somehow—I wanted to be buried on our own soil—but the torture, the flames— and to end it all, to end it, *quickly*—I nosed into the ground."

CRASH!

The small burning coffin was soon a charred wreckage but McKeown, thrown clear, lay near by and when picked up by the Germans was still breathing. A miracle. His seared body was put on a manure pile until—hours later— in the back of a horse-drawn wagon it bumped over a dirt road. For a second, conscious, he opened his eyes and two Huns, holding rifles over his head, were zealously guarding their human prize of half dead misery.

Two months passed; months of delirium and agony. His leg, face and hand were burned to the bone. Amputate the leg? Why trouble the doctors? Useless waste of energy! Soon he will die. *He heard that.*

"Doctor . . ."

"Ja, Ja."

"My locket—my picture, doctor!"

A locket, a little golden locket with the miniature of a girl, was in an inside pocket of his uniform. He wanted it —to die with. He wanted it—to hold—to hold within his hand when he was going.

"My locket, Doctor!—please . . ."

But the Germans refused to let him have it.

By cheating certain death, he saved his leg and recovery was probable. Luck! Six weeks passed and the first dirty bandage had never been removed; the leg was tor- turing McKeown and other men in the hospital insisted on some treatment. Finally, after bitter complaints, a doctor unrolled the bandage. The leg was alive—with squirming maggots.

"Good feed for the dogs," laughed the Doctor proceeding to scrape the maggotty mass from the tender bone. McKeown heard *that*, too.

Oblivion again. Then hot delirium and, with illusions of the Germans trying to kill him, he tried to leap out of the window. Time and again Allied comrades held him, saved him from himself. Rational, he fought for life. His superhuman spirit and the help of his friends pulled him through his greatest battle.

"I'm fine now," he tells us.

God bless such a man!

"Want to escape, get back to the squadron and fly again."

Weak, half-healed, far from well, he would settle with the Huns. Later McKeown was credited with shooting down two of the three Fokkers which had attacked him. A costly victory. *Another war hero!*

Lawson, Foster, McKeown and I; four American prisoners in a prison courtyard . . . four aviators, four pilots shot down in action. Four men who once were fighting in the air are now, together, fighting for a mere existence. A bond of friendship is a treasure of life as this compensation of war springs into a reality. Precious companionship! Priceless moments of throbbing ecstasy. Twenty minutes; time is up; no dallying. The guards are taking us away.

"Good-bye . . . Good-bye." Lawson and Foster are dragged off.

"Good-bye, Archibald," McKeown smiles and, held tight by a guard, hobbles off.

"Cheerio! . . . Cheerio!" The voice of the Englishman is almost God-like.

Rushed up four flights of stairs, I am again in my dark room, alone.

Hunger, half-forgotten, returns. How long will they

starve me? Hunger? Bosh! Think of McKeown. Solitary confinement; isolated from fellow man; how the room stinks after the fresh outdoors. The pail in the corner . . . putrid. When will they empty it? God! what a filthy hole . . . !

Early that afternoon a guard comes for me. Where now? A pleasant surprise as, shoved through a door, I am in a room with Lawson and Foster. Lawson, buoyant and cheerful, is a different person than when in the courtyard.

"What's happened?" I asked, wondering what could so exhilarate him.

His eyes, wet with happiness, twinkled. "This place is only temporary. We're going to be moved to the main camp tomorrow," he beams. "An Englishman in the yard told me so."

Could it be true? Perhaps; we three were together; there was a reason. Foster, eyes shut, lying on the bed, says nothing. His face is flushed, his forehead damp and his body limp.

"What's the matter?" I go over but he does not speak.

"He's ill," whispers Lawson, "says he's been sick for days. Was lying down when they came for him but felt better outdoors. Climbing up the stairs finished him; he just collapsed."

We decide he has the flu.

Long into the night, sitting in the dark, we discuss our chances of moving. Foster, restless, his head hot with fever, worries us. We must watch him; we will not sleep. But contemplating good news in the morning, we unwillingly doze off.

CHAPTER XX

DAYLIGHT, grim through the grating. Foster, eyes shining and cheeks burning, wonders if we will go. The door opens about ten o'clock. As we walk out of this dark, smelly room Hope again walks with us. The main camp; at last we are going to the main camp; the large permanent camp at Karlsruhe! Air, companionship and walking privileges are again dreamed of. It will save Foster; he is weak and trembling.

Twenty Allied prisoners line up.

Twenty-four guards, shouldering rifles, form a cordon around us. Their uniforms are immaculate; their spiked helmets, green vizored and emblazoned with the crowned, spread eagle, are tightly strapped under their chins. An officer is in command. His helmet is brightly polished; his boots are shined to a mirrored gloss; his uniform is perfection and a scabbard dangles at his side. We are about to depart. The leader twirls his mustache, draws his sabre and, with great pomp and military splendor, gives a command. Through the streets of Karlsruhe he leads the Mock Triumphant Procession.

They strut—on parade. We shuffle—on exhibition. They kick a military goose-stepped escort. We drag a weary-limbed obedience. They, with heads held high and bodies stiff in spotless uniforms, are inflated; for them it is a gala pageant. We, weak, ragged, dirty, sick, emaciated and with bearded faces, are humiliated; for us it is a mortifying business. We feel the contrast! We are woebegone relics of the war.

Through the streets of Karlsruhe, the conquering guards kick high. Through the streets of Karlsruhe, so the German population may see. Civilians line the streets. They gaze, gape, point and laugh. The glitter blinds! They drink it in. They believe this gaudy pretense means safety for the German Empire. Through the streets of Karlsruhe —let no one miss the spectacle. Through the streets of Karlsruhe—will Foster drop in his tracks? Through the streets of Karlsruhe—McKeown on his raw-boned leg. Through the streets and, at last, we arrive.

We halt.

A small wooden building, an integrant part of a high board fence, is before us. Guards parade back and forth; talking is within. One by one, each prisoner is individually taken inside. We stand outside—waiting. Fifteen, twenty, sometimes thirty minutes elapse. Spent, some wilt and are about to fall; the prod of a bayonet. Waiting, waiting, waiting, one man faints—what about it, he will come back. Fully three hours pass. It is my turn. Two soldiers, gripping my arms, lead me inside where, in three adjacent rooms, more guards and German officers intersperse.

"Take off your clothes!" orders an officer.

Naked, I stand before them. They search my clothing. My Sam Browne belt is thrown into a pile already confiscated; my metal mirror adds to a collection of leather and metal articles; my diary, started in solitary confinement, joins papers, compasses and maps on a desk; my boots, carefully scrutinized and found worthy, are stood up in the corner; my French francs, twice counted, are put in a table drawer; German prison money is handed me; worn-out Russian shoes are thrown at me and, told to dress, I am sent through a door into a large prison yard, perhaps three hundred feet square.

An array of color. Scottish plaids, British browns and pearl grey; French sky-blue, deep blue and scarlet; Canadian and American khaki.

An Australian stands near. "You are an American aviator!" He looks at my wings.

An execrable scream of agonizing torture intermittent with cursing, yelling and ill-omened silences, tears the air.

"What is that?" I ask.

"They are amputating a Frenchman's leg." The Australian shudders.

Another wail of insufferable pain; a dead stillness; a low moan and the courtyard is quiet . . . awe-stricken.

"They strap him down and saw it off without an anæsthetic . . ." Excruciating sobs drown his voice. It is heartbreaking. The cries are unbearable and I hold my hands over my ears.

A guard, grabbing my arm, leads me across the yard and into one of several barracks where wooden-slatted beds line the walls of a room about twenty feet long and ten feet wide. Lawson, Foster and McKeown are inside and with four others and myself we are eight.

Foster is sick. McKeown's leg is bothering him and he sits on the edge of his bed to take off the bandage. We watch as he unrolls it, tenderly. Running pus covers his ankle; yellow and purple pus oozes from the foreleg and we wash it with cold water to cleanse it as best we can. Only tender bone and some fast-clinging matter remain. Refolding the paper bandage but unable to find a clean spot we wind it around. His burned finger, although crooked and stiff, is healed; his face, although blue and transparent where new skin tissue-papers the bone, is painful but not raw. It is his leg. If he keeps it we will have seen another handiwork of God.

Porter, a little Scotch lad from Glasgow, is eighteen and a member of the Royal Flying Corps. Childlike, whimsical, he is as young as Peter Pan and old as Methuselah. We love him.

Preston, also of the Royal Flying Corps, is a handsome young Englishman from Keyhley, Yorks. Captain Edler and an Infantry officer, both Britishers, have been prisoners for nearly a year. They look it. A year, an eternity of suffering, has left them intrepid. They are branded but unflinching; weak but stout-hearted; drained but game to the finish and although physical wrecks they are mental towers of strength. Edler, who contracted malaria on the Salonica Front, is a very sick man.

At four in the afternoon we are issued Red Cross food. Canned beans, hardtack, *real* coffee and jam. What a sight! What a feast! Carloads of Red Cross food have been sent through Berne, Switzerland, to the prisoners in Germany and for a wonder we get some.

McKeown forgets his leg. Foster, too, is interested. "Heigh-Ho! a can of beans for the four of us." We heat them on a low brick stove but the coffee . . . smell it . . . just smell it . . . what can we brew the coffee in?

"An American who was here left a coffee pot," says the infantryman. "He said it was for anyone who came. I'll get it."

He produces the pot, we open it and find a note which reads:

GOOD LUCK FELLOWS—PURYEAR.

Puryear! from my squadron, a prisoner since July 26th, wonder how he has fared? Gone but a few days, no one knows where; damn it all, just missed him.

The coffee steams. The beans sizzle. The banquet is spread.

"Hey, Foster, here you are," handing him beans.

What a dinner! What dissipation! What unbelievable luxuries! "We are living like Princes, nothing less." Food, fresh air when we wish and the delightful friendliness of the Englishmen intoxicates us with precarious bliss.

Six o'clock. Lawson and I go for a walk. McKeown, limping on his bad leg, joins us. We stretch. We breathe. Simple animal movements are voluptuous: the black, starving, lonely days are behind; this . . . this is elixir! We are alive!

The other prisoners, captured before America entered the war, stare at us but do not speak. We are strange people. Apparently the only Americans here. We walk around unmolested. It does not seem real. The guards, pacing, pacing, pacing back and forth watch us suspiciously. Their furtive glances spoil the illusion and back in the barracks we discuss the war. The end is doubtful. We tell of America's strength, food-power and men, and although not contradicted we feel the Englishmen doubt us. Darkness comes and we go to sleep.

.   .   .   .   .

Awake and refreshed we make coffee. Hardtack, jam and coffee . . . what a breakfast! We smile, foolishly, at each other. A rap on the door. A Frenchman enters saying that for five marks apiece he will clip our heads. Our hair is long, dirty, we have had no way to comb it and here is a use for the prison money . . . sure, clip away. I am the first customer. Clip, clip, clip, the clippers run; clip, clip,

clip, from my forehead to the back of my neck; clip, clip, clip, matted bunches of filthy hair fall off.

"Voilà, Monsieur—c'est bien n'est-ce pas—c'est mieux—" sniffs the barber.

Everyone laughs heartily and even McKeown, grinning weakly, holds his sides. *Le barbier—Mon Dieu*—this is a serious business—hands me a mirror. *"On peut s'inspecter sans frais,"* he says. I look.

Smooth, but not as round as a billiard ball, is my head. Bumps, little ones and large ones stand in bold relief above a bewhiskered face, yet in spite of my uneven pate the others succumb and it is my turn to laugh.

A safety razor is another Red Cross gift. We shave. Clean faces slapped with cold water are a delight. Pleasure for us but McKeown who also decides to shave suffers self-inflicted punishment as each stroke of the razor tears away tender bits of skin. Slices of flesh are jerked out by the dull blade; blood trickles down his cheeks; scraping, scraping, with dogmatic grit he hacks away until his face, like a slab of raw beefsteak, is flabby and sore but shaven.

McKeown has other troubles. A Russian, who brought him soup, had a warm woolen undershirt. By some ruse McKeown got it, put it on and a fuzzy softness caressed his body. But now it wiggles, he takes it off—it is lousy. Naked to the waist with the garment on his knees he picks them off with tedious precision and one by one, kills each louse. Crack, crack . . . they hide in the deep piled down. Crack . . . what a big rascal! Congeries of them, grey ones, red ones, cluster rebellion in the arm pits and crack . . . crack . . . crack . . . we will be glad when they are ejected.

Scotty is a clown. His clipped head is also shaven yet one need not look at him to laugh for the mere thought of Scotty brings a smile. But he is so young—still in his 'teens.

Youth solves his shaving problem. He is beardless. Carefree, with no knowledge of fear, he is a natural born aviator who flew pursuit at the Front in a Sopwith Camel. Alone, this child soared into the air and single-handed fought against veteran German Aces. It seems a crime. On the Somme Front, at fifteen thousand feet, four Fokkers dove on him. Four experienced wily Huns against a Scottish schoolboy. He was shot down . . . crashed . . . but lived.

A deep scar snakes above his right eye. Marveling how he was so gashed without being killed I question, "How did you get that scar, Scotty?"

He grins. So waggish is his little face that I cannot help but laugh. He pouts. It is difficult to convince him that I am not joking but seriously interested, and then, appeased, he confides.

"Weel, I will a tell ye. I was dooin' m' acr-roobatic stunts i' England for-r m' instructor-r. An' he was a watchin' me too. When I hae finish an' cum doon he said, 'Hoot Mon! I can har-rdly see ye, dinna go oop so high.' So oop again I gae. An' I was over-r th' hoose tops, too. I was doin' m' stunts. Hoot Mon! somethin' wint wr-rong. I hit th' hoose. The next thin' I knew m' nur-rsee says 'Sit oop, m' lad, and take this.' An that is th' wae I got th' scar."

He laughs. To him it is a big joke.

Funny, quizzical, innocent little Scotty.

Captain Edler fights. The ravages of malaria grip him as hypochondria, the dreaded result of this disease, tears him to pieces. "It's got me!" he yells, "it's got me!" and in the throes of melancholia he paces back and forth. He is a doctor who knows the symptoms so, grinding his teeth, he battles with Herculean strength against a mania for self-destruction. It is piteous. His body shakes uncontrollably;

his face distorts with anguish; he puts on an overcoat, turns up the collar and, white as chalk, with his blue lips trembling, walks up and down. Chills convulse his body. In a flicker his cheeks are scarlet, his eyes bloodshot and he is burning up. Fever racks his system. He stands, still, to tussle with demon Suicide. He walks, fast, to outwit the Devil. He wins and, prostrated, lies down in dread of another call from Satan.

He tells us about malaria patients. On the Salonica Front hundreds of them were loaded into cars and sent in "Suicide Specials" to the rear for medical treatment. "Suicide Specials" because so many by jumping off the train or killing themselves in other gruesome ways never reached their destination. Soldiers—self-destroyed. *Martyrs in the cause of war.*

When Captain Edler is well he recites. "On the Road to Mandalay," "The Pink Garter" and scores of other selections hold us enthralled by the hour, for he is a master of recitation. Often he is lying down too ill to talk and then Scotty volunteers to entertain. We try to dissuade him. "Please Scotty, please, not tonight." We argue; we threaten; we tell him we will not listen but is he downhearted? Not he, the persistent magpie. His talented generosity is munificent and, clearing his throat, he begins. We pelt him with every loose article in the room but nothing can quell his artistic efforts. He has a "Repertoire." Try and stop it! "Gunga Din," his favorite, begins and closes each program which consists of nursery jingles, love sonnets, poems, ballads and memorized snatches of Captain Edler's recitations. He finishes. Then, without hesitation, he starts over again and only sheer physical force prevents him from repeating the entire list.

Scotty—the pet and the pest of the barracks.

·　　·　　·　　·　　·

Nearly every day English bombing planes raid Karlsruhe. Sometimes they come in the afternoon but mostly at night when the bright moon is high. These raids thrill us. With the first warning shriek of the sirens we eagerly dash to the door.

Fire-flashes, from hundreds of exploding anti-aircraft, like harmless twinkling stars, hang in the sky. Searchlights, from many turrets, like long white arms supinely graceful, fondle the heavens. Defense guns roar a terrible din; shells burst a blanket of steel over the city and in a transport of delight we watch the recalescent galaxy of fireworks.

A powerful explosion! A certain hit! The raiders, unloading their bombs, are destroying Karlsruhe! They are getting the Germans! Each mighty explosion is music to our ears. We cheer! Like college boys at a football game we cheer and yell approval. Hurrah! hurrah! hurrah! for our side. Our lusty yells bring the guards who force us into barracks and warn that further demonstrations mean severe punishment. "Hope they get the railroad yards," we whisper. The Germans, petrified, tell us the bombs do no harm. We know better. These frequent raids with tons of explosives do their damage.

We eat, walk and sleep. A new dish of rice is prepared; nice white rice and the crackers too are made from white flour. The food, scant in quantity, is rare and tempting. We prize each grain, each swallow, each crumb and are satisfied. We think we are living well but a short while ago would have despised our condition. All is comparison. Our outlook has deteriorated. To live, that is the problem, not how. Habits we once would have deemed shameful are commonplace. One gets used to anything. We have changed.

.   .   .   .   .

The courtyard is a sorry sight. Heads are swathed in gory bandages. One soldier, his right arm gone, clumsily uses his left; he cannot manage it. Another, a leg missing, hops about, falls and hops again; he has no crutch. Faces, grotesque from shell-fire, stare at us. Eyes are gouged out. Boys, young men and middle-aged soldiers are confused, wary and suspicious. Some—have forgotten.

      .   .   .   .   .

A tall, spare Frenchman is always out. Regardless of the weather he prowls around. Night and day he walks and walks. Always, he wears a heavy sky-blue overcoat; always, the deep turned collar covers the back of his head; always, he is alone. He speaks to no one. No one speaks to him. Now—he stumbles. Now—his body catapults across the yard and hits the fence. He seems so sad. We ask about him and hear that when at the Front, with his collar turned up, a piece of shrapnel struck his head and the steel, piercing his skull, carried with it a bit of the dyed blue cloth. They took out the shrapnel but the cloth is deeply imbedded near the base of his brain. "It won't be long now," we are told, "before he is out of his mind." He totters past. His eyes are those of a hunted deer. He falls and screams. "It won't be long now." . . . No, not long . . . his brain is going . . . let's get away . . . not long, now . . . God! . . . Look! . . . he's gone mad!

CHAPTER XXI

GOOD news! Rumors that we are to be moved.

Here, we have fared the best but the camp is far back in Germany and so guarded that escape is beyond the scope of reason and—escape is our goal.

It is seven o'clock in the morning. We are in the courtyard. A German officer and sergeant approach so we stand at stiff attention, for here in Karlsruhe the rigid rules are enforced at the point of a bayonet.

The officer speaks to the sergeant who in turn translates: "You are leaving here in thirty minutes; you are to make no noise; you are to conduct yourselves as gentlemen; you will assemble by the gate at seven-thirty and you are warned to take nothing away from this camp."

"An' wher-re ar-re we a gayin'?" propounds Scotty.

The officer glares at him . . . icily.

The Imp looks up . . . naively. His guileless baby face saves him for only Scotty could have so spoken without calamitous results.

"Dismiss!" orders the Sergeant and they walk away.

"You must be careful, Scotty, you'll get in trouble . . ."

"Hoot Mon! Dinna ye want to know wher-re we ar-re a gayin'?" and with a comic squint he hop-skips into the barracks.

Twenty minutes later, we four Americans, Scotty and twelve Englishmen are grouped around the gate.

"Where are we going?" . . . "Where, do you suppose?" . . . "What part of Germany?" . . . "Where now?" . . . we speculate.

An officer enters the yard. Thirty guards, with spiked helmets and shouldering rifles, follow him in military formation. They march to the gate. The officer gives an order. He is slight, fair and undersized. He gives another order. His helmet, with the motto *"Mit Gott Für König und Vaterland,"* is fancier than the others and swallows his head. He gives a command. He is groomed and faultlessly dressed. He gives another command. His sabre dangles and a foxy waxed mustache is high under his nose. It is red. This fidgety runt flits around giving orders first to one guard then to another. He pulls at his coat . . . "You—do this." He adjusts his helmet. . . . "You —do that." He brushes non-existent particles of nothing off his black, polished boots, fingers his collar and . . . gives an order. He twists his carroty mustache, then . . . gives another order. We are highly entertained. Even the guards show disgust.

Nine o'clock. Assembled in columns of fours we are corralled by guards. The gate swings. Outside are nine Americans, all aviators just out of solitary confinement. They join us. The officer gives a final command, our journey is begun and we again tramp through the streets of Karlsruhe.

The officer is in a paroxysm of effervescence. Now—he struts ahead; now—he runs from side to side; now—he skates behind giving orders, orders, orders, all useless and unwarranted. A minute here, a minute there and he jumps . . . like a parched pea.

The guards are fine examples of Prussian militarism.

Their helmets gleam, their rifles tilt evenly, their goose-steps are picked with precision and they look straight ahead. Civilians, lining the streets, are proud. "See our fit and wonderful soldiers!" "Look!—the worn-out, dilapidated Allies." Again, this pomp and pretentious display is, to the majority, a stimulating potion.

An elderly German gentleman stands on the sidewalk. His face is fatherly, kind and understanding. This ceremonial gaudery does not deceive him for he shakes his head in disapproval and walks away, sadly. His son, perhaps— or maybe two fair boys—did march away to war, and war to him is what it is . . . a tragedy.

We arrive at the railroad station. The officer, galloping ahead, shouts arrogantly for a clear passage so his guards may enter triumphantly. A few soldiers, near by, step aside but one husky Boche does not stir. Big, raw-boned, probably on leave after fighting in the front line trenches, he has no intention of giving way to a priggish little officer and a bunch of bedraggled prisoners. The officer, about half the size of this grizzly warrior, yells at him as if he were a dog. Our sympathy is with the soldier, who takes a long-stemmed pipe out of his mouth, spits, and yells back. The officer is rampant. His mustache twitches and foaming with rage he orders two guards to arrest this *"ungehorsamen Soldaten!"*

The soldier, to our surprise, does not resist but peacefully walks away with his arresters. They are his comrades but he loathes the officer and swears future vengeance with vile oaths.

Another rebellion against Boche discipline.

The soldiers, fed up on the war, are cracking. Tyrannical and overbearing Prussian officers are no longer submissively obeyed. The great German military machine is crumbling.

During the mêlée a peasant, old and dressed in remnants

of civilian clothes, wedges through the crowd. A gunny sack with carrots, beets and turnips rests upon his stooped back and sidling close he whispers, "Cheer up, boys! We'll soon have you out of here."

A spy!

He risked the chance of being caught to give a word of courage.

We board a train. Prisoners on one side and the alert guards opposite. Windows and doors are locked. We remove our shoes. The guards, taking off their heavy, uncomfortable helmets, sigh with relief, rub their heads and don grey cloth caps bordered with red.

Noon. The train stops in open country and we get off. For about half a mile we plow through a meadow of long green grass and then, herded like so many cattle, go into an old barn. Musty hay covers the floor; mold and cobwebs cling to the weather-beaten rafters; the owner left his peaceful farm to learn the game of war. *"Mit Gott Für König und Vaterland"* he went . . . never to return. Two guards flank the door, others encircle the building and bats fly near the roof.

A large kettle is brought in and a plate of cold soup is apportioned to each one of us. The Germans have a good luncheon. Our soup is heavy and rancid but experience has taught us to eat whatever we can whenever we can and we swallow the rotten liquid. We lie on the straw wondering where we are bound.

An hour later on another train we speed across unknown enemy territory. Hours pass. Rain beats on the panes and it is cold. Darkness comes. More hours. Twinkling lights, dim through the rain-bespattered windows, show we are entering a town and the officer, perpetual motion, again gives orders and bustles about. His self-importance is astounding. The guards put on their helmets. We put on our shoes but are not allowed to move until the guards have taken strategic posts both inside and out.

We step into ink.

The rain is pouring. The guards, black objects in the wet night, circulate around us and with only their bright helmets and shiny bayonets visible we feel hemmed in by murky demons.

Groping . . . we stumble through the black streets.

Bells! Ding!-Dong! Ding!-Dong! Church bells are ringing.

Crowded so close together we can hardly walk. Ding!-Dong! Ding!-Dong!—what glorious bells! A drenching rain still falls. Ding!-Dong! . . . Ding!-Dong!—cathedral bells, ringing, ringing, ringing and we are soaking wet. Bells!—why do they ring tonight?

"Halt!"

We are separated and in a few seconds the Englishmen melt into the black. Out of sight. Gone. Yesterday we were together, close association made us friends and now, Scotty and all, they are taken away.

"Marsch!"

On narrow, cobblestoned streets ever turning in and around we plod through the storm. Where are the lights we saw from the train? It is pitch dark. A brick-paved pathway is so narrow that we go in single file through a gate which leads into a secret passage with high stone walls and after fully twenty minutes of a steep climb stand before a large iron portal.

Its jaws open—spookily. Bells! Ding!-Dong! Ding!-Dong!—louder, together, bells for a bride on her wedding day. It is late. Chiming, chiming, chiming, they ring in a symphonic poem of vibrant tones. Ding!-Dong! Ding!-Dong!—why such special chimes before the midnight?

We enter a courtyard and in a wooden building we thirteen are jammed into one small filthy room. Bunks, three tier deep, are built on the walls. We are cold, sneezing and drenched to the skin. Later, taken into a larger room, we stand before a fat Hun, a Medical Officer who sits behind a table strewn with various instruments. He is a doctor, but looks like a butcher and his fat would tip the scales at three hundred pounds or more. Told to take off our clothes, we strip. In sodden piles our uniforms lie on the floor. The corpulent Bull, with a long needle, inoculates us in the chest.

We are afraid of the serum. In—goes the needle. Stories of Hun atrocities are well known. In—goes the needle. One by one he jabs us while the others, naked and shivering, dread their turn. In—goes the needle.

"Disease germs! . . .

"He is filling us full of poison!" . . .

This brute and the guards do not understand English and openly he is accused of inoculating us with a deadly fluid. In goes the needle. He is rough and in a hurry. Deep— goes the needle. No antiseptic washes his instrument between the vicious thrusts.

"Disease germs! I tell you they are!"—

Some believe he is actually performing just such a ghastly crime; others, although shaky, are doubting, but a few of us ridicule their fears.

The gorilla finishes. We are told to dress, quickly. Our garments are so wet we can hardly pull them on. Chilled, we re-enter the room and lie down. We are freezing cold. The serum takes effect. Nausea and retching follow. The room, about twelve feet square, is airless. A terrible odor. A few, who otherwise could have withstood the sickening aftermath are also ill. Everyone vomits. The stench is appalling. No place to sit . . . the bunks reek with bile. No place to go . . . the corners steam. Endless hours upon hours. Some, from over-straining, are in a stupor; others, hurrying, throw up and slip in their own spew. Our clothes, soggy with rain, are covered with slime and the room is one pungent mass of coagulated body refuse. The night is hideous beyond description. No one speaks. We are horribly ashamed. We are utterly debased.

The cold dawn seeps through a barred window.

Bells!   Bells!   Ding!-Dong!   Ding!-Dong!   bells of jangling silver. Ding!-Dong! Ding!-Dong! ringing, ringing, ringing, in discordant clanks. Can these metallic jarrings be the chimes of yester-night? Ding!-Dong! Ding!-Dong!—harsh and clear in a grating sacrament. An Italian prisoner brings *ersatz*, holds his nose and runs. A room not fit for a hog is a sewer of incarcerated men. We are grey and haggard. A few sip the coffee, thinking it might help but generally it is untouched and even now, squeamish and enervated, we are ordered to another room and again told to undress.

In pretense it is a physical examination, but they are looking for maps, compasses or other contraband goods. One fellow has a map pasted with adhesive tape to the sole of his foot. There he stands on a map of Germany and the astute Huns, feeling around his naked body, miss it. They keep our clothes for further searching and give us a coat and thin cotton trousers with a wide yellow stripe which runs down the back of each coat and braids the trousers. Typical prison raiment. With these worn, germ-laden clothes next to our skins we huddle together all day long in our bare feet, too cold to sit down and too weak to stand up. No bunks. This inoculation room is our quarters. We are miserable.

Night comes. The bells ring. Ding!-Dong! . . . Ding!-Dong! No food. The bells ring! Ding!-Dong! . . . Ding!-Dong! We lie on the floor. The bells ring! Ding!-Dong! . . . Ding!-Dong! Wish they would stop! It is drafty and, chilled, we catch cold. Ding!-Dong! . . . Ding!-

Dong! A cacophony of discords and the bells ring and ring. They baffle us; we flinch at each stridulation. My God! why are those bells ringing? Ding!-Dong! . . . Ding!-Dong! . . . Ding!-Dong!

Morning. The bells still ring—nothing to eat. Noon. The bells still ring—nothing to eat. Our clothes are returned and we walk into the prison pen where towering stone walls of an ancient castle fortify the courtyard. Other prisoners are here. All are Americans, all are aviators and we learn that only airmen have the pleasure of this confinement camp in Landshut, Bavaria, forty kilometers north of Munich.

The castle, resting high upon a hill-top above the city, rises in the baronial hauteur of a forgotten era. Built in the eleventh century by the Duke Ludwig, it was a residence of splendor for the Dukes of Lower Bavaria, but magnificence has gone and mute grey walls which once sheltered Kings now guard American aviators.

Puryear left here a few days ago for Villingen, so again I have just missed him. Many have tried to escape, with the result that we are jealously guarded. They will have no more of it, we are warned. Puryear and a French aviator named Conneau escaped from Rastatt and tramped for three nights in a torrential squall towards Switzerland but they went too far west and upon reaching the bank of the Rhine realized their mistake. Conneau knew of a Boche aerodrome near the Swiss border and about a night's walk further so, planning to steal a Boche plane and fly to France, they went ahead but had no sooner started than they were recaptured and put in solitary confinement.

Wardell, another American aviator, was on a train going from Karlsruhe to Landshut. He tried to escape, was caught by a guard and brutally handled. Tucker, Miller and Strong got out of this courtyard but once safely over the inner walls they were enclosed by yet another wall and forced to surrender. Four others escaped but were also found a few days later. All were punished with solitary confinement.

The commanding officer here is a Prussian major about sixty-five years old. Short, squabby, white haired, he is the most contemptible brute we have yet encountered. Every evening he has our shoes taken away and all night long, with each change of the guards, we are awakened and counted. Each visit means a lecture on discipline; he threatens us, without cause, with every sort of punishment. When the Major calls there is Hell to pay. We tremble at the sight of his bull-dog face; the mere sound of his voice and we are afraid, for he lectures, bullies, threatens and during these sessions we must stand at attention. We do, but it never quite suits him. We must salute differently, according to his taste and with more subservence. He is as mean as a human being could be. He is cruel. The slightest noise and, taking it as a personal insult, he flies into a rage. We are told of rules so rigid they could never be enforced but to break one means terrible castigation. He demands penal servitude. Confinement, here, is a mild chastisement; if we disobey he promises us solitary death in Northern Prussia.

Fortunately, he spends most of his time at the British prison in another part of the city and his cowed henchman, a German sergeant named Capp, supplants him. "Mister Capp," as we call him, acts as interpreter for the Major, is a slave to his slightest whim and, although a natural born liar—like all we have met—he is otherwise fairly decent. Servile and cringing, he obeys from fear and often is ashamed to carry out his master's drastic orders. Born with half a chance in life he might have been a reasonable fellow but, handicapped, he is a lying puppet. We do not dislike him; we are sorry. He is a soul in bondage.

Thoughts of escape no longer tempt us. We prize our lives too highly to buck the Major. Also Landshut is two hundred and forty kilometers from the nearest point in Switzerland and this, with the series of doubly guarded walls, is a forbidding factor.

Bells! Ding-Dong! . . . Ding!-Dong!—clanging for mourners.

More inoculations! Three for typhoid, two for cholera and one called the "Five-in-One," which consists of cutting our shoulders in five places with a knife before the serum is rubbed in. The physical pain is nothing compared to the mental dread. . . . Sickness again.

Bells! Ding!-Dong! . . . Ding!-Dong!—hammering at sepulchers.

Several days drag by and another group of aviators arrives.

"They will never inoculate me!" boasts one. "I've had them all; they make me deathly ill. You wait, I won't have it."

"That's right," we encourage him jokingly. "Just tell the doctor you refuse. That will be sufficient."

That night the newcomers stand stripped. We watch. The boaster is examined for wounds. He allows that, of course. The medico reaches for the needle, placidly. The flyer steps back, defiantly. "Oh no, you don't! . . . you don't inoculate me!" . . .

The doctor, not understanding nor for the moment imagining a rebuff, beckons. The patient does not budge. The Hun, seeing the light, roars in such rage that the once courageous and resisting prisoner goes meekly over. He sticks out his chest. The doctor looks at the unethical paunch and, flattening it with a blow, sticks in the needle. Apparently this aviator has not been a prisoner for long.

.   .   .   .   .

Bells! Ding!-Dong! . . . Ding!-Dong!—they ring continually.   Chimes on the numerous city churches never stop.   They are supposed to peal forth every quarter of an hour but manifestly no clock is ever set by another and the result is an unceasing tintinnabulation.   Bells!   Bells! Bells!   The ever-ringing bells of Landshut.

Days upon days drag by and life at Landshut is frightful. Interminable days. Hideous nights. Not a chair; no bunks; we sit or lie on the floor of a drafty room and wind blows through the cracks.   Our hunger is maddening.   Food—is our one thought.   Food—is our only desire.   Food—for we are almost starving.

We know that the Red Cross sends food supplies for the prisoners in Germany.   But—not a scrap arrives for us! We know, also, that other American prisoners who were here before we arrived have already received Red Cross rations.   They have a surplus.   Do they divide with us? Never.   Not a bite do they offer!   We know who they are, we see them in the courtyard, they do not seem to mind Landshut—why should they?—with plenty of Red Cross food which they keep for themselves.

The Germans issue a round loaf of black bread to each one.   Our eyes bulge and our mouths water at such bounty but—it is to last ten days and the man does not exist in Landshut with will power enough so to ration himself.   At times we get soup.   It is far worse than any before and so rank that despite repeated efforts many cannot swallow it. We try, mightily, for food is so precious that as long as it does not poison us we try.   Today it is foul; made from the entrails of fish.

Two so-called meals a day.   An Italian brings an earthen pan with a watery mixture of cabbages and turnips or sometimes added bits of potato.   It is a treat.   He places the container on the floor and we scramble for it like a pack of hungry wolves.   Afterwards, we realize our uncouth actions.

Where is our self-respect? Are we but animals? We will be men! One fellow is appointed to apportion out each meal but as we are never nourished, never free from poignant cramps of hunger, and always harrowed by famishment the plan is not worth a straw. When the fodder arrives hunger rides rough-shod over reasoning power. Another barbarous rush!

To make my loaf last as long as possible I ration myself but this afternoon, yielding to temptation, I cut a thin slice. This is a choice pleasure and toasting makes it more palatable, so putting it on our low brick stove I replace the loaf and return for the bread. It is gone! Someone, when my back is turned, has stolen it. *My* slice of bread! Mine! How I had hoarded it, saved each crumb, been strict with myself and now some dastard takes it. We all have the same amount and he, the contemptible thief, filches mine. The loss is of vast importance. I stand, shaking with hot rage, as crumbs brown on the bricks. Someone is joking . . . of course . . . just a joke . . . no one, no one here would seriously do such a thing . . . so I laugh and say, "Where is my bread? Come on . . . give it up."

No one speaks. Then it is true! Someone, actually, took it to keep and eat! The shabby sneak! And the hurt! An aviator, one of us! Perfidy where honor is unquestioned.

Methodically I speak to each man. "My bread has been stolen . . . did you take it?" My anger is boundless. Each one answers, "No." Someone lies! Let him! Many, to appease me, offer to replace it but bread is not what I want now. Who amongst us is a dirty cheat? With primitive fury and promising retaliation if ever his name is known I go out. Some certainly could tell me but knowing what they would do in such a case do not dare, for they feel as I do and fear to let me know. It is well. In this heat of anger I would strangle him.

Evenings and all night long electric lights burn in our

room. Our bodies line the floor. In rows, heads to the wall and feet towards the center, we try to rest but sleep is thwarted as the guards, in heavy boots, pace the bare planks. They delight in making noises. A stockinged foot protrudes a bit . . . they kick it. They are bound we shall not sleep and are so provocative that our bodies writhe with discomfort, nerves and lack of calm. We are wretched. Talking boisterously they exchange ribald jokes, snort raucously and stamp on the wood.

"Quit that damned racket! I can't sleep," yells a prisoner, distracted.

A guard rushes at him, points a bayonet at the pit of his stomach and threatens to kill. We are breathless.

"Be quiet," we caution. "Do not move."

The Hun, snarling and showing his teeth like a cur, waits for the slightest excuse to kill him. We sit up. The prisoner, motionless, does as we tell him and the guard, finally, lifts his bayonet.

A fitful night of spasmodic dreams. I reach and reach to grab a piece of roasted meat which hangs upon a fork held by an armless hand. A dog, hungry too, claws fiercely at my leg and chews and chews and chews.

The bells! Ding!-Dong! . . . Ding!-Dong!—ringing, ringing, ringing. Ding!-Dong! . . . Ding! . . . "Jim, get up, it's time for Sunday school" . . . Dong! The light in my eyes. Sunday school! . . . in the basement of Saint Mark's church . . . every Sabbath . . . that's what we did . . . went to Sunday school. She had a silly leghorn hat with a blue ribbon and I had a serge suit with a starched Eton collar. Ding!-Dong! . . . Ding!-Dong!—the memory bells of Landshut.

Now the guards are worse than ever. Nights are pandemonium. Relief guards, aware of a prisoner's recent insolence, look for trouble. They bang about. Their manner dares us to show the least sign of unruliness and they pester us, malevolently, in hope some one will protest. They court disaster. Like vultures they watch the man complained of and hoping to do bodily harm annoy us to exasperation. We hardly dare move.

.   .   .   .   .

Balconies on the castle overhang the prison yard. The townsfolk come to see. Leaning on the balustrades they watch us, avidly. No admission here. This sideshow is free and with mouths agape, they stare at the freaks. They look and whisper; they look and jeer; some glance and quickly turn away; others, with morbid curiosity, stay by the hour and girls, with rosy cheeks, smile at the guards.

.   .   .   .   .

October.
A rumor that Bulgaria has surrendered, but, traced to a Hun, the story is discredited. We also hear that the Germans will soon move us to a prison camp at Villingen, in the province of Baden, less than thirty miles from the Swiss border. We pray to be sent. Only thirty miles from Switzerland! We will escape, somehow. "The train for Villingen passes within twenty miles of the border." Twenty miles from freedom! With a half a chance we will jump off the train.

McKeown draws a map. On a small piece of paper he copies the one pasted on the other fellow's foot and hopeful of escaping from Villingen he draws and draws. He finishes. We will be searched again, that is a foregone conclusion and where, where can he hide it?

"On your foot, put it on your foot, Mac," suggests one. But we have no adhesive tape.

"In your ear . . . try that," suggests another.

"No, it won't cram in, they would spot it," says McKeown.

"Your mouth . . . way back and up behind . . ."

"But don't they always examine mouths?"

"Do they? . . . ask me! One doctor tried to get his whole dirty fist in mine."

McKeown treasures his map for he plans to escape and return to the squadron for another crack at the Huns. The spirit! We all love McKeown. He thinks, plots, fingers his map tenderly and finally finds a safe place.

"They will never find it there," he tells us.

He decides to hide it in the other natural cavity of his body.

.   .   .   .   .

Days and days. Ding!-Dong! . . . Ding!-Dong! The bells, ringing, ringing, ringing, rack us to pieces. Nights and nights. Ding!-Dong! . . . Ding!-Dong! What if we are not sent after all? Ding!-Dong! . . . Ding!-Dong! Wish we had a pack of cards. Leaves blow into the courtyard, autumn leaves, dead and brown which we roll into cigarettes and pasting scraps of refuse paper with spit, try to smoke. One puff—we are reeling.

Some are sullen. Some are sad. Everyone is weak and shaky and our morale is going. The nights are chilly and lately it has been raining.

Half past two in the morning. Bitter cold and pouring rain.

"Get ready to leave!" we are told.

All we have to do to "get ready" is to stand up. We huddle by the door but a guard prevents us from passing until the sergeant arrives. Mister Capp appears.

We arrived in Landshut at night and in a storm. We leave in the black of early morning with the rain pelting. Bells! Ding!-Dong! Ding!-Dong! They rang when we

came. Bells! Ding!-Dong! Ding!-Dong! They ring as
we go. Rain, slanted by the wind, drives through the dark.
Again we will be water-soaked.

"Mister Capp! Will you get us some umbrellas?"

"Yes, Mister Capp, we'll get drenched walking to the
station."

"If you have time to wait I'll order you a taxi-cab," and,
smiling, Sergeant Capp tells us to follow him. We turn up
our coat collars, duck our heads and go across the courtyard
where an officer and guards wait to take us to Villingen.

Roll Call. Mister Capp gives some papers to the officer,
the guards assemble and thoughts of leaving the fiendish old
Major and his musty castle-prison brace us up. We are
pitiably buoyant.

"Good-bye, Mister Capp."

"Good-bye."

Again through slashing rain and driving wind we are
single file on the narrow brick path. Again the gates of the
iron portal open—slowly. Again the bells. Ding!-Dong!
Ding!-Dong!—leaden chimes of Hell!—raw, mixed with
fury, as if rung by devils' claws. Ding!-Dong! Ding!-Dong!
—louder, together, bells for a murderer on his day of execution. Ding!-Dong! Ding!-Dong!—the hideous bells of
Landshut! Ding!-Dong! . . . Ding!-Dong! Pray God
we never hear them again.

On through the winding cobblestoned streets. The light
from a guard's flashlight. The railroad station. And in a
fourth class coach we start the journey with the same pre-
cautions of guards, rifles, locked doors and windows. Our
shoes, this trip, are put in a car ahead with the officer. They
take no chances with us Americans.

CHAPTER XXII

DAWN. Grey skies. Soggy ground. Hours . . . hours
. . . hours . . . we are cold, thirsty, hungry and our last
meal, at four yesterday afternoon, was a bowl of thin, sour
soup. Hours . . . hours . . . hours . . . it is three o'clock
in the afternoon and the guards munch at raw turnips. We
crave food. They chew tobacco and spit on the floor. We
watch them. The smell of feet, wet clothes and smoke from
the guards' clay pipes fill the coach where for twelve hours
we have squeezed together while even the twist of a sore
muscle was watched with suspicion. We are ill-tempered
and unstrung. We convince a guard by argumentive threats
that we must see the officer. It is imperative we say and,
as he goes to the car ahead, we appoint a spokesman to ask
for something to eat.

The officer arrives. He is a Bavarian. Young, perhaps
thirty, his sad face is handsome and his expression that of
one whose heart is heavy. He knows grief. He stands as
if waiting to be spoken to.

"We are hungry!" our mediator tells him. "We thought,"
he hesitates, "we thought . . . perhaps . . . you might
get us some food."

The Bavarian offers no comment but listens, politely.

"At least he is listening," we whisper.

Cognizant of the caliber of this officer the spokesman tells of the horrible treatment at Landshut, of the old Prussian Major and of the sickness and lack of food. "We are hungry, sir!" he pleads. "Just a carrot . . . a raw turnip . . . anything."

"Did the Major at Landshut give you any food for this trip?" the Bavarian asks in perfect English.

"No!" we chorus.

He turns away.

"I'll wager he gets us something to eat."

"Have you gone crazy, too? Did he say he would? And just what have you got to 'wager'? You're a Hellish optimist!"

We are silent. The train rumbles along. The guards talk and spit tobacco juice. It is after five o'clock and we pull into a station. About five minutes pass when the Bavarian enters our car and behind him are two boys carrying a basket. The officer hands us each a bottle of pop and we gulp it down.

"Thank you, sir!"—"Thank you very much!"—"Thank you!"—"Thank you!" we all cry.

He looks pleased and, paying the boys from his own pocket, leaves. The guards have a fit. They jabber, jabber, jabber back and forth in disgusted surprise.

"What did I tell you? This officer is a Bavarian; the Bavarians aren't too damned strong for this war anyway and they hate the Prussians like poison."

"You're right! Guess the description of that old Buzzard at Landshut did it."

The train jerks.

The landscape, strange to us, is familiar to the guards, who point excitedly to barns, houses and distant villages. It looks like any other country but the atmosphere is tense.

The train rattles on.

Now a fence runs along the embankment. A lone soldier, leaning against it, watches the train go by. The guards point, astonished. We look. The "soldier" is a child. He does not look a day over twelve and the pack he carries is nearly as big as his immature body. His uniform, much too large, hangs on his still growing frame and as he labors under the weight of his equipment even the guards are impressed by his extreme youth.

"Das ist bloss ein Junge, der Soldat spielt!" explains a guard. He is ashamed to have us know that this small boy is really in the German army.

It is seven o'clock in the evening when we leave our seats for the first time to get our shoes, now dumped in a corner. The train stops and we are in the city of Ulm. A slight mist is falling as, shivering, we crowd together on the platform. The Bavarian, inside, calls to the guards and we are taken into the waiting room. The air is warm, a large stove is in the corner, and we tingle from the heat.

A half hour passes . . . thirty minutes of warmth . . . thirty minutes of stretching our aching bodies, when the officer enters followed by two German Red Cross women. Solemn, glum, middle-aged, they view our presence with disfavor, shove a plate and spoon at us and, disgruntled, stalk out. Returning, each carries a large bowl and a tempting odor fills the room as wisps of steam rise from the contents. Food! . . . The good Bavarian! Hot stew! They spoon it out and fill our plates to the brim. Hot stew with real potatoes! We wolf it down. The officer speaks to the women who, shrugging their shoulders, pay little attention. He speaks again, severely and with authority. Frowning and with wry faces they again fill our bowls with the steaming stew and we eat a second plate with gusto. The Bavarian, responsible for this wonderful feast, watches us intently. He knows that we are grateful. Our plates are licked clean and assembling on the platform we march through the dark streets of Ulm.

I am on the inside near the curb and now and then crowded onto the sidewalk. The guard, poking me in the ribs, shoves me back. Again and again it happens. Each time the guard takes delight in jabbing me and I am mad with rage. If the officer knew he would stop it but remembering the stew I grit my teeth and stumble along. Why cause him trouble . . . he has been so kind.

We halt before a white stone building.

The Bavarian rings a bell, a door opens and we go inside. A large court stretches its walls up to a roof of glass. Each floor can be seen, seven in all, with iron railings completely encircling each level and doors of individual cells opening into narrow intervening walks. A dreary building of confinement, this city jail, but it is warm, clean, dry and we are fortunate.

"This is war," says the officer. "But I thought it would be better to sleep here than sit up all night on the train."

We smile our gratitude.

The jail-keeper stands waiting. A baggy, black suit enshrouds a crooked back and jelly-like legs. Poppy, blood-shot eyes bulge from a face raddled with red, distended veins. An upper tooth, decayed and yellow, touches his lower lip. He is a repulsive thing. A pawlike hand with long dirt-filled finger nails holds a large ring from which many keys dangle. A tumefacient growth is rooted to his throat and a loose bag of glabrous flesh hangs down to his chest. A hideous, pitiful creature.

One by one he takes us away. My turn comes and we climb a winding iron stair-case to the fourth floor. The cell doors are solid steel. I peer over the railing and countless similar doors, like crypts in a mausoleum, dot the walls. The jailer shoves at the heavy door, over a foot thick, and slowly it swings on the hinges. I am thrust into a small cell, the door re-swings and a sibilant swish of air, like the closing door of a large safe, startles me and for a second I wonder if the room is air-tight.

As a blind man I grope in the black and feel—a bed. It is iron with a mattress and two blankets. I run my hands along the walls and feel—cement. I fall over an iron stool, find a small iron table hinged to the wall, see a spot of greenish light and, feeling it, discover a cut in the door about six inches square which tapers through the thick steel to an outside peep-hole so one could look in but not out. What a cell! Cased in steel and cement I feel hermetically sealed. What type of law breakers were put in here? . . . fit for murderers, but were ordinary thieves and petty offenders so punished? Hope they remember where I am!

My clothes are still wet . . . guess I'll take them off, and undressing I pile my things on the table and, finally, find a pail. How strange to have my clothes off! My bones ache and lying down I wearily pull up the blankets. They smell . . . my clothes are off . . . how strange . . . nice though . . . the smell . . . better than the train . . . fine fellow that Bavarian . . . drowsy . . . warm . . .

    ·   ·   ·   ·   ·

A hand shakes me. A candle flickers in the darkness. Rubbing my eyes I see the distorted face of the jailer. He leans over to see if I am awake and the hanging flesh-pot brushes my face. He puts the candle on the table and goes out. I put on my damp clothes . . . seems like night . . . how tired I am! . . . how terribly tired! The jailer returns, we go to the main floor, the others are there and it is but three o'clock in the morning.

Our officer is in an anteroom signing papers. The guards watch him, intently. When he comes out we nod "Good

Morning," almost imperceptibly. The guards watch us. Were they certain of our gratitude or his graciousness they undoubtedly would report him. They must never know. The Bavarian, seemingly, ignores us but a transient illumination of his sad eyes reveals a soul of understanding as he calls the roll, gives orders and prepares to leave. The half-human jailer fumbles with a key and ultimately claws open the door. We assume formation and march toward the railroad station. The air is cool. A bright moon shines on the guards' helmets and the thud of tramping feet resounds in the early morning stillness.

We board a train. The guards are circumspect. Dawn approaches and the landscape is a weird grey. We are speeding and the train roars through a world wrapt in solemn silence. The sun, bursting with fresh radiance, lights the earth as we rattle along. A shrill whistle! We swing around one curve, swerve around another, thump in juxtaposition to a gravel embankment and tear into open country.

We are nearing Tuttlingen.

Twenty miles to the Swiss border! Twenty miles to Liberty! McKeown casts cryptic glances at the guards who, clenching their rifles, keep a sharp lookout and rivet their lynx-eyes on us. These are the most menacing guards yet and a move means death. The train stops. Rifles point at us. Ideas of escape are given up. McKeown is despondent.

We look out the windows. Sentries pace the Tuttlingen station platform and men, women, and children, hurrying to and fro, pass beneath our window. We wave to the little ones who giggle, smile and wave back until their mothers, scolding and whacking them for noticing us, jerk them along.

Two Red Cross Sisters follow our officer who walks

briskly toward the car. One carries a large pan, the other dishes, and presently guards hand us plates of boiled spaghetti. Another windfall due to the good Bavarian and we start to eat. It is salt as brine. The German women, forced to give food to prisoners, have spitefully saturated the spaghetti with salt, but we eat it without comment, for it is food and furthermore we would not have our officer know.

Whistles. Voices. Cries. The train slowly pulls away and soon the uneventful landscape glides past.

Hours later, on the outskirts of Villingen, we trudge along a lonely dirt road. To be jostled together and hemmed in by guards is natural. Our movements are cramped. Our thoughts are limited. Our world is small. Food, prisons, prisoners and guards . . . that is all. Maybe we will know someone here for Puryear left Landshut for Villingen some time ago.

Ahead and on the left are a few barracks in a place of dismal grey with guards scattered outside the barbed wire fencing. This is the prison all right. To the right, a bit further on and back from the road, is a red brick building. We walk by the fence and halt before a boarded section where a door of large dimensions is flanked by armed sentries. Our officer shows his credentials. One sentry, with unnecessary care, reads them over and over and this foolish delay vexes the Bavarian who, although he shows impatience, avoids a rumpus. The doors open, the sentries are rigid and we walk into an enclosure which is separated from the prison yard proper by another fence.

The Bavarian goes into the Commandant's office to report our arrival. We wait. Through the barbed wire, about a hundred feet away, we see Americans. Our officer returns, walks quickly past and then turns, abruptly . . . "Good-

bye," he says.   Just two bromidic words but his glance is a
tender farewell.

"Good-bye," we answer, loath to see him go.

He walks through the gate.   The large doors meet behind him and we know we shall not see him again but in
each grateful heart is a place for one of the finest men who
ever served his country.

.   .   .   .   .

In a barracks in the center of the courtyard we are
searched and the examination of our clothes and naked
bodies takes over two hours. McKeown still retains his map.
We dress and go into the courtyard where the other American prisoners, waiting to see us, look for familiar faces and
seek new friends.   Strangers all, but we have known each
other . . . always.

"How is the food?" is our first question.

"We receive rations from the Red Cross," and they tell
us that bulk supplies of both food and clothing come
through Berne, Switzerland.   This assurance of food whets
our appetites.

"You are our guests for supper tonight."—"Yes, we
knew some prisoners were coming and waited to eat with
you."—"We've got plenty, come along!" So, they delayed
dinner to share their rations with us! What a welcome!

I am to be the guest of Jefferies and Hardesty; Lawson
and McKeown will eat with others in the same barracks
and already we feel better and already we are friends.

"Dinner is ready," Jefferies announces.

Canned beans, water biscuit, coffee, jam and rice pudding
are put before me.   I eat and eat.

"Have some more . . . here." He piles up my plate
and as there seems to be plenty I eat until satisfied.

"Now have a cigarette."   And with a smoke to top off

such a banquet I feel really full for the first time in Germany.

Jefferies, known by everyone as "Jeff," was brigaded with the British, has been a prisoner for eight months and tells of many amusing incidents since his capture.

"Is Puryear here?" I ask. "He left Landshut for . . ."

"Puryear! My God, do you know him?" breaks in Jeff.

"Know him! . . . he was in my squadron . . . just missed him at . . ."

"You just missed him here all right."—"Missed a Hell of a riot too and—" "He escaped!"—they all talk at once.

"ESCAPED!" we chorus.

"Yes, just last night . . . right out that window." Jeff points to a window in the barracks and laughs.

"What!"

We marvel that, from all places, an escape was actually made from here where more than a hundred Germans form a watchful personnel to guard about one hundred and twenty prisoners. They boast that this camp is the strongest, safest prison in Germany and brag about its impregnability. Amazed, we listen.

"It's true, they got away. Puryear, Battle, Tucker, Isaacs and Willis are free, so far."—"Others were caught and are in solitary confinement."—"They watch us like hawks now."—"Yes, no one else better try it."

This prison camp at Villingen measures about two hundred by four hundred feet and has a center court. Barracks, their outer windows tightly barred, line the edges; a high board fence, topped with barbed wire, connects the barracks in places where they do not join together and a few feet further out a low barbed fencing runs around the camp. Beyond that is a ditch about five feet wide filled with sharp-pointed wire entanglement and it, also, encircles the enclosure. Edging the ditch still another fence girds in a final barrier of barbed wire which stretches up until, at a height of ten feet, pointed steel arms curve inwards. Outside this supposedly invincible barricade rifled guards pace all day long. Before dark the guard patrol is doubled. As a last precaution a row of electric lights, which completely encompass the camp, burn all night.

"Puryear tried to escape from Rastatt, they put him in solitary confinement for fourteen days and . . ."—"He had only served five when he came here . . ."—"Yes, so they locked him up for the other nine," they tell us.

Released from solitary confinement Puryear was pregnant with plans. So were many others. They talked and talked. If one escaped, an inspection would follow which would catch those preparing, so they decided on one wholesale break—they would all break together. Liberty or Death! All had an equal chance. The lucky ones would make it; the others would take their medicine; the plot was widespread, the work begun and everyone in camp had a finger in the pie.

"A Russian here will get you anything for a price . . ."

"That's right. Knives, compasses, caps, overcoats . . . how the devil he does it is beyond us . . ."

"But he does. Give him the cash and back he comes with the goods. They got tools, equipment and countless odds and ends from him."

Barracks lights are out at ten-thirty. How to put the entire camp in darkness? Chains of wire, with lead weights at either end, could be thrown over the uninsulated wires where they entered the camp. This would make a short-circuit but it was a high and difficult throw. A miss meant failure. To insure success several chains were made to be thrown by those not escaping.

"Tell about the disguises, Jeff."

"Oh, yes. They got Russian overcoats and in the dark they looked just like German uniforms."

Day after day, while someone stood watch, Puryear took the planks from his bed. He cut the pieces, bored in holes and when wired together they formed a ladder.

Willis, carving tediously on a block of wood, made the exact replica of a rifle. He painted it black and when polished it shone at night like real steel.

They were about ready. That was Saturday. Final details for a dash to Freedom. Window bars would be cut the last day; a messenger assigned to report when all were ready; short-circuiting of the lights was to be the signal; each man knew in what turn he would climb out a certain window and every move thereafter. They decided on Monday night. Then—they heard that the Russians were to be moved Monday. The Germans would surely inspect the camp after they left and again they feared that their groundwork and tools would be found. The next day was Sunday. Could they all be ready? Yes . . . well, the better the day the better the deed . . . they would go Sunday night.

The Sabbath passed, peacefully.

The sun shone and went down. The twilight came. Lights in the barracks and the guards paced back and forth. Eight . . . nine . . . ten o'clock and the camp was still. Ten-thirty . . . the lights in the barracks went out . . . the prisoners were in darkness . . . the guards knew "All was Well."

Puryear pulls the runway to a window, puts on a Russian cap and overcoat and slings a haversack of food over his shoulder. Others, in different barracks, also prepare. The messenger reports each man is at his post. All are ready.

The time has come. All wait . . . breathlessly. Ten minutes pass. The outside lights sputter . . . sputter . . . sputter—and go out. The entire camp is in total darkness.

Willis, wearing a Russian overcoat, runs to the guard house.

"*Raus! Raus! Raus!*" he yells. "*Raus! Die Amerikaner fliehen,*" and he brandishes his wooden rifle. "*Garde Raus!*"

The Germans, never suspecting him, pour through the gate to surround the camp. Willis goes with them, but— he keeps on going.

Russians at their end of the yard throw bottles against the fence, yell and raise other false alarms to distract the Huns. A guard, just outside the fencing, stands directly opposite Puryear's window. He had been there all evening. Evidently, earlier in the day, he had noticed the bars had been tampered with and when the lights went out he fixed his rifle for action.

The wire screeched!

Someone has gone over; now is the time.

A rifle shot!

The guard does not budge and Puryear . . . hesitates.

Whistles blow!

Now or never! Delay means failure. Puryear shoves the ladder partially out of the window and jumps to the ground eight feet below. The ladder is pushed out after him so Puryear, throwing it against the fence, starts up.

"*Halt!*" yells the guard.

"*Ja, schön,*" answers Puryear, climbing.

"*Halt! Halt! Halt!*" threatens the guard.

"*Ja, gut. Ja, Ja!*" and poised on the top of the fence . . . Puryear jumps.

Now outside the barbed wire only a tree is between them.

Puryear runs around it. The guard chases him . . . around
. . . around . . . around.

"Halt! . . . Halt! . . . Halt!"

The dry crack of rifles fill the air. Puryear can no longer
trifle with the guard. He runs! He runs for his life! The
guard fires . . . point blank, but Puryear, zig-zagging in
the darkness, keeps running and disappears. Battle, Tucker
and Isaacs went out other windows.

The impossible was accomplished. Five men escaped.
Several others, caught at the fence, were brought back but
not one was hit by rifle fire. Now, much to the chagrin of
McKeown, we are guarded more than ever.

Lawson, McKeown and I occupy a barracks with about
twenty others. The beds are made of eight-inch planks but
proficient in lying on wooden slats I pull up the covers and
go to sleep. A few hours of bliss and pains wrench my
belly. All night I am up intermittently, vomiting. It was a
good dinner but my bedraggled stomach could not stand the
shock of such a treat.

CHAPTER XXIII

THE days go by.

When Puryear and the others escaped they took canned food with them and now Red Cross rations which were formerly issued once a week come daily. Cans are first opened and then we get the contents. McKeown, Mitchell, (an aviator from Mississippi) Lawson and I pool our rations for in this way we get a variety. Others do the same. Occasionally prison money buys shrivelled apples and onions. We make sauce with the apples and boil the onions. Twenty lumps of sugar a week. This is the first we have had in Germany and we crave sweets. Also a piece of chocolate a quarter of an inch thick, not an inch wide and about four inches long is supposed to last two weeks. I gobble all mine at once. In exchange for scraps of Red Cross food a guard smuggles in saccharine tablets and one fellow, starved for sweets, eats too much. He is a mass of red blotches.

The Germans still give us black bread and soup. The soup is made at the end of the yard where a filthy orderly, standing on a ladder, stirs the brown liquid with a long pole. How they manage to make it taste so sour and smell so frowzy is beyond me, but we need quantity and get it down. However, were it not for the Red Cross food, we could not live.

McKeown is too generous.   The greedy ones, and they
are plenty, impose on his unselfish nature and take food
from him all the time.   He, who needs more care than any
of us, goes without to give to others.   He shows it.   His
health is suffering and it riles me.

"Keep your own food, Mac," I tell him, "or you'll be
sick."

"I'm all right," he smiles.   "They need it more than I
do."

McKeown has a heart of gold.   He is the finest character
I know.   He does not seem real; he is so splendid.

A newspaper, by some subterfuge, gets into camp.   A
socialist publication, it accurately prints any Allied suc-
cesses.   One fellow translates and when it arrives he becomes the most popular man in the barracks.   We crowd
around.   "The Allies are making great gains," he reads
and we listen, avidly, to every item on the war.

The nights are very cold and the damp mornings white
with fog.   One blanket means little.   We get up stiff, chilled
and, hunching our backs, hug our bodies and shiver like a
lot of sick cranes.   The winters in Villingen are severe and
we feel we never will be able to weather it.   We plan to
escape, continually.   McKeown talks of nothing else.   But,
since the last break, things have changed.   At night large
flood-lights make the camp as bright as day; extra guards
now patrol inside as well as out; roll call is made both morning and evening; the surrounding barbed wire fence is
charged with high-voltage electricity; an officer makes frequent inspections, but we never know when he is coming,
and when he does suddenly appear we stand at attention
while our quarters are minutely examined.

With another prisoner I stand in the courtyard.   A German officer, fully two hundred feet away, enters the gate.

His stern profile looks straight ahead, and we do not salute. But, from the corner of an eye he has watched us.   He strides over.

"Why did you not salute me?"   He is bombastic.

"You were so far away, sir, I did not deem it necessary," explains my companion, politely.

"You did not deem it necessary, eh?—*you!*"   The officer goes into a tirade.

"Do you wish us to salute you at long range, sir?"   That finished him.   Five days alone in a black cell.

The least offense means solitary confinement and so sweeping is this punishment that one is not a full fledged prisoner until he serves a sentence.   Not to endure a term of solitary confinement in Villingen is a breach of etiquette. In fact, the isolated cells are always full and others, sentenced, are on a waiting list.

A makeshift shower is installed in a hut at the end of the camp.   We bathe beneath a trickle of cold water.   At first it is a treat, but to put on clothes sticky with filth lessens the pleasure. McKeown examines the bathhouse. His thoughts are neither of cleanliness nor dirt . . . only escape.

"I must get back to the squadron!" he tells me.   "Just once more!   I've got to fly over the lines . . . just once more."

I believe if he did get into the air he would deliberately ram into a Hun, for he is lost in but one thought—escape.

He stares into space, thinking, thinking, thinking.   "I've found a way, Archie!"   His eyes shine.   "I've found a way at last."

In the bathhouse is a loose floor-board.   A foot below is the ground.   From there it is about twenty feet to the electrified barbed fence and McKeown's plan is to dig an underground tunnel starting at the bathhouse and running beneath the fence. We talk it over. We must get out of

Germany before the winter sets in and we decide to do it, somehow. The sacred plans must not leak out; we confide in but a few.

"What can we dig with?" I ask.

"A spoon—I have a spoon." McKeown, weak and sick, is dauntless.

We lift the floor board and start. One digs while the other, outside, warns when a guard is coming. We dig and dig. Each day we scatter small amounts of earth in the near-by garbage cans. We dig and dig. But we dare not dispose of much at a time for fear the Germans should notice it. We dig and dig. One spoonful, then another, careful not to spill or leave a track. We dig and dig . . . wish the damned spoon were larger for at this rate we figure it will take over a month to complete the tunnel.

"You see," McKeown burrows the spoon, "when we finish, the others can go, too."

He always thinks of others . . . always.

"They'll scamper out of here like rabbits." He smiles and digs, digs, digs.

We are on our way to freedom. We will escape! To dig at the tunnel is a daily religious duty. To see McKeown with his burned face, his horribly burned leg and his tortuously burned finger, feverishly spooning out the earth is a sight never to be forgotten.

Digging to liberty—with a spoon.

.   .   .   .   .

A flu epidemic threatens the camp.

Many are sick and two, seriously ill, were wheeled away from the barracks several days ago. We hear they have died. The Germans take away only those who will die. Otherwise, they do not bother. When that time comes they wheel in a long wicker basket, dump the patient in and . . . that is the end. Jeff calls it the "Baby Carriage." He has been here long enough to know what it means.

"Believe me," says Jeff, "when they wheel up that baby carriage it's all over; that's the last ride you get from here."

Men, frail and ill, who should be in the hospital lie on the hard boards fighting to get well. Little chance . . . in here.

Several days pass. Death hangs over the barracks. No care, no medicine, it is cold, dank and the sick ones need attention. We do all we can but are so helpless. We dread the basket.

Jeff gets the flu.

For days he has lain on his bunk. Last night he was so weak—could barely turn his head. Today he is worse and does not move at all. He is very ill and we are worried. To collect myself I go out for a walk. Returning across the yard I see the baby carriage before our barracks and two orderlies carrying someone out. They place him in the basket. I run over and there—pale as death—is Jeff.

"Jeff!" I say, "how are you?"

He is motionless. With effort he rolls his glassy eyes and stares at me. His blue lips open but he does not speak. His drawn face is set, determinedly.

"Jeff!" I bend over to encourage him . . . a lump fills my throat . . . I cannot speak.

He knows he is in the baby carriage! We look at each other. His lips tremble and he whispers . . . faintly. I do not hear so leaning over put my ear close to his parched lips.

"I'll . . . come back . . . Archie." Such a fragile gurgle. "I'll . . . come back."

"Sure you will Jeff!" I force a smile. "Sure you will!"

His eyes shut. They wheel him off in the sinister basket.

Jeff . . . too! God damn them! Why do they wait so long? I walk and walk and walk . . .

.   .   .   .   .

Great commotion!
"Heard the news?"
"What?"
"Battle and Tucker are back!"
"No!"
"There they are, by the gate."
We rush over and crowd around them. Escaped, recaptured and here they are. What rotten luck! Haggard and worn, uniforms caked with mud, they are fagged out. We all talk at once. "What happened?"—"How did they catch you?"—"Where have you been?"—"What about the others?" We are frantic with curiosity and excitement.

The turmoil dies down and we hear their stories.

Battle, under cover of darkness, traveled by night. He hid by daylight but it was difficult to find places. One day he came to a haven of refuge, a haystack, where, sleepless, he could rest as well. He crawled in deep under the straw and felt safely hidden.

The bark of a dog. Then someone walked past. Thank God, they were gone! Another bark, nearer this time and a man's annoyed voice. Battle held his breath. The hound, scenting him, yapped and sniffed at the haystack. The man called again and again but the dog paying no attention yelped and jumped around the straw. The animal's noisy persistence brought his master, who was a hunter and, investigating with his gun, he poked out Battle and turned him over to the military authorities.

Tucker, his feet so swollen that he could no longer walk, slumped to the middle of a road. Crippled, helpless and with no choice but to sit there he was picked up and brought back under guard.

The fate of Puryear, Willis and Isaacs is unknown and Battle and Tucker are sent to solitary confinement. The commandant, flushed with confidence at the recapture and wise in his own conceit, tells us what fools we are. "If you try again the guards will kill you." He is calmly nonchalant. "Why attempt to escape just to be caught? It is foolhardy! Your two *brave* men," he sneers, "are in solitary confinement and the others, too, have been captured. You cannot get away."

We treat all Germans as natural born liars and do not believe that Puryear, Willis or Isaacs have been caught.

.   .   .   .   .

The days crawl. We dig at the tunnel; eat Red Cross food; answer roll calls and listen insatiably to news of the Front in the socialist paper. All agree that the war will last until Spring. We must get out! A winter here will be fatal. We must get out!

I dig and dig and think of home. Home! . . . the soft magic of the word is gone. Home! . . . my thoughts juggle with the spoons of dirt. Home! . . . it does not mean what it used to, somehow. I dig and dig and dig—a fat worm—quit wriggling—get out. Home! . . . where are the thrills that made the visions of home a giddy joy? Home! . . . where is the feverish excitement which at the end of a school year made the thought of my room at home an inspiration for future ambitions? Ambitions? . . . I was too ambitious. Distorted values . . . striving and striving . . . for what? A sensible man wants happiness . . . nothing more. And happiness is food, a bed and two blankets . . . nothing more. Home! . . . just a place to eat and sleep in—is that all? But, I am right . . . yes, absolutely right . . . and yet something is wrong . . . quite wrong . . . and I dig and dig and dig. Another worm, a slimy thing, is cut in half by the spoon. To eat and sleep and be warm—that is home. What more could one want of life . . . yet, something is wrong . . . and sad . . . Home!

.   .   .   .   .

Today a handful of new prisoners arrive.

Dirty, haggard and tired they wait outside the commandant's office and peer through the barbed fence. How well we know what they have been through! One fellow wears a long, faded, loose Russian overcoat which reaches to the ground. His back is all we see; he does not look through the wire; he stands a bit apart and for some reason I watch only him.

The gate opens. They file in and still my gaze follows the figure enveloped in the Russian coat. He walks slowly, there is nothing familiar about him, yet I cannot take my eyes away. His face turns and my heart beats, heavily. Can it be? I dare not trust myself so, lagging beside, I scrutinize his profile—can it be? Dropping behind, I stare at his shoulders and wonder—can it be? Running ahead, I watch him. His white face, closer, closer, closer, grows until it fills the courtyard and only his face is there. My pulse pounds! There is no mistake and tearing towards him I yell, "Woody!"

His own name startles him. His head pivots in every direction as he searches for the source of the call. He does not notice me—yet.

"Woody!" I am hysterical with joy. "W-O-O-D-Y!"

He sees me, stops still and gapes in stark amazement.

"WOODY! How are you?"

But he only stares, bewildered.

My throat fills; my heart sinks; is Woody ill or—worse?

"Archie!" his voice chokes. "Archie! . . . thought you were killed."

We throw our arms about each other and cling, speech-less. A guard takes him away.

I chase around in circles. Then finding McKeown, Law-son and Mitchell I spread my good news. "Woody is here!" I tell them. "Woody is here!"

"Who?"

"Woodard of the First Pursuit Group. Woodard of the 95th. Woody! . . . my roommate at the Front."

We know he is being searched and wait anxiously until it is over. He comes out.

"Woody! This is McKeown; this is Lawson, Woody, and here is Mitchell." They shake hands. "You're eating with us, Woody; we have a fine mess," and we five walk across the courtyard.

"Tonight we will have a great meal, Woody, the very best for you . . . a Red Cross banquet. Woody! How are you?"

Dinner is over. We smoke, talk, stroll around the yard and Woodard pulls a cigarette case from his hip pocket. "Here's a good souvenir," he laughs.

The case, in two pieces, was cut in half by a bullet.

"But it must have hit you, Woody . . ."

"Just a furrow where it scraped my backside; healed up now."

Woodard, patrolling over the lines, was surprised by three Fokkers. They dove in attack, bullets zipped by and his plane, riddled by the first few bursts, became clumsy and unmanageable. The controls were hit and his ship started down. Phwit! A stinging sensation and he squirmed in his seat as streams of smoke whisked past. He dropped fast. The ground was rushing up and he tried to level out but the elevator control was damaged and his plane veered and bucked like an angry bull. He saw a fence—*crash!*—and was in a heap. He snaked his way through the tangled wreckage and was taken prisoner.

"It was Sunday, September 29th, and I was north of Verdun," he says.

"September 29th? Exactly three weeks to a day, Woody, after I was shot down."

"Yes, I remember well, Archie. It was Sunday morning, September 8th. Avery and Heinricks came back and we thought you would be along. We waited all day. When night came I began to wonder but McGucken, your mechanic, was certain you would return and hung around the hangar long after dark. The next morning I hardly knew what to think but McGucken insisted that you would be back. That day an observation balloon reported that an Allied monoplace machine crashed one kilometer east of Étain about ten o'clock in the morning and at one o'clock the enemy were seen to drag the wreck to the nearest road, take it apart and haul it away. The report tallied with the time and location where you were last seen and we gave you up for dead. But McGucken was still hopeful and waited and waited and waited; would not admit nor believe that anything could happen to you. Finally he said, 'Well, I guess Lieutenant Archibald is gone.' It hit him hard; he felt pretty blue."

To hear my own roommate tell of the report of my death, to know of my mechanic's faith in me and his sadness, is uncanny.

The days of flying! . . . a thousand years ago. The days of flying! . . . yesterday. I see the white hangars; I touch my plane; I watch McGucken testing the control wires; I am back . . . back with the squadron. "Archibald, you fly number one on the left . . ."

"Heinricks is a prisoner, somewhere." Woody's voice is

far away. "When last seen he was gliding towards the earth with Fokkers on his tail; we hear he was severely wounded."

Heinricks! So they got him, too! When I joined the squadron it was Heinricks who took me on my first trip to the lines; Heinricks and I who practiced on the lake, that day; Heinricks who led the formation the morning I was shot down and now, he's down . . . a prisoner . . . or dead . . . Good God!

"Remember Luke?"

"Luke? Why of course, Woody. We four, Luke, Beauchamp, you and I were on the train together the day we joined the group. Do I remember, why I can see the little crossroad where we parted. Luke and Beauchamp bound for the 27th and you and I for the 95th."

"Well, Luke is the sensation of the Front."

"What do you mean?"

"Just that! Luke is the most talked-of man in Europe! He's the Ace of Aces; known everywhere as 'The Great Luke.' He got fifteen official victories in less than two weeks. He'll get killed at the rate he's going, though. We gave a banquet for him and he was told to take it easy, that he was worth more alive than dead. But Luke just laughed. Said he was a different person the minute he got into the air. Wehner used to fly with him, remember, but after eight victories was shot down in flames. Luke goes it alone now. He's a wild man in the air! He's gone crazy! Why, he told his commander that with protection he'd clean up the entire German balloon line!"

"Luke? . . . well I'll be . . ."

"On September 18th he shot down three Fokkers and two balloons in less than seven minutes!"

"What? . . . Five in seven minutes!" I am dumbfounded. Luke, that little Arizona towhead, had told the truth and fooled us all.

"Yes, and all confirmed. It's the greatest record ever made at the Front! No aviator of the entire Allied Armies ever equalled his victories. His name blazes the headlines of every Paris paper. He's the idol of France."

.   .   .   .   .

One of the new arrivals walks—alone.

He wears a uniform of the Royal Flying Corps and walks —alone. Others in the courtyard, singly and in twos and threes, stroll and chat together but the Englishman walks— alone. Now he steps before one fellow who, with a blanched look of horror, hurries away. Again he walks—alone. Then one by one he timidly approaches different prisoners but each, with a grimace of compassionate loathing, leaves him. With head bowed he walks and walks—alone. Finally his back stiffens and with hopeful determination he joins a group of laughing men. They look, stop talking, stand cringingly appalled and desert him. He is shunned as if he were leprous and, with drooping shoulders, resumes his walk —alone.

I start towards him. He hears me and as he turns a body with arms and legs comes to meet me. I am petrified. Between his flying cap and collar, where his face should be, is . . . something else. I want to run away but digging my nails into my hands keep walking until we are but a few feet apart. My flesh creeps at the horrible, hideous, pitiful sight, for his face, a twisted, shapeless mass of scarlet flesh, is burned beyond human semblance. His nose is gone; his bead-like eyes swim in purple; his lower eyelids are missing and instead are watery, bloodshot sockets. He has no mouth or lips but from a writhing hole come guttural sounds. Sweat is wet on my forehead but I decide to stick it, somehow, and talk rapidly. He tries to answer and, gulping to keep from being sick before him, I give an excuse to leave. "Sorry," I say. "Glad to have found you! Had a cousin flying with the British, nothing like the Air Service, after all . . ."

He chews out a murmur. This time I catch a word, distinctly. "Cheerio!" he gurgles as I walk away.

"Cheerio!" I call back, without looking. "See you again . . ." My conscience burns. But is it my fault if I am not burned? My throat sticks. What courage! What strength! An aviator, fighting for England, shot down in flames, to be a repulsive thing for the rest of his days. God! much better if he were dead. He haunts me; my ears ring with his "Cheerio" and his gallant soul has cut my soul in half.

.   .   .   .   .

McKeown is quiet and stays by himself. He sits alone, for hours, pensive and brooding. The progress of his tunnel and escape interest him but otherwise he is melancholy.

"What's the matter, Mac?"

"Nothing, just planning to get out. One more crack at the Huns . . . that's all."

I know differently. The sight of the burned Englishman persecutes him and he looks in a mirror. He pictures himself far worse than he is and imagines he is horribly disfigured. Another flight and I feel it purposely would be his last.

"My parents are old people, Archie," he tells me, "why let them see me like this?"

He does not want ever to go home; he is not himself.

.   .   .   .   .

It is dinner time. Lawson, Mitchell, Woodard and I sit down to hot Red Cross food but McKeown is not here.

"Where's McKeown?" I rap out but no one knows. "Wait!" I demand. "Not a bite until McKeown comes."

We find him, half hiding, in a corner of the barracks, eating his cold, miserable soup.

"Dinner is ready, Mac." We are casual.

He stays in the corner and does not speak.

"Mac!" I cry. "Come and eat . . ."

"Now listen, Archie," he argues plaintively, "please go ahead with your dinner. I'm going to escape soon and want to save all the food I can . . ."

"Why Mac!" I appear surprised and hurt, "when you decide to break you know we will give you all the food you can carry and anyway you must eat hot food to keep in condition until you go. Come on now!"

"NO!" He is adamant.

"All right," I say, sitting on the edge of my bunk, "if you won't eat neither will I."

"Now Archie," he pleads, "go ahead and eat; I'm fine and . . ."

"Not a mouthful until you come with me."

He looks at me disconsolately. He knows I mean it and is cornered so, rather than have another sacrifice, he surrenders. That is McKeown.

"You old stiff!" I whack him on the back. "Are you getting goofy?"

"Perhaps . . . Archie . . . perhaps." And he smiles.

CHAPTER XXIV

November.

Turkey surrenders. The terms of the Armistice are known. The surrender of Bulgaria over a month ago is confirmed and the Allies are driving ahead on the Western Front. The prospects of crippling the enemy for effective organization during the winter and an early spring advance into Germany look promising.

Several days later Battle and Tucker are released from solitary confinement. Their pale faces are dirty, their cheeks sunken, but they are cheerful to have finished their sentences and we hail their deliverance with open arms.

Then, we hear the awful truth. The penalty for escape is not over; there is yet another price to pay; the worst of all. They must atone for their daring in the most dreaded spot in Germany; they are to be sent to Northern Prussia.

Northern Prussia! The thought freezes us to the marrow.

Stories of venomous dungeons and the gruesome treatment of prisoners, fed on but bread and water, have filtered into camp and Northern Prussia is a symbol of death. We whisper among ourselves, solemnly. Battle and Tucker, speechless, stand in the courtyard waiting to go. Our words of encouragement fall on deaf ears; they are comfortless.

The guards appear and lead them toward the gate. We follow and awkwardly wish them Godspeed but they are crushed, their throats are full, they are facing a tragic end without further hope and cannot speak. Their thin, suffering faces betray a prayer for immediate death rather than the dragging hell of torture and starvation. They know they are doomed and, silently, they pass out the gate.

Glowing accounts of Allied success!

Tremendous offensives of the French, British, Belgians and Americans fill the socialist paper. All along the Western Front the Germans fall back in full retreat. The Americans sweep ahead on a fifty-mile front above Verdun. We believe the Boche will retreat to the Hindenburg line and then hold out, indefinitely.

November 4th.

With five hundred thousand troops taken prisoners, Austria surrenders to terms more rigid than either Turkey or Bulgaria.

News! News! News!

Revolution breaks out in Germany.

In the harbor at Kiel the Red Flag is hoisted on the battleship Kaiser. Mutiny, like a scarlet octopus, spreads over the shipyards and stretches its arms to suck in the shore workshops. Councils of soldiers, sailors and workmen form the mutineers, flaunt possession of the town and the movement is reaching to the industrial centers. We hear that Karlsruhe is taken. A few revolutionists, after appropriating the city, charged to the prison camp and demanded the sword and insignia of the Prussian Commandant. He refused to surrender and was promptly killed. They control the railroad stations and German soldiers, as fast as they arrive, are stripped of all arms.

·   ·   ·   ·   ·

A red autumn sun shines on the courtyard. The brisk wind is cold, and after a jog-trot we stop, shivering, to discuss the revolution.

The gate opens. An American walks in. We wonder who it can be as his hand flutters in a wave and he shouts, "Hey! What do you think of this?" We rush over and there, standing before us, is Jeff.

Jeff! . . . back from the death hospital! Jeff! . . . back from the baby carriage! We are so flabbergasted that our joy is smothered in surprise.

"Good work, old man! Good work . . ."

He is thin, weak and the color of parchment but he grins, victoriously.

"Jeff! God! . . . this is great!"

He says nothing, just smiles; he is, himself, astounded. This is the first time that anyone, wheeled away in the wicker basket, has ever returned.

.   .   .   .

November 10th.

I walk from the barracks into the courtyard where laughter and talking of excited men permeate the camp with some unexpected joy. Many swell around the gate, others rush to join them, everyone rejoices, all are buoyant and slipping through the crowd I see two men. They stand, wreathed in smiles, while the hilarious mob welcomes them as conquering heroes.

"Battle and Tucker, can you beat it!"

Battle and Tucker who, defeated, left with a prayer for death return as happy men throbbing with life and animated exhilaration.

"Say!—this isn't Northern Prussia."—"No! You're in the wrong place."—"What in the devil happened?"

At Cassel, a city almost due north of Frankfurt, they

were waiting for a train to take them on the last lap of their wretched journey into Northern Prussia. They stood there, surrounded by guards, broken-hearted and silent with voiceless woe.

Suddenly, the revolutionists swooped upon them. Surrounding the guards they took away their rifles, ripped the Prussian insignia from their uniforms, put the red ribbon of mutiny on their tunics and, slapping Battle and Tucker on the back, called them "Comrades" and told them they were free men.

Free men . . . in the heart of an enemy country. Free men . . . with Germany afire with a red revolution, with hordes of disorganized, antagonistic troops retreating in chaotic disorder and with the possibility of travel dangerous. Free men . . . but a freedom filled with peril and, accompanied by their four guards, unarmed and wearing the red badge of sympathetic mutineers, they returned to Villingen. Free men . . . they came home . . . to prison.

The Commandant orders the guards back on duty. They smile and, pointing to their flaming ribbons, refuse. This bloodless revolution, for there is not much killing, is swift, far-reaching and successful. All officers, when seen, are stripped of their insignia and given a red badge.

The revolutionists take possession of the camp!

Our Commandant, now, obeys their orders. The daily routine of life is the same but the very air is charged with news. We hear that Puryear and Willis reached the Rhine, swam to Switzerland and successfully escaped.

The rumor of a proposed armistice between the Allies and Germany! Agog, disbelieving, yet hoping, we gather in the courtyard and there, pasted on a pole, is a bulletin. We read. It verifies, in bold print, the longed-for news, but the iron-clad terms so far exceed in severity those granted to Austria and Turkey that we feel Germany will continue the war rather than yield to such demands. The words, AN IMMEDIATE REPATRIATION WITHOUT RECIPROCITY OF ALL ALLIED AND UNITED STATES PRISONERS OF WAR, leave us untouched, quite unmoved and cold.

Freedom! . . . we do not want it now!

An Armistice, so prayed for, is a sick illusion.

What of our comrades who paved the road to victory? Dead. Did they give their lives that an enemy, smelling defeat, could cry "Peace"? What of our friends who held back the foe? Gone. Did they grit their teeth and, dying, drive on that the Boche, when they had enough, could yell "Quits"?

Victory is at hand!

A well-earned, blood-soaked victory. Men, sobbing in agony, left the world too soon. They died on battlefields, in hospitals or fell from the air in a country war-torn, shell-ridden and devastated. They died—for victory. That victory is almost accomplished. They died—aiming for a goal. That goal has not, quite, been reached. Only a few feet more and a sacred pledge to the dead is fulfilled.

We are the winners!—must we stop before we have won all?

We are the winners!—must we turn at the very threshold?

The Germans know they are beaten! But, *Das Vaterland* must not be touched! Are our men to be forgotten? The Germans, whipped to a pulp, surrender as we near their undemolished gates. Did our soldiers sacrifice in vain? Will the Allies listen? How, with the glassy eyes of thousands of dead watching them, can they halt at the very portal? Heaven prevent! Will they, standing knee-deep in the blood-soaked ground of a destroyed, defiled, ravaged and prostrated country, acquiesce? God forbid!

We are the winners!—shall the vanquished leave a demolished country and return to one intact? Shall they walk from barren, shell-blown fields into meadows fertile and green? Shall they turn from cities they have riddled, from villages they have blown to bits and from towns where not a building stands or a thing lives to a land unspoiled and a place apart? Shall they leave a desolate mass of filthy twisted ruins and return, submissively, to a country untouched? To a country where streets are clean, where cities loom in the old splendor and where in every town and hamlet their homes, still standing, await them?

Vengeance is mine . . . and every man here feels the same: every man prays the war will go on: every man wants the Allies to force a crushing and everlasting defeat upon the enemy. To march—march—march—triumphantly into Germany!

.   .   .   .   .

November 11th!

The war is over!

Germany accepts the terms of the Armistice. Of course! Hostilities cease . . . the war is over! The Kaiser, with an inglorious flight into Holland, ends his grotesque career.

Every captain does not sink with his ship!

The war is over!—we are dumb!

The war is over!—we are in a frenzy!

The war is over!—we chew at the words but cannot digest them!

The war is over!—all is havoc!

.   .   .   .   .

Uniformed students from a military school across the road pour out of the red brick building. The institution is a thing of the past and piles of helmets, *"Mit Gott Für König und Vaterland,"* will gather dust. The boys, heretofore forbidden to come near the prison camp, look through the barbed wire and watch us, curiously.

"You are free," they yell. *"Mit dem Kriege sind wir jetzt fertig. Der Krieg ist aus! Der Krieg ist alles fertig!* Comrades go Home!"

Comrades—Hell! But, after all, they are just kids, what do they know?

.   .   .   .   .

We attend evening roll call.

Consumed with an impatience to leave we are irritable and on the tiptoes of expectation.

"When will we be released?"—"Yes, when do we get out of here?"—"We are prisoners no longer!" . . .

The Commandant promises us release in a few days, warns us to make no demonstration, and we return to our barracks.

I get into bed and pull up the blankets but sleep will not come. The war is over. The fight is finished. All is quiet . . . everywhere. Guns are silent, the venomous skies are clear and Peace, who hid in shame during the four years of hideous warfare, floats above the world and with tears in her eyes spreads wide her gossamer wings. Peace! The old Fiddlediddles are still at it. They scratched their beards to have a war; they scratch again to stop it; they are through and now—God's Will be done!

Time goes by and still we are held. Encouraged by rumors of release we try to be calm but as days upon days creep along we are restless. Everything becomes unbearable and now, still prisoners a full week after the Armistice, we are on the point of hysteria.

An assembly is announced.

We rush to the center of the courtyard, stand in a long

straight line and wait, breathlessly, for the good news. A German, red-faced and fat, is before us. He smiles benignly and his attitude is one of sugary friendliness. "Comrades!" he begins. "We are friends together."

With forced patience we await further remarks.

"Comrades!" We cringe at the word. "Germany has won the war!"

We rivet our eyes on him.

"Because," he explains, "we have won the freedom of our people."

We stare.

He jabbers on, cleverly plays with words, gives a false coloring to our situation and, although his choice of sentences attempts a false submissiveness, there is no sign of a battle lost. He claims, repeatedly, victory for Germany. He uses, repeatedly, the word "Comrades."

We are riled. Comrades! The sacred word comes sour from his lying mouth. Comrades now, are we? What fools they think us! A fiendish enemy, unmerciful and tyrannical at a sign of victory; submissive and quitters in face of defeat; to call us "Comrades" and say they won the war. Good God!

We let him blabber on, why not? We know, he knows— and the thing we want now is to be in France for Thanksgiving. His long speech is contradictory, vague, meaningless and childlike.

"Return to your homes, my friends . . ."

He is nearly through . . . we will be in France by Thanksgiving!

"Carry love and kindness in your hearts for the German people!"

We listen, silently; we stand, quietly, wondering how long he will keep us.

"Comrades, you cannot leave, yet. You must wait and be patient."

Patient? . . . our patience is exhausted! We have waited; we have swallowed it all; we have borne the delay; we have listened to lies; we have been told Germany has won the war and now, incensed beyond further tolerance, we are bitter, wrathful, defiant and filled with hatred. We all talk at once, demand consideration and, with the flashing thought that we might be held as hostages, insist on a definite date for our release.

The German says he does not know and calmly starts to leave. An American colonel, afire with wrath, jumps in front of him and blocks his path. "You lie!" he yells. "You are a liar! We want our release!"

Frightened and trying to pacify the Colonel's rage the German, in desperation, offers an explanation. "Millions of soldiers are streaming back from the Front," he seems confused. "There is no transportation and it is impossible to let you out."

"We don't need transportation!" roars the Colonel. "We'll walk out! We demand our release! We want action, not lies and false promises!"

Cowering under the tirade the German nervously calls a guard, pushes past the Colonel and sneaks away.

We hold a mass meeting.

We decide to break out in a body and walk to Switzerland. The Germans, sensing our attitude, place machine guns around the camp, fire them as a warning and, guarding us as never before, warn against an outbreak. We are held by the revolutionists and uncertain of their attitude cannot understand the situation.

The socialist paper carries accounts of America sending shiploads of food to a supposedly starving population in Germany. We draft a cablegram to the United States; we request a postponement of all food shipments until our release is effected. Well aware that such a message will never be sent we hope that since it must go through the hands of the Commandant our drastic thoughts may hasten a release.

The Commandant, plainly disturbed, stalks into the court-yard. "Do you want to starve the women and children in Germany?" he demands.

"Absolutely!" answers an angry voice. "We want to starve the whole damned German nation until we get out of here!"

The Commandant, with nothing more to say, hurries away.

Another day sinks into night. Another, another, still others and we treat the many rumors of release as jokes, for lies are so consistently told by the Boche that we seek the truth by direct contradiction.

Iron crosses, spiked helmets, revolvers, belt buckles and countless other German what-nots are offered by the guards in exchange for some of our Red Cross food. We want none of their junk and tell them so. We smile and point to *"Gott Mit Uns."* They, deceived and disillusioned soldiers, nod approval and agree that the blatant motto is a fallacy.

November 26th.

Fifteen days since the Armistice and still we are pris-oners. Helpless, fretful, hemmed in by machine guns and with the hope of a Thanksgiving in France but another shattered dream we go to bed, disconsolate.

CHAPTER XXV

A HAND pulls at me and, startled, I jerk from a sound sleep. Lights blaze, rain hits the roof and a German soldier, hurrying through the barracks, wakens other sleeping men. Jumping up, excited and wondering, I stand in the open doorway and stare into the darkness.

"*Raus! Raus!*" The German shakes them one by one but some, stupid with sleep, refuse to get up.

"*Raus! Sie fahren nach der Schweiz!*"

"Are we leaving?"—"Say!—Are we *really* leaving?"

"*Ja, ja. Sie fahren nachhause!*"

Leaving! . . . It is cold and my teeth chatter as I watch the rain, slanting steel, bounce on the earth and splash into ground puddles.

Leaving! . . . The word is staggering . . . I stand . . . hollow . . . and then through the sheets of grey-white water I see my sister . . . laughing.

We are leaving for Switzerland! The barracks hum; the hour has come. My right boot will not go on my left foot; it is three o'clock in the morning; where is my bread?

We scurry around and chattering like magpies tie up our scanty possessions including cans of Red Cross food. Each man is aware that a longed-for hour of life is here. Each

man talks, rushes, buttons his coat and arranges his little
bundle. Each man is tense. Each man . . . but Jeff.

Jeff does not move.

He lies in his bunk, tucks the blanket close about his
neck and watches our enthusiastic preparations with sarcastic amusement. Suspicious and mistrustful of the Boche
at all times, even now he disputes their word.

"Hey, Jeff! . . . get up. Hurry! . . . we're leaving!"

"Who said so?" he grunts. "You don't believe these
damned Germans do you? We're not leaving, don't fool
yourself, never believe a German! If they say we're going
that means we're not."

"Get up, you damned fool . . . get up!"

"Jeff! . . . shake a leg, we're going right now! It *is*
true."

"I'll believe it when we're gone, not before," and he re-
fuses to stir.

Roll call.

As prisoners we line up for the last time and Jeff, still
challenging the now obvious truth, joins us. It is dark
and the rain is pouring. Tingling with joy we hold tight
to our parcels, listen for our names and answer . . .
hoarsely.

Silence.

We wait.

The drenching rain pelts down, we are soaking, but it falls
unheeded on bodies intoxicated with feverish delight.

"Marsch!"

We swing through the gate! OUT! The road is feather
soft; our feet are bubbles, barely touching, as we walk on a
strip of winding black satin into Villingen.

At the station a train of coaches stands ready. We hop
aboard and even as the train pulls out Jeff insists we are not

leaving Germany. A German officer and guards are with us. They sit drained of feeling. The coaches bump and jerk; the wheels race on slippery tracks and the train, speeding on and on and on through the night, rattles and rumbles. Noises, but not a human sound for our hearts so throb that we are voiceless.

The rain stops. Clouds, grey and apathetic, dissolve before a rising sun and we look at each other in the light of a new dawn. A whistle blows! blows! blows! The shrill sound, as it screeches in warning for a clear track, pierces our very souls. A clear track! A clear track . . . from Bondage to Emancipation.

The sun, high in the heavens, lights the world as the train with a final jolt drags to a stop. We are in Constanz, Switzerland, and picking up our bundles we scramble through the car and jump down the steps. How fresh the air! How warm the sun and how quiet, how very quiet!

We follow the officer to a long wooden barracks and file in. Formerly a hospital, rows of iron cots line the walls and a large stove is in the center. This half of Constanz is policed by the Germans and we are therefore still under guard.

A civilian tells us we may send a message home.

A message home! I stand, trembling, and repeat to myself, "A message home . . . a message home . . ." Then with shaking hand take the paper and, scrawling two words, "Free Again," hand it back.

A strange feeling grips me. I have sent a message home! My mother, father and sister will read it. After months of suspense, over and over and over again, they will read it. "Jim is free!"—"My boy is coming home!"—"Jim is out of prison!"—they will say, and my mother will cry, my father will cough and my sister will run upstairs, quickly. How happy they will be! Through a blue mist I see them, so very plainly, and my boiling blood is full of crackling ice. I have never felt this way before—I do not understand it and struggle to control myself.

.   .   .   .   .

We go to bed and sleep like tops until morning.
It is Thanksgiving Day.
After a breakfast of *ersatz* coffee and black bread we go for a walk, led by the German officer. The sky of opalescent blue is strewn with drifting clouds, snow-white and pink. A delicate wind, gentle as the breeze from a butterfly's wings, fans soft blue ripples across the tranquil surface of Lake Constanz. Green is the earth from autumn rains and tumbled leaves of pink and gold are everywhere.

We look and look with eyes fresh-washed and wonder at the novel loveliness of nature. We see her in new glory and, transported by such exquisite enchantment, are timid before her beauty. The wonder of her; the sweetness of her breath; the amber earth, like musk and myrrh, in love with hidden violets, sighs and we are bathed in perfume. I never knew—alas, I never knew—or could it be that somehow one forgets—I never knew that nature was so beautiful.

At a glance we see Germany, Austria and Switzerland. Germany is back of us . . . BACK of us! Germany, the Germans, the prisons and Hell are behind and back of us forever. The international boundary line and, ahead, the other half of Switzerland. The impulse to run!—to dash across!

Young German soldiers, all boys under eighteen, serve our dinner—Thanksgiving dinner!
We are thankful! Typical German soup, a bowl for each, and we are thankful for, in a few hours, as free men,

we will walk in a free world. Only a few hours more! We
are truly thankful!

*Oh Lord! I give Thee thanks. Hear me, dear Lord,
and look into my grateful heart for I am thankful. Our
Father in heaven, listen to my plea. Make me to remember! Make me to forget! Oh God, I pray Thee
help me to walk in peace.*

Our meal is over and the arrogant German youths order
us to wash the dishes. We laugh at them! We are no longer
prisoners of war, it is too ridiculous; but they, stubborn and
ignorant, complain to the officer who, although disrelishing
the fair judgment, decides in our favor.

The next morning is November 29th.

The Swiss government has provided a train for our
transportation and we are told to get ready. For the last
time we collect our few possessions; for the last time we
leave the barracks; for the last time we walk, under guard,
to the station and board a train. The too-toot of a whistle,
the coach shunts and we move, slowly, away from the platform.

France! We are going to France!

We sit, mute as stones, and watch the gliding landscape.
Faster now, faster . . . faster . . . and the trees are
whirling past. A lone Swiss soldier, young and handsome,
smiles at us. He is our friend.

The boundary line!

We cross the line and a rare emotion surges through me.
Hot and cold . . . bitter and sweet . . . blind and hitherto unfelt . . . I swim in shell-pink waters but cannot
see.

We are free!

Men, women and children, standing on the embankments,
wave and cheer as the train slides by. We pull open the

windows and lean out. The men, throwing their caps into the air, yell a welcome; the women, some cuddling tiny babes, flutter their hands and toss white aprons; girls and boys, offering us apples, shout and run to catch the train, and little children with American flags held high above their innocent heads, jump with glee and laugh as we wave at them.

Zurich . . . and the train slips on.

We skirt the Lake of Zurich, thunder through a tunnel and into the valley of the Sihl. The snow-capped Alps, like white-hooded sentinels, spread guard above the picturesque farms and green meadows. We cross the Lorz and through the western windows the beauty of Switzerland unfolds as a graceful flower.

Lucerne . . . and the train stamps on.

The Emme River, running crystals, and we cut through rich pastures caressed by wooded slopes. The village of Hassel, so prettily situated, as if it grew alone and blended, unaided by the hand of man, into the countryside. The day is grey but clear, blue lakes of limpid turquoise are precious gems set in resplendence.

Berne is headquarters for the American Red Cross and we speculate about our arrival.

"Is it much further?"

"We ought to get in during the afternoon . . ."

"Think the Red Cross will meet us?"

"Perhaps . . ."

"If they do it will mean something to eat . . ."

"Chocolate and cigarettes, maybe . . ."

We swing around a curve and through a slight drizzle the mountain ranges, with long brown skirts and white kerchiefs, cut sharp silhouettes against the sky. Another curve, another, then another and ahead in the distance is the city of Berne. Taut are our nerves; tight are our throats and again, except for the rumbling coaches there is not a sound. Nearer—we cram our heads and shoulders into the windows. Nearer . . . nearer . . . nearer . . . beautiful Berne with her shoulders high above the sea and beneath her feet the winding Aar. Nearer . . . nearer . . . nearer. The train slows and a tremendous roar—as if the universe were one gigantic waterfall with a human voice in every rushing drop—drowns the noise of the car wheels and we jerk . . . to a dead stop.

Cheers! Cheers! Cheers!

A solid mass of joy-crazed humanity; a passionate world let loose; a human pandemonium of cheering, yelling, screaming people stretches from the platform into a vast half-circle beyond. Thousands upon thousands of human beings crush together in an uncontrollable tempest of savage happiness.

"Vive l'Amérique."

"Vivent les prisonniers."

"Vive Wilson."

Cheers! Cheers! Cheers! They shout, shout, shout and pictures of President Wilson are everywhere. American Flags! They wave from every conceivable spot and the Stars and Stripes—*our* Stars and Stripes—rise and fall, curl in and out and despite a gentle rain unfurl their welcome.

We are lost in excitement!

"Vive la Suisse," we yell. *"Vive la Suisse,"* and our throats are split as we yell and yell.

We are steeped in exultation!

"Vive la Suisse," and we laugh. *"Vive la Suisse,"* and we cry, for our hearts are torn to shreds by the unexpected reception.

McKeown, his voice already gone, still moves his lips in a silent effort to vent the emotion of a soul infused with joy and gratefulness.

We are the first prisoners to be released through Switzerland. **Our** train is late and for hours these patriots have waited in a drizzling rain to greet us. To prevent the frenzied multitude from swarming in, all gates are closed and only members of the Red Cross are allowed on the platform. They, racing back and forth, wait anxiously to board the train.

The doors are open!

Men, women and girls rush in. The girls, tears streaming down their animated faces, deluge us with chocolate and cigarettes. Food, shoes, overcoats and money are offered. The Red Cross has everything and to request is to receive. A few, badly wounded, accept overcoats but the rest of us ask for nothing. We are more than satisfied.

"Will you have some tea?" proffers a dear old lady.

"No, thank you."

"Some tea, my boy, some nice hot tea will do you good."

I am stuffed with chocolate and, to refuse her insistent kindness politely, I say, "Thank you, but I am not feeling well."

"*My! my!*" she exclaims. "You are ill . . . my poor boy! I must get you some cognac right away," and setting down her teapot she hustles out.

The excited crowd mill around and when she returns about ten minutes later I am in the center of the jammed coach.

"Where is my poor boy who is not feeling well?" She looks about worriedly. "I have some cognac for him."

"Right here!" calls a fellow near the door.

Tender is her smile as she hands him the cognac; bright is her wrinkled face as she watches him drink it and as, with smacks of pleasure, he graciously thanks her, she is contented.

The train whistle blows. A mad rush. The Red Cross workers, with "Good-bye!"—"Good Luck!"—"Good-bye!"

hasten out and the coach is clear. We hang from the windows and the continuous noise of the fomenting mob swells into an uproar.

"*Vive l'Amérique! Vive l'Amérique!*"
Cheers! Cheers! Cheers!
"*Vive la Suisse! Vive la Suisse!*"
Cheers! Cheers! Cheers!
The train, noiselessly beneath the mighty outcry, shuttles and pulls away, slowly. Cheers. Tears. Strained faces. A sea of flags wave accompaniment to the rising cadences of a final farewell. Faces blur and pass. The noise rends the air, hangs quivering and, as we gain speed, echoes and dies under the grinding coaches. Faster—faster—at full speed and far away but "*Vive l'Amérique! Vive l'Amérique!*"—rings and rings and rings in our ears.

I finger my cigarettes and chocolate, pile them together and look at a postal card which a pretty blue-eyed girl gave me. Through a sun spot on a blue world is thrust an arm; a giant hand holds an American Flag and below this bright-colored picture is a little verse:

> *Our flag, the flag of liberty*
> *The flag that flies for you and me;*
> *Upheld by right from day to day,*
> *The Stars and Stripes are here to stay!*

Wondering who she was I put it in my breast pocket and look up to find a new man at the end of the car. He stands by a window; wears a loose Russian coat and meticulously cuts small pieces from a large red apple. He can barely open his mouth and with difficulty pokes the pieces in.

"Avery!" I shout. "Avery!"

He sees me, rushes over and smiles, crookedly. A big red lump bulges from one cheek; he is thin, deathly pale and evidently in pain.

"My jaw is broken . . ." he tells me.

Avery returning from a patrol saw a tempting string of German balloons and leaving the formation turned back. He was alone. "Thought I'd get two or three," he says, "wonderful chance, dove on them and from God knows where a formation of Fokkers pounced on me . . ." He was taken to a hospital at Trèves. "My jaw was broken. The Germans never set it." It healed, all askew, and Avery is a sorry sight.

"Maybe," he is hopeful, "when we get to France they can rebreak the bone and set it properly."

Avery! from the 95th. Avery! from my own squadron. So happy am I to see him that to ask when or how he got on the train never occurs to me.

Late afternoon.

On—on toward Lausanne.

The sun is burnished copper and rays of red, of purplish red—like thickly flowering fuchsia all entwined with heliotrope—enwrap the mountains all around, up and down and all around, in shaded, deep chiffon.

A curve. The train stops on the side of a steep incline and cradled just below, in a golden mountain crevice, is the little town of Bellegarde. We get off, stretch ourselves and dig our boots into the soil of France! On the track ahead a Red Cross train waits to take us to a hospital and beneath is a bridge which spans a roaring river between us and the town.

A long line of girls, in double file and led by a man, starts across the bridge. Slowly, as if in some religious procession, they reach this side and begin the winding climb up the slope. Nearer, and we see they are laboring with some heavy load. Nearer, and we discern that between each two girls sways a large wicker basket. They arrive. Bottles

upon bottles of champagne fill some baskets and others
are piled high with glasses. We line up—respectfully.

"Je suis le Maire de Bellegarde."

The Mayor introduces himself, shakes hands with each
one and, after offering the *"Félicitations"* of the town, tells
the girls to fill our glasses.

Corks pop.

Champagne flows.

We drink to the Mayor. We drink to the girls. We
drink to Bellegarde. We drink to France, America and
Freedom. A glass to a toast and we thank the Mayor—
most heartily.

*"Encore un verre. Mais oui. Regardez, beaucoup, beau-
coup."*

Corks still pop.

Champagne still flows.

We drink to the *splendid* Mayor! We drink to the *beautiful* girls! We drink to *wonderful* Bellegarde! We drink
to *unequalled* France, *glorious* America and again we thank
the Mayor, the *worthy* Mayor—most, most graciously.

*"Encore un coup. Oui, oui, oui, encore. Encore un
autre."*

The champagne, but half gone, pours into our glasses.
The supply seems endless, the corks pop, pop, poppetty pop,
pop and two empty bottles roll down the hill. They roll
and roll down the hill—the funniest bottles that ever rolled
down a hill . . . and we drink to the bottles that roll down
the hill.

It is dusk.

Good-bye to the Mayor! Good-bye to the girls of Bellegarde! We board the hospital train.

An electric bulb, dim and small, hangs from the ceiling.
Iron bunks, one above the other, line the car and the doors

are doubly wide for loading and unloading the wounded. My bed is a lower and opposite me is McKeown. Poor Mac, he seems different lately and on the verge of a breakdown. A faint whistle, an answering toot from the engine, and we are off.

.　　　.　　　.　　　.　　　.

On through the dark. The train jerks, stops frequently, starts, stops again and the night is long. Daylight. Morning, and an orderly gives us a bowl of oatmeal, coffee and white bread.

"Archie!"

"Yes Mac . . ."

"What's this?" He holds out two slices of bread.

"Bread, Mac—*white* bread."

He studies the pieces, doubtfully, and shakes his head. "But it's too white for cake," he says to himself.

The train stops at Allerey. It is a city of barracks as far as the eye can reach and we are led to the delousing station where we undress, take a hot shower and, wrapped in a blanket, follow an orderly to a barracks. Inside are rows of white cots, white curtains hang between and snow-white sheets are tightly spread.

McKeown puts something under his bed, cautiously.

I go over and find hidden cans of Red Cross food and pieces of the white bread. "Why Mac, you'll get plenty of food now," I tell him. "No use saving those things."

He shakes his head; he is doubtful. "I'll keep it for a while, Archie . . . just in case . . ."

The contentment!

The warm wave of weariness; the kind of tired that lulls one to rest without a single thought. Clean pyjamas, clean bodies and I rub the whitest sheets that ever were against

my face. Sheets!—imagine! The comfort and the tender
care! France! France! France! Here we are, like babes
in cribs, and a whimper brings attention. Here we are . . .
at last. Here we are . . . it is hard to believe—quite hard
to believe—but good, oh so good! Clean, clean, clean and
spotless white . . . everything so clean and spotless white.
France! . . . and I am sinking . . . softly soothed . . .
sinking . . . sinking . . . into sleep.

Dinner time.

Refreshed, we all sit up. The trays of food! We stare,
watch and wait our turn, then stare and stare again for on
each tray is steak, deep brown gravy, potatoes, creamed
carrots, apple pie and coffee. We eat our first real meal;
the trays are gone; then down I slip . . . and deep I slide
. . . and back I go to sleep.

Three days have gone.

Our day nurse, a spinster past her prime, is proficient in
her duties but lacks an ounce of sweetness. Her sour face,
with nary a smile, is hard to look upon and Red Tape—tied
in knots—is her only motto. Men, to her, are horrid things
and when she is on duty—such a rigid, freezing duty—we
are cross and ill at ease.

But our night nurse! You should see our little night
nurse! Young and pretty, full of life, she comes with the
dark and the whole place is bright. Efficient, quick, she
whisks through her tasks and then sits down to talk and
laugh with us. All fighting men, to her, are heroes and when
she is on duty—although strict, she's warm and glowing—
we are happy for, being men, we love her.

Our uniforms are returned. They are badly shrunken
and wrinkled but deloused, sterilized and thoroughly clean.
We walk around the hospital. Wounded—wounded—

wounded.　This base hospital, one of the largest in France, is overspilling with the wounded.　Board walks, stretching over the mud, are filled with men.　Men with an arm gone; men with a leg gone; men with an eye missing and some, in wheel chairs, far worse.　Crutches, sticks, empty sleeves with safety pins and bandages in an "After-the-War" parade.

We visit the wards.

Thousands of wounded men, separated according to the nature of their injuries, lie in the wooden barracks. Smashed jaws, crushed heads, nose, ear and neck wounds. Shattered lungs, torn intestines, pulp-like shoulders, hips and knees.　Double amputations and blind ones.　The barracks next to ours is a veritable maze of arms and legs, pulleys and ropes.　The limbs are tied up and strung; pulled here and there; held in place by heavy weights and dangle in every conceivable direction.　Recuperating—in a torture chamber.

How senseless it all seems.　Once, whole and free from pain—they went to war.　Now, shot to pieces and in agony —they are back.　The splendid doctors and nurses with untiring patience and skill are performing miracles, but the miracles of skilful men who mend them can never reach the miracle of God who made them.　And this is but one hospital.　The thought of countless others in France, Germany, England, Italy and elsewhere makes one shudder. The green boys who sailed away on a great adventure are ripened now—mature—and some, too ripe, are rotting. *The fruit of war.*

Some pray to live but will die.　Some pray to die but will live.　Others do not know nor care.　They cry to be sent home; they sob to be left alone; they scream in pain and then, apologizing, swoon away forever.　But—we have won the war!　Each afternoon at two o'clock a funeral cortège passes our window. Yesterday only two or three rode to the cemetery in wooden boxes. Today there is a long line . . . boxes . . . boxes . . . boxes—so many died in the night. Yes!—we have won the war!

     •   •   •   •   •

Almost two weeks have passed; we want to get away from here. A final examination. Our pulses and temperatures are taken; our throats and noses swabbed and, according to our conditions, a doctor grades us with A-B-C- or D for official records. He finishes with me.

"What letter did you give me, Doctor?"

"Why . . . er . . . you're all right, son . . ."

"You wrote a D." I grab his coat. "I saw you . . ."

"Yes, I gave you a D . . . but . . ."

"But what? I want an A, Doctor. Why mark me D? I want an A to show on my record . . ."

"Now let me explain. You're weak, just out of Germany and a little upset, so . . ."

"Explain nothing! A! A! A! I want an A! I'm not weak! I'm fine! I don't deserve a D." and I argue . . . argue . . . argue . . . until, spent, I start away, shaking.

He pats my shoulder. "You're right," he says, "I'll give you an A. Here it is—look," and scratching out the D he prints an A beside my name.

     •   •   •   •   •

Fretful, we long to leave. Eating, sleeping, walking or talking with the patients is monotonous and we chafe for action. We write letters home. One to my father and mother is posted and I scribble another:—

My darling Sister:

We are still in Allerey but hope to leave in a few days. I am well and happy but my heart aches to see you. What joy it will be. How is Ginger? Will take

the first boat possible, then a train for Seattle. How I
long to hear you play again. You must play and play
and play, old pieces, new ones, everything. Why try
to write when soon I will be with you?

All my love

Jim.

I call on the Commanding Officer of the hospital and tell
him of my desire to leave. He explains he cannot let me
go now; says we must wait a bit. Wait—wait—wait—for
what? We are under no special orders. Wait! It is impossible to wait another day!

I decide to run away.

It is midnight.

All are asleep. The barracks is still. A solitary light
at one end of the dark room shines a halo above the nurse's
head while she, the angel, sits knitting.

I dress, stand by my cot, and feel like a traitor. Mc-
Keown stirs in his sleep, uneasily. The others, dead to the
world, are quiet. Leaving them . . . I am leaving them!
My throat pulls . . . this is the end . . . I am leaving
them all. Good-bye, Mac—Good-bye—everybody—and
the nurse, putting down her yarns, goes into an adjacent
room. What a chance! On tip-toe I sneak down the aisle,
quietly open the door and, with a last look, go out into the
night.

Over the narrow walks I run . . . slip to the side . . .
stick in the mud . . . back on the boards . . . and run,
run, run to the railroad station. The Paris train, due fifteen
minutes ago, will be in any moment. What luck! Almost
missed it and out of breath I sit down. Thinking, thinking,
thinking—of Paris—New York—Home, and jumping up I
ask, "Where is the train?"

"It's late. Won't be along till four . . ."

Damn it all! Well, I'll wait until four and, pacing up and down the platform, see a light on the track ahead.

An engine glugs into the station. An American officer and three privates, smeared with coal dust and dirt, are on it.

"Where are you going?"

"We're taking this engine to Paris."

"May I go with you?"

"Sure! Come along . . ."

I climb up and sit on the coal in the tender. Away we go! At a furious rate of speed we tear down the track and the engine jumps like a grasshopper. At every station a brakeman sidetracks us for the late express but each time, as soon as his back is turned, we throw the switch and, with the distracted Frenchman waving his arms and yelling, race away. What a ride! Bumping . . . swerving . . . tearing at top speed and the coal spilling out.

Early morning and we pull into the Gare du Nord.

"Thank you, Lieutenant," and I start up the streets of Paris.

Strange—how strange I feel!

Walking, walking, walking—the same old streets but nothing seems familiar.

Different—how different everything is!

Walking—walking—walking—and entering a small café I try to eat some breakfast.

The city now begins to stir. Garbage men and flower girls, yawning, go to work. The men wheel their cans and the women sprinkle small chrysanthemums.

Alone—how terribly alone I am!

Walking, walking, walking—where? Oh, yes—the quartermaster's office to get some money and I turn into the Champs Élysées. The Champs Elysées! Yes, this is the

Champs Elysées . . . but there is a change. An American Colonel stops me. I salute.

"What army do you belong to?" he blusters.

"The American Army, sir . . ."

"What service?" he roars in disgust.

"The Air Service, sir!"

"What do you mean?" He glares at me, infuriated. "How dare you be seen in the daylight like this."

Instantly, but for the first time, I realize my grotesque appearance. My uniform, like crumpled crêpe paper, is covered with coal dust. The tunic, shrunken and far too small, is without a Sam Browne belt, half buttoned, open at the neck and the tight sleeves show inches of bare arm. My breeches, with holes in the knees, are skimpy; bulky cloth leggings wrap round my legs and shoes, old Russian shoes, are far too big.

"What is your name?" he snorts.

"Lieutenant Archibald," I answer in embarrassment, "of the 95th squadron, First Pursuit Group. I just got out of Germany, Colonel, have been in the hospital at Allerey and am going to the quartermaster's to get . . ."

"I'm sorry." His look is one of contrite astonishment. "If anyone stops you just refer them to me," and he shakes my hand, warmly.

Afternoon.

Along the streets of Paris I walk as in a dream. Unconscious of direction, unseeing and not caring, until suddenly I pass the *Café de la Paix*.

"Archie!"

Three aviators, all instructors, sit by a sidewalk table. They gape at me, amazed.

"Why, Archie! We heard you were dead . . ."

"Yes, we were just drinking to you . . ."

"Sit down, Archie! Sit down and have a drink . . ."

"Sure, sit down and tell us the news . . ."

Tell them the news! What news? Good God! They are enthusiastic and mean well, but I refuse and walk on.

Paris!

The streets are full of people; the taxis honk! honk! honk!—and children, laughing, roll their hoops and clap for Punch and Judy. Cafés are full of customers; the Tuileries fountains play and mothers, young, in widows' weeds, lead small sons by the hand.

Paris!

The theatres are jammed at night; *Louise* is at the Opera; the maimed, the sick, the halt and blind go walking through the gardens. Red Cross girls are everywhere; soldiers of all nations; and now and then a small parade chalks down the avenue.

Paris! To get away! To get away—at once.

.   .   .   .   .

Three days later I arrive at the Aviation Center in Tours; register with the Military Police; hire a room at the Hotel Universe and go shopping. A uniform of special order hangs finished but much to the dismay of the tailor has not been called for. It fits me to a nicety and after flourishing some extra francs it is mine. Thrilled at this coup I buy underwear, boots, shirts, collars, every known accessory and a suitcase.

It is evening and happy as a lark I stand before a mirror, trying on my clothes. A rap at the door.

"Come in!" and I whirl around.

A military policeman salutes, stiffly.

"Sir, you are under arrest!"

My temples pound. What now? My God! What is it now, and almost crying out in rage I ask, "What for?"

He hands me a telegram, smiles knowingly and disappears.

I read it.

It cannot be true! Again and again I read it. How is it possible? Over and over and over, aloud and to myself, I read the words but do not believe them. How could she be in France? . . . just wrote a letter to her from Allerey . . . some mistake, and rushing out I wire back for verification of the message. The answer arrives:

> Your sister left this P. M. for Paris am forwarding your message to her there care Red Cross Hdq. where she will report in the morning.
> Operator Allerey Dec. 14th, 1918.

My sister is in France! My sister!
I send another wire.

> Take first train for Tours and I will meet you.
> Love
> Jim.

"*Concierge! Concierge!* I want another room."
"*Comment?*"
"*Une autre chambre—Vite, vite, il me faut une autre chambre.*"
"*Une autre—Pourquoi?*"
"*Ma soeur vient! Ma soeur des Etats Unis—elle arrive demain.*"

Each afternoon, at three o'clock, the train from Paris reaches Tours. Tomorrow . . . tomorrow . . . what a good thing I have a new outfit! Terrible if she had seen me before.

Two o'clock. I dress with care and meet the train, trembling. She is not there. For three days, at three o'clock, I meet the train but still she does not come. Did the wire get through? Maybe she is ill! The fourth day and with burning cheeks again I meet the train.

Down the track, far down the track there is the little figure of a girl. She is in a Red Cross uniform. I look and look, it may not be, but as a French civilian picks up her *heavy* suitcase I surmise, somehow, it is. She trots beside; the man has long black whiskers. The way she walks! The quick, short steps and perky head—for no one ever walked like that but her . . .

"HAZEL!"

"JIM!"

.   .   .   .   .

Two days pass.

My sister is under Red Cross orders and must return to Paris. She begs me to accompany her and so we go together. Arriving, we hail a taxi and hand in hand ride to a Pension on the Avenue MacMahon.

"Here we are!—Jim's here!" She races up the stairs.

"Here's Jim!—I brought him back!—Jim! come on— Hurry!"

And following her—'twas ever thus since childhood—I go into a room, a drawing room which fronts the street below, and standing there in Red Cross uniforms are her two friends.

Tippy and Elma—girls from home—to greet me.

A fire in the grate burns low; the afternoon is late; a sputtering light from red hot coals glows through the dusky twilight. We talk, we laugh, we reminisce, and in the half dark room we know—a lot of things—which need no words at all.

My sister plays!

The yellow keyboard, white against the black. Her lovely face, enhanced and brightened by a dying flame, looks up. A first caress and with the softest notes a laughing tear rolls down a rocked slope. She plays and plays! Her hands, so young and strong, press deep—deep—and deeper yet, until, with soul inspired skill she pulls from out the aged keys a boy and girl who skip along—skip along—and peek with awe into a thicket green where cedars tall grow by a mountain lake.

She plays—of Home!

She plays—of virgin forests; wooded hills; and sunshine through the rain.

She plays—of moonlight on the Sound and now, her hands are still.

I try to speak.

No sound will come. My hands are ice; my throat is fire. I struggle hard to laugh . . . to move my lips . . . or to relax and get away but all of me, except two quivering knees, is paralyzed. The music from my sister's hands has left me dumbly powerless and tears run down my face. Tears! With lowered head, ashamed, I reel and stumble from the room to break out sobbing.

Strength—my strength is gone. Between two velvet hangings I am crying.

Strength!—My squadron!—Conflans!—Solitary Confinement! — "Cheerio! . . . Cheerio!" . . . I hear the faintest "Cheerio" just across the hall. Prison courtyards! Hunger! Death! The face of the burned aviator at Villingen! He looks at me . . . he haunts me . . . he mumbles . . . "Cheerio."

If *they* can carry on—and they *will* carry on—then all must carry on and I fight with all my might until I whisper, "Cheerio."

A sniveling weakling wipes his eyes and listens to a song,

> *Three musketeers in iron boots*
> *Guarded old Paris town*

Beauchamp! . . . Beauchamp! . . . I forgot to write his mother in Princess Anne.

Library of Congress Cataloging-in-Publication Data

Archibald, Norman, 1894-
Heaven high, hell deep, 1917-1918 / Norman Archibald.
p. cm. — (Wings of war)
Reprint. Originally published: New York : A. & C. Boni, 1935.
ISBN 0-8094-9616-X (trade). — ISBN 0-8094-9617-8 (library)
1. World War, 1914-1918—Personal narratives, American.
2. Archibald, Norman, 1894- .
3. World War, 1914-1918—Prisoners and prisons, German.
4. Fighter pilots—United States—Biography.
5. Prisoners of war—United States—Biography.
6. Prisoners of war—Germany—Biography.
I. Title. II. Series.
D570.9.A7 1992   940.4'8173—dc20   91-33957 CIP
[B]